Democracy for Sale

How Corporate Greed is Corrupting Democracy and Endangering the Planet

By Robert Cain

Democracy for sale

Copyright 2024 by Robert Cain

All rights reserved. No part of this book my be reproduced or copied without express permission from the publisher.

Published in the United States by -
Artwurks Creative Media Company
1739 Franklin St. Suite D Santa Monica, CA 90404
contact@Democracy4Sale.com

Written and Edited by Robert Cain
Cover Design by Artwurks Creative

Paperback
ISBN- 979-8-9927084-0-0

The views and opinions expressed in this book do not reflect or represent the authors or institutions cited herein. This book is intended to reflect the author's views and observations based on his experiences and publicly available information.

AUTHOR'S NOTE

Whether it's the language we speak, the sports we follow, or our political preferences, much of our understanding of the world is shaped by what we've been taught. Our parents, friends, and the places we grow up all contribute to what we perceive as knowledge. Knowledge is like compound interest—it builds over time. A wise man once told me, "If you truly want to understand something, you must read books."

Unlike newspapers, magazines, or online articles, books often take years to research and write, offering a depth and breadth of understanding that other media simply cannot. That's not to say there's no value in other forms of media, but a good book has the power to open up the world like nothing else. The pages can transport us to distant places, allowing us to see through the eyes of people we may never meet.

I recognize that people lead busy lives. Many work long hours, and at the end of the day, they just want to unwind, watch a game, or spend time with family. In our fast-paced, high-tech world, reliable information is often buried beneath corporate media noise and an endless stream of online misinformation.

I originally set out to make a documentary, but I quickly realized there was too much information to fit into a 90-minute format. So, here we are. I didn't read my first non-school-required book until my late twenties, but I've read hundreds since. Those books opened my eyes to serious issues facing our country and the world—issues that often

Democracy for sale

provoke either glassy-eyed indifference or conspiracy theories fueled by social media. Just as a house needs a strong foundation, understanding the complexities of our political system and its corruption requires foundational knowledge. Social media and corporate news aren't in the business of educating the public, so I've compiled key insights from some of the most impactful books, along with countless articles, podcasts, and lectures on government, finance, and history. My goal is to provide an enlightening look behind the scenes of America.

My intention is that, through the incredible work of brilliant authors and many hours of research, readers will gain a clearer understanding of the corruption in our political and financial systems—and how, by working together, we can restore the American dream for future generations. I love my country, and I am deeply concerned that it is being eroded from within by greed and the pursuit of power. For decades, moneyed interests have fought against the progress that the American people—those of us who want a better, cleaner, and safer world—have worked so hard for. Unfortunately, they seem to be winning.

Throughout my life, I've worked in a variety of fields, before eventually settling behind a camera in film and television. My career has allowed me to travel, meet remarkable people, and witness extraordinary stories of courage and wisdom. Those experiences have inspired me to write this book. There are a lot of words in these pages, and I apologize for that. But hopefully you'll find inspiration here as well. More importantly, I hope we, acting together, can live up to the original promise of America.

Democracy for sale

"What an astonishing thing a book is. ~ Writing is perhaps the greatest of human inventions, binding together people who never knew each other, citizens of distant epochs. Books break the shackles of time. A book is proof that humans are capable of working magic."

Carl Sagan , Cosmos (1980)

Contents

   Author's Note:
   Contents:
2 Introduction:

Part 1: History:

6   The Founding Fathers:
    A Perfect Union Didn't Include Corporations:
11 It's a Tea Party: The British East India Company.
15 The Gilded Age:
    Industrialization and Corporate Power:
17 The 20th Century: Pushing Back on Corporate Power.
18 The New Deal: Post-War: Corporate-State Symbiosis.
21 The Modern Era: Corporate Political Influence in the 21st Century.
23 The Great Myth of Free Markets: The Brain Washing of America:
30 What is a Corporation? Are Corporations Really People?
34 Understanding Corporate Charters:

Part 2: Governance vs. Economics:

39 Capitalism, Socialism, Communism - Oh my!
44 The Rise and Fall of Neoliberalism:
50 TAXES, Uh! What are they Good For?
52 Government and Corporations - A Love story:

Part 3: Government - It's a Family Affair:

60	How the Trump Family Cashed In: A Masterclass in Rigging the System.
65	Trump's Inauguration: A study in buying influence:
68	Trump 2.0: Monetizing the Presidency (Again!):
68	The Gospel According to Grift:
68	Crypto Chaos: The MAGA Meme Coin:
68	The Emoluments Clause? Never Heard of It:
69	The Presidency as a Personal Brand:
70	Insider Trading: How to Make Big Bucks in Congress:
75	The Revolving Door: Government, to Corporate Lobbying, and back again.
81	The World is full of Cheaters: Taxes? What Taxes?
82	Papers, Papers Everywhere: The Panama and Paradise Papers and other revelations.

Part 4: The Billionaire Class:

87	"Winners Take All" - Doing good without doing much.
90	How the Wealthy Use Charities as Tax Shelters:
94	Hidden Wealth: How the Ultra Rich are Robbing the American People... Legally.
94	The Millionaire's Guide to Evading Taxes:
98	The Right's War on the IRS:
99	The Ideological Battleground:
101	Carrying Water for the Rich:

103	Greed-flation: Why US Corporations Are Raising Prices Despite Surging Profits.
106	How Oil Corporations Work Together to Keep Prices Painfully High:
111	Big Ag's Big Scam:
113	Supersizing Profits, Supersizing Waistlines:
116	Corporate Consolidation: The Road to Market Manipulation and Price Gouging.

Part 5: The Military-Corporate Complex:

122	The Black Hole Where They Throw Our Money:
123	Military Contractors - Keep the Money Flowing:
127	The Military Money Machine and the $400 Toilet Seat: Cost-Plus Arrangements.
132	The Federal Trash Can: Waste and Abuse in the Military Budget:

Part 6: Public Money, Private Profit:

138	The Great American Sell-Off: How Privatization Screws the Public.
139	Selling America by the Pound:
139	The Privatization of Everything: How the Plunder of Public Goods Transformed America:
145	Water, water everywhere... The Privatization of Pennsylvania's Sewer System:
149	Flush with Cash - The Importance of Utilities:
153	Chicago Sold Its Parking Meters...

153   No Parking Anytime, Anywhere.
154   Selling the Crossroads of America:
156   Prisons: Crime Is Good for Business:
162   Lock Em 'Up and Cash In:
168   The Great Disruptor Hustle: How Uber, Airbnb & Friends Privatized Profits and Socialized Costs.
172   They even want to own the weather:
174   Your Opinion Literally Does Not Matter... Unless You're an "Economic Elite":
175   The Princeton Study: A Harsh Reality:
175   Represent.Us: Shedding Light on Systemic Corruption.
176   Democracy in Name Only!

Part 7: The Courts:

179   Justice is Blind... Deaf and Apparently Dumb too: The Supreme Court: Where "Justice" Takes a Backseat to Bad Decisions:
185   Key Legislation and Court Decisions:
185   The Supreme Court Rules Overwhelmingly for Corporations:
186   The Rise of Corporate Personhood:
186   The Aftermath.
187   The Burwell v. Hobby Lobby Decision:
190   The Right-Wing's Decades-Long Project to Pack America's Courts:
195   The Federalist Society:

195	Leonard Leo : The most powerful man in America you've never heard of.
201	What's the matter with the 5th?
206	The Poisonous Influence of ALEC on Our Politics:
210	Shock Politics: How the Right Seizes Power During Troubled Times.
211	Case Studies in Shock Politics:
214	The Corrupting Influence: Corporate Approved - Politics, Education, and Science:

Part 8: The Media - Bigger is Better.

219	Mys-Story:
221	Media Consolidation - Corporate Pac-Man:
225	The Great Shrinking of Investigative Journalism: Or How Media Got Sold to the Highest Bidder:
231	How Corporate Media Has Abandoned Journalism for Sensationalism:
234	The FOX "News": A Propaganda Machine for the Republican Party.
239	The Right-Wing Echo Chamber: When Repetition Creates "Truth".
244	Manufacturing Consent: How "Think Tanks" purchase an Alternative Reality.
246	Anti-Social Media: How Corporations Are Selling Our Souls for Profit.
251	The Media's Obsession with "Both Sides-ism":

255 Deals with the Devil: How Hedge Funds are Warping Journalism.
259 The Merchants of Doubt: Corporate PR Campaigns and the Distortion of Truth.

Part 9: On Sale - Everything Must Go!

266 Owning Knowledge: How Journals and Public Research became a profit center.
271 Vulture Capitalism: A System Feeding on the Vulnerable.
276 What's the Matter with U.S.? Why People Vote Against Their Own Best Interest.
281 The Consequences of a Corporate-Driven Society:

Part 10: Some Bright Spots

285 Media that Matters:
287 It's Funny but True!
291 Business Unusual: Yeah, we built that!
296 Guaranteed Basic Income or UBI:
299 Choices, Choices, Choices!
302 Increased funding for the IRS:
303 How to be Grassroots: Joining the Fight for Reform.
303 Solutions for Reclaiming our Democracy:
305 **Conclusion:**
306 Addendum:
312 Acknowledgements:
315 About the Author:

Democracy for Sale is a call to awareness and action—an urgent plea for citizens to reclaim their political power from corporate elites so we can protect life, liberty, and the pursuit of happiness and safeguard the planet for future generations.

"Alone we can do so little, together we can do so much."

Helen Keller

Introduction

Imagine waking up one day to discover that your country had been hijacked by a secret cabal of elites whose only mission was to squeeze every last cent from the people. Oh, wait—you don't have to imagine. Welcome to America, where the rich keep their tax loopholes while the rest of us foot the bill. Where public assets are sold off like clearance items at a going-out-of-business sale, and basic services—once considered a given—are now premium, pay-to-play luxuries.

Health insurance? Sure, you can have it—until you actually need it, at which point, surprise! You're on your own. Gas prices? Magically high, even when supply is abundant (but don't worry, it's probably your fault for not driving an electric car you can't afford). Education? It's still available—if you're willing to take on a lifetime of debt. Auto insurance? More expensive than your actual car. Groceries? Well, let's just say eating is quickly becoming a privilege, not a right.

Meanwhile, the public is distracted by an endless loop of mind-numbing media and pointless culture wars, too busy arguing over trivial nonsense to notice the great American wealth heist happening in broad daylight. If a foreign power had pulled this off, we'd be in the streets, demanding justice. But since it's coming from within, half the country shrugs, and the other half cheers it on.

For decades, the price of everything has risen—**except paychecks**. Bridges are falling apart, roads resemble obstacle courses, schools are underfunded, and "trickle-down" economics? Yeah, turns out we

were just being trickled **on**. Meanwhile, the richest Americans have hoarded historic levels of wealth, while working-class wages have remained stagnant since, oh, around 1980. The stock market is soaring—fantastic news if you're already rich! But for everyone else, credit card debt is at an all-time high, and the gap between the ultra-wealthy and regular people is the largest in American history.
And here's the kicker: This didn't happen by accident. It wasn't some tragic economic fluke. It was planned, it's just that you and I weren't in on it.

The story of this country is complicated. America has accomplished great things. We've advanced science, made strides in civil rights, and even cleaned up some of our environmental messes. But we've also invaded countries under false pretenses, caused a global financial meltdown, and turned a blind eye to the suffering of millions of our own citizens.

What does it mean to be a "citizen"? Most would default to the legal definition of being a resident of a country, but maybe we've lost the deeper meaning. The word originates from the Latin "civitas", meaning "community member." Citizenship implies not just rights, but responsibilities—working collectively to manage resources, protect the environment, and provide for the common good.

Unfortunately, at some point, we stopped being **citizens,** people with a stake in our communities and a responsibility to each other—and became mere **consumers**, tricked into competing with one another for goods and services, where the only thing that matters is fulfilling personal needs and desires. And wouldn't you know it, this mindset has allowed corporations to strip away everything that once made this country great, all while convincing people it was for their own good.

Politics, which shapes nearly every aspect of our lives —the air we breathe, the water we drink, where we can live, and whom we can love—all shaped by decisions others make on our behalf. Yet, American politics has been reduced to a mindless spectator sport, much like football. Most people don't even know the names of the key players, yet they cheer for their "team" as if watching the Super Bowl. And just like in the NFL, the real winners are the billionaire owners.

Many have grown disillusioned with politics, perhaps because it has failed to solve the nation's problems or meaningfully improve their lives. Social media has carved us into tiny, disconnected bubbles where meaningful participation feels pointless, making us feel disengaged and disinterested in our government.

The United States of America stands at a crossroads. The foundational principles of democracy—government of the people, by the people, for the people—are increasingly undermined by a different set of interests: powerful corporations and wealthy elites who have worked for decades to shift the country from its founding principles to a system ruled by oligarchs. This book explores how corporate influence has permeated American politics, how business elites exert their power, and what this means for our democracy, economy, and the survival of the planet as we know it.

Democracy for sale

"We cannot seek achievement for ourselves and forget about progress and prosperity for our community... Our ambitions must be broad enough to include the aspirations and needs of others, for their sakes and for our own."

Cesar Chavez

Part 1:

History

The Founding Fathers:
A Perfect Union Didn't Include Corporations.

The Founding Fathers of the United States are often celebrated for their vision of a democratic republic built on principles of liberty, justice, and limited centralized power. While much attention is given to their debates on government structure and individual rights, their views on economic power—particularly corporations—reveal deep-seated skepticism. Why were they wary of corporations, and what were the implications of their views on the early development of the U.S.?

In the late 18th century, corporations were vastly different from today. They were chartered by governments for specific public purposes—such as building infrastructure or engaging in trade—and their activities were heavily regulated. The British East India Company, with its enormous power and influence, served as a cautionary tale. This semi-governmental entity not only controlled vast territories but also had its own private army and played a significant role in colonial exploitation. The abuses and corruption associated with such corporate power were fresh in the minds of American revolutionaries.

The Founding Fathers were influenced by Enlightenment thinkers who warned about the dangers of concentrated power. Adam Smith, often called the father of modern economics, cautioned against monopolies that could distort markets and harm public interests.

Democracy for sale

Thomas Jefferson was particularly wary of centralized economic power, fearing corporations could become a new form of aristocracy. In 1816, he expressed his hope to "crush in its birth the aristocracy of our monied corporations, which dare already to challenge our government to a trial of strength and bid defiance to the laws of our country." Similarly, James Madison, the "Father of the Constitution," described corporations as "at best a necessary evil only."
These concerns were not just theoretical. President Andrew Jackson saw firsthand the growing influence of corporate power and, in his 1833 message to Congress, questioned whether the American people would govern themselves or "whether the money and power of a great corporation are to be secretly exerted to influence their judgment and control their decisions." Later, in 1888, President Grover Cleveland warned, "Corporations, which should be the carefully restrained creatures of the law and the servants of the people, are fast becoming the people's masters."
Despite early restrictions, corporate power expanded in the 19th century. The Industrial Revolution and legal changes loosened corporate restrictions, shifting economic power from democratic oversight to private interests—a trend that continues today.

These issues are particularly relevant now with billions of corporate dollars flowing to our politicians.
The Concerns of the Founding Fathers can be boiled down to five major issues:

Concerns About Corporate Power: The Perspective of the Founding Fathers

1. Concentration of Wealth and Power

The Founding Fathers believed that concentrated economic power could lead to concentrated political power, threatening the democratic system they sought to build. Corporations, with their ability to amass substantial wealth, could exert undue influence over government policies and elections. This concern has not only persisted for decades but has been exacerbated by the Supreme Court's radical decision in Citizens United, which allows corporations to contribute unlimited funds to political candidates.

2. Monopolistic Practices

There was a fear that corporations could engage in monopolistic practices, stifling competition and innovation. The concern was that such entities would prioritize profits over public welfare, leading to exploitation and economic inequality. Over the past 50 years, consolidation in major industries—including oil and gas, groceries, insurance, and healthcare—has dramatically reduced competition and driven price increases.

3. Lack of Accountability

Early corporations were often granted special privileges and limited liability, which could lead to irresponsible behavior. The Founding Fathers worried that corporate leaders, protected from personal liability, might engage in reckless or unethical actions without facing consequences. These concerns have proven prescient, as seen in the banking sector during the Great Recession, when reckless financial practices crashed the global economy, and in environmental disasters caused by chemical and oil companies that have severely damaged ecosystems and public health.

4. Impact on Small Businesses and Farmers

Many Founding Fathers, including Thomas Jefferson and James Madison, championed the agrarian ideal, valuing the independence of small farmers and businesses. They feared that corporations could dominate markets, making it difficult for small enterprises to survive. Today, a handful of large agribusinesses control much of the food supply and receive the bulk of federal subsidies while failing to adequately protect the public from food-borne illness outbreaks.

5. Corruption and Influence

The potential for corruption and undue influence was a major concern. Corporations could use their financial power to bribe officials and manipulate legislation in their favor, undermining the integrity of the democratic process. Recent pro-corporate rulings by the Supreme Court have made prosecuting corruption more difficult, with some legal experts arguing that these decisions have effectively legalized bribery and entrenched "pay-to-play" politics.

Historical Responses and Evolving Corporate Power

In response to these concerns, the Founding Fathers and early legislators imposed strict regulations on corporations. Charters were granted sparingly and for limited durations, corporate activities were closely monitored, and stringent rules were implemented to prevent monopolistic practices. Many states even included constitutional provisions to restrict corporate power and influence.

Democracy for sale

Despite these early restrictions, the landscape of American business and corporate power began to shift in the 19th century. The Industrial Revolution brought significant economic changes, leading to the rise of large corporations. Over time, legal and political developments loosened many of the original restrictions on corporate activity. However, the Founding Fathers 'skepticism was rooted in a desire to protect the young republic from the dangers of concentrated economic power and inequality. Their concerns about monopolistic practices, lack of accountability, and the potential for corruption reflect a cautious approach to balancing economic power with democratic principles. While the role of corporations in America has evolved dramatically since the 18th century, their warnings remain relevant in contemporary discussions about corporate regulation and economic justice. Their vision serves as a reminder of the need to remain vigilant against threats to the democratic ideals upon which the United States was built.

> *"If men were angels, no government would be necessary".*
> *James Madison*

It's a Tea Party
The British East India Company

The Boston Tea Party of December 16, 1773, remains one of the most iconic acts of defiance in American history. This event—marked by American colonists dumping British tea into Boston Harbor—was not merely a spontaneous protest but the culmination of growing tensions between the American colonies and the British Crown. At the heart of this conflict was the British East India Company (EIC), a powerful commercial entity whose actions and policies inadvertently became a catalyst for revolutionary fervor.

The British East India Company: A Global Powerhouse

Founded in 1600, the British East India Company (EIC) was granted a monopoly on English trade in the East Indies. Over time, it evolved from a commercial trading venture into a quasi-governmental entity with its own private army, governing vast territories in India. By the 18th century, the EIC controlled much of the tea trade between Asia and Europe, making it an economic powerhouse deeply tied to British imperial interests.

As tea became a popular commodity in Britain and its American colonies, its consumption symbolized not just a daily ritual but social status and British identity. However, the EIC faced financial difficulties in the 1760s and 1770s due to military expenditures in India and fluctuating demand for its products.

Colonial Resistance and the Tea Act

To understand the Boston Tea Party, one must consider the broader context of colonial resistance to British taxation. The end of the Seven Years 'War in 1763 left Britain with massive war debts, prompting Parliament to impose new taxes on its American colonies. The Stamp Act of 1765 and the Townshend Acts of 1767 were met with widespread protests and boycotts, as colonists resented being taxed without representation in Parliament.

The colonial mantra of "no taxation without representation" encapsulated their grievance. Colonists argued that, lacking direct representation in the British Parliament, they should not be subjected to its taxes. This principle fueled a growing sense of American identity and resistance to British authority.

In an effort to rescue the struggling East India Company and reinforce British control over the colonies, Parliament passed the Tea Act in May 1773. This Act allowed the EIC to sell surplus tea directly to the American colonies, bypassing colonial merchants and eliminating duties on tea exported to America. In essence, it was a tax cut for the EIC, giving it a significant advantage over other tea importers.

While this may have seemed beneficial to consumers, colonial merchants and citizens saw it as a direct attack on economic fairness. The Tea Act symbolized everything the colonies despised about British rule: taxation without representation and the intertwining of corporate and governmental power. To put it in modern terms, it was akin to granting Starbucks a massive tax break while raising taxes on all other coffee sellers—essentially handing the EIC a near-monopoly over the tea market.

The Boston Tea Party: A Bold Act of Defiance

Tensions were particularly high in Boston, where resistance to British policies was strong. The Sons of Liberty, a radical group led by figures like Samuel Adams and John Hancock, orchestrated protests and boycotts against the Tea Act, warning that any attempt to unload British tea would be met with fierce opposition.

The Boston Tea Party was not just a routine protest—it was a dramatic and calculated act of defiance. On the night of December 16, 1773, a group of colonists, disguised (poorly) as Mohawk Indians, boarded three British East India Company ships in Boston Harbor. They proceeded to dump 342 chests of British tea—worth approximately £10,000 (millions in today's dollars)—into the harbor. While it may sound like a wild tea party gone awry, this was a deliberate demonstration against corporate greed and government overreach.

British Retaliation and the Road to Revolution

The destruction of the tea shocked the British government, which responded swiftly and harshly. In 1774, Parliament passed the Coercive Acts—known in the colonies as the Intolerable Acts—to punish Massachusetts and reassert control. These included:

- **The Boston Port Act**, which closed Boston Harbor until the East India Company was compensated for the lost tea.
- **The Massachusetts Government Act,** curtailed self-governance in the colony.

Rather than quelling dissent, these measures galvanized colonial resistance. The colonies convened the First Continental Congress in September 1774 to coordinate a unified response, calling for a boycott of British goods and organizing militias. Instead of suppressing rebellion, Britain's heavy-handed response united the colonies and accelerated the push toward revolution—a classic case of unintended consequences.

The Lasting Legacy of the Tea Party

The Boston Tea Party and the British East India Company are forever linked in the narrative of American independence. The EIC, a symbol of British economic power, found itself at the center of colonial resistance. The Tea Party was not just about tea—it was about governance, economic control, and the right to self-determination. It demonstrated the lengths to which American colonists were willing to go to defend their principles against unchecked corporate and governmental power, ultimately paving the way for the birth of a new nation.

Just as the colonists resisted corporate influence through the Tea Party, modern America faces similar battles against corporate dominance in politics and the economy. The fight against concentrated economic power continues, proving that the lessons of the Boston Tea Party remain relevant to this day.

The Gilded Age
Industrialization and Corporate Power

The rise of Corporate tyranny in America:
The intricate dance between corporations and American politics is as old as the republic itself. While the term "corporate influence" might evoke images of modern-day lobbying and campaign finance, its roots are deeply embedded in the nation's history. From the early days of the American Revolution to the contemporary political landscape, corporations have consistently wielded substantial influence over the nation's political and economic directions.

The influence of corporations on American politics may have been at a high point during the Gilded Age of the late 19th century, when industrial magnates like John D. Rockefeller and Andrew Carnegie wielded enormous economic and political power. Using their money and influence to pressure politicians to pass favorable legislation in the hope to inoculate them from any laws or regulations..

After the 14th Amendment, ratified in 1868, significantly expanded civil rights protections, lawyers for the Southern Pacific Railroad Co. tried to use it to avoid a tax assessed by Santa Clara County, Calif. Southern Pacific said it was a person under the 14th Amendment and the tax on railroad property was not equal because it was not assessed to other persons, which violated its rights.

The case went to the Supreme Court, which in 1886 ruled in favor of the railroad based on California law, not on the premise that a corporation is a person under the Constitution.

What followed was a slew of Supreme Court cases in which big corporations demanded constitutional rights. They were trying to protect themselves from increasing calls to break up monopolies, ban corporate giving to politicians, and protect workers and the environment.

Still, the power of corporations, particularly monopolies or trusts, continued to grow. The 19th century witnessed the rapid growth of industrial capitalism, which significantly expanded corporate influence in American politics. The era of the "Robber Barons" saw industrial magnates like John D. Rockefeller, Andrew Carnegie, and J.P. Morgan amass unprecedented wealth and power. These industrialists wielded considerable influence over political decisions, often ensuring favorable legislation and government policies through lobbying and other means.

One notable example is the establishment of the Standard Oil monopoly by Rockefeller, which was supported by favorable state laws and railroad rebates. The political clout of such corporations often led to regulatory capture, where industries effectively controlled the agencies meant to regulate them. This period also saw the rise of powerful lobbying organizations and trade associations, further entrenching corporate power in the political sphere.

The 20th Century:
Pushing Back on Corporate Power

The turn of the 20th century marked the beginning of the Progressive Era, a time of significant social and political reform aimed at curbing corporate excesses. The public outcry against corporate monopolies and political corruption led to landmark legislation, such as the Sherman Antitrust Act of 1890, which sought to break up monopolies and restore competitive markets.

In 1901 President Theodore Roosevelt took on corporations which earned him the nickname "trust buster". He was able to pass legislation banning on corporate political contributions as well as measures prohibiting misleading labels and harmful chemicals. Roosevelt aggressively pursued antitrust cases against major corporations, including Standard Oil and the Northern Securities Company.

At the time, progressive era reformers were demanding an end to the practice of children as young as two years old working in textile mills, factories, and mines. The business community fought against reforms, not by claiming that child labor was "great" but by constructing an argument about freedom. They claimed, "If you let the government tell businesspeople what to do, it would encroach on their freedom to run their businesses" and deprive fathers of the right to raise their children in the way they wanted.

In 1913, Citizens of both parties came together to pass the 17th Amendment requiring that the people directly elect U.S. senators.

Prior to that, senators were appointed by state legislatures, a process rife with corporate influence. President Woodrow Wilson, from 1913 to 1921, and Franklin Roosevelt, from 1933 to 1945, passed more regulations limiting corporate power. During Roosevelt's term, Supreme Court Justice Hugo Black struck down the idea that corporations are people with rights under the Constitution. After that, corporate personhood was a dead issue for decades, until 2010 when the Robert's Court, under chief justice John Roberts, issued the "Citizen's United" decision, reviving the "zombie" idea.

Even though Presidents Roosevelt and Woodrow Wilson championed progressive reforms, targeting the undue influence of corporations, despite their efforts, the incestuous relationship between corporations and politics persisted, adapting to new regulatory landscapes.

The New Deal:
Post-War: Corporate-State Symbiosis

On the surface, everything was great in the summer of 1929. The total wealth of the United States had almost doubled during the Roaring Twenties, fueled, in part, by stock market speculation. When the bubble burst in spectacular fashion in October 1929, and the decade-long Great Depression that followed, most viewed the banks as victims not culprits. The familiar narrative places banks among the institutions that suffered fallout from the crisis. In fact, the crisis was all about the banks—from the central bank (the Fed itself), down to the smallest savings institutions.

The runaway speculation that triggered the 1929 crash and the Great Depression that followed couldn't have taken place without the banks, which fueled the 1920s credit boom. New businesses— making new products like automobiles, radios and refrigerators— borrowed to support non-stop expansion in output. They kept it up even as business inventories soared and Americans 'wages stagnated. The banks, ignored the warning signs, and kept subsidizing them.

The banks also funded the speculation itself, providing the money to investors needed to buy stocks on margin. Bank lenders discounted or downplayed growing signs that Americans were overstretched. Farm incomes, in particular, plunged in the years leading up to 1929, and others found their wages stagnant. By 1933, the wave of bank failures forced the newly elected president, Franklin D. Roosevelt, to declare a four-day banking "holiday" while Congress debated and passed the Emergency Banking Act, which formed the basis of the 1933 Banking Act, or Glass-Steagall Act. Legislators required banks to join the Federal Reserve system and approved the creation of deposit insurance, so that future bank failures couldn't wreak havoc on family savings.

The Great Depression and the New Deal of the 1930s further reshaped the relationship between corporations and the American government. President Franklin D. Roosevelt's New Deal policies which aimed to stabilize the economy and provide relief to those affected by the Depression, lead to increased government intervention in the economy. This period saw the creation of numerous regulatory agencies and social safety nets, fundamentally expanding the role of the federal government to protect the public from reckless corporations.

Despite initial resistance, many corporations adapted to this new regulatory environment and found ways to influence it. The wartime economy of the 1940s further cemented many partnerships between the government and large corporations, as industries ramped up production to support the war effort. The post-war era saw unprecedented economic growth, with corporations playing a central role in shaping domestic and foreign policies. Even with a high marginal tax rate, this became a renaissance for corporations, largely shaping American life with a free hand. The Oligarchs were back!

Then came Earth Day 1970...
Across America 20 million people took to the streets to demand that corporations stop polluting the air, soil and water and destroying wildlife, forests and rivers. Within a few years, with bipartisan support, Congress created the Environmental Protection Agency and passed the Clean Water Act, the Endangered Species Act, the Toxic Substances Control Act and many others.

In 1971, a corporate lawyer from Virginia, Lewis Powell, whose client was the U.S. Chamber of Commerce, outlined a plan for how corporations could strike back. Powell, a director of several international corporations including the Philip Morris cigarette manufacturer, wrote a memo to the Chamber saying corporations had to organize and plan long term and pool their money. Most significantly, corporations had to find "activist" Supreme Court judges to grant them rights, Powell's memo said.

In 1972, President Richard Nixon appointed Powell to the U.S. Supreme Court.

Corporations did what Powell recommended. The U.S. Chamber of Commerce established a National Chamber Litigation Center. Corporate executives funded "legal foundations" around the country, such as the "Federalist Society" to pound their message into every court -- that "the Constitution gives corporations the same rights as people" in fact, they would be "Super People" in that they never die. Finally, in 2010, the Supreme Court decreed just that.
It overturned decades of campaign-finance laws and ruled that Citizens United, a Virginia corporation that advances conservative causes, could air an anti-Hillary Clinton documentary during the 2008 presidential race, which until then violated campaign finance laws. But the court didn't stop there. It said that corporations, in protection of their free speech rights, may contribute <u>unlimited</u> "independent expenditures" to candidates' Super PACs.

Now, in the 2024 presidential election, money is flooding into Super PACs to pay for the campaigns and television ads of the corporations chosen candidates. A few billionaires spent more than 400 million dollars in the effort to elect Donald Trump.

The Modern Era:
Corporate Political Influence in the 21st Century

The formalization of corporate political influence began in earnest in the 20th century, with significant milestones such as the formation of political action committees (PACs) and the lobbying industry's growth.

The late 20th and early 21st centuries have seen a dramatic escalation in corporate political influence, driven by changes in campaign finance laws and the rise of lobbying. The landmark Supreme Court case Citizens United v. Federal Election Commission (2010) significantly altered the landscape of political spending, allowing corporations and other entities to spend unlimited amounts on political campaigns through independent expenditures.

This decision has led to the proliferation of Super Political Action Committees (Super PACs) and dark money organizations, which can raise and spend vast sums of money with little transparency. Corporations now wield enormous power in shaping political agendas, funding campaigns, and influencing policy through lobbying efforts.

Today, corporate influence in American politics manifests in various ways, including lobbying, campaign contributions, and regulatory capture. Major industries, such as finance, pharmaceuticals, energy, and technology, have significant sway over legislative and regulatory processes. This influence often leads to policies that favor corporate interests, sometimes at the expense of public welfare and our democratic principles.

This imbalance undermines the democratic process, as corporations can exert more influence than individual citizens or grassroots organizations. Issues such as climate change, healthcare, and economic inequality are often shaped by corporate interests, highlighting the ongoing tension between public good and private profit.

The influence of corporations on American politics is not a new phenomenon; it is a deeply entrenched aspect of our nation's history. From the early days of the republic to the modern era, corporations have exerted influence in shaping political and economic landscapes. While efforts to curb corporate power have met with varying degrees of success, the dynamic relationship between corporate interests and political authority continues to evolve. Understanding this historical context is crucial for addressing the very real challenges of creating a more balanced and equitable political-financial system.

"What is government itself but the greatest of all reflections on human nature?"

James Madison

The Great Myth of Free Markets:
The Brain Washing of America.

During the 1920's when the people began demanding that government force business to clean up it's act, there were a group of people, very rich, and powerful people, who were crafting plans to gaslight the people into believing that the so called "free market" and unrestricted capitalism were the only way to have a free country. After the deadly industrial age, where as much as six percent of the workers were dying each year in work place accidents, where children as young as three were put to work in factories and the widows and families were left on the streets if they didn't have family to support them. Those that didn't die on the job would often succumb to diseases such as "Black Lung" from the coal mines or other chronic illness from toxic exposure. European countries began to mitigate these problems with insurance programs paid for by taxes on the companies, but America was slow to catch on, but it did eventually begin to act and regulation of capitalism's worst impulses became popular as it saved lives and provided for fairer working conditions and better wages. Unions were once suppressed by company executives often with the help of hired thugs (strike breakers) as well as the local police forces, but with the help of laws designed to protect workers rights, the working class began to have the power to demand change. The American people rested some power away from corporations and we saw the greatest expansion of the middle class in our history. In short, unrestrained capitalism was bad for the people and for the country and people realized that only through collective action could we all have healthy, happy and productive lives and that the shared economy added great wealth not only to the people but to the companies as well, but that was not good enough for the Titans of Industry.

In the early 20th century, Ludwig von Mises, a noted Austrian economist and historian, issued a sharp critique of the Soviet central planning system and argued in favor of limiting the government's economic role. Mises concluded that "any kind of centralized planning is going to devolve into a totalitarian state." A protégé and colleague of Mises was Austrian-British economist and Nobel Prize winner Friedrich von Hayek who advanced the idea of free market capitalism with his publication of the 1944 book titled, The Road to Serfdom. He won rave reviews in Britain and the United States when he argued against socialist economic policies and claimed the government would inhibit rather than promote freedom. The businessmen who brought Hayek to the U.S. were excited by his message, but they thought it was too sophisticated for an American audience. It also contained a number of exceptions to the argument against government intervention, identifying the benefits of the government regulating pollution and deforestation, ensuring sanitary working conditions, and the need for social security. He allowed for a rather wide space for government action and that didn't fit the narrative these businessmen wanted to portray. So when the Reader's Digest version of the book was published in 1945 for a consumer audience "they stripped out all of the caveats, all of the exceptions, and [sections] where Hayek says you actually do need government, creating a false impression of the book's meaning. During the late 1940s and early 1950s, a small group of pro-free market businessmen funded the Free Market Study project at the University of Chicago's School of Law and Economics. Adam Smith's Wealth of Nations, first published in 1776 received a similar treatment with Economist George Stigler given the task of producing a revised edition of Smith's seminal book. Adam Smith had a very extensive discussion in The Wealth of Nations on the need for banking regulation and noted why you cannot have a successful capitalist economy unless you regulate banks for all the reasons we are familiar with today. There are sections in The Wealth of Nations on why workers have to be paid fair wages and why it's reasonable for workers to have "collective agency" (unionize), and how factory owners would pay starvation wages if they could get away with it. All of that is removed from the Chicago School's version of Adam Smith's book.

The shift in America's economic and political thought began to take hold in the 1920s when leaders in the electricity industry successfully waged a massive propaganda campaign to fight government involvement in electricity markets by making the case of 'creeping socialism 'and 'a threat to the American way of life. '

Thus began the project to convince people they had to choose between "Free Market" Capitalism or a soviet style organized economy.
Beginning in the early 20th century American business interests, such as the National Associations of Merchants, sought to influence public opinion through educational content, twisting curriculum to promote "free market" capitalism. Business leaders and conservative think tanks launched a systematic campaign to promote this ideology, largely as a response to the increasing popularity of progressive ideas and New Deal policies, which business leaders viewed as threats to their economic interests. These efforts have been instrumental in shaping the economic and political landscape of the United States today.

One of the primary strategies employed was infiltrating the education system. Businesses and their advocates recognized that shaping the beliefs of young people was crucial for the long-term success of their agenda. They provided funding and resources to schools and universities, often with strings attached that ensured the promotion of pro-market narratives.

Democracy for sale

In the 1930's the electricity industry hired academics to rewrite the textbooks that were being used in American high schools and colleges. The goal was to influence the curricula in burgeoning business schools to be pro-market, pro-capitalist, anti-regulation and anti-government. Very early on we begin to see the overt misrepresentation of American history with the "Tripod of Freedom" campaign. They asserted that America was founded on three essential principles that are like a tripod, and if you undermine any leg of the tripod, the whole structure will collapse. The three legs are representative democracy, the Bill of Rights, and free enterprise, or capitalism.

Corporate-funded foundations and think tanks played a significant role in the development and dissemination of educational materials that emphasized the virtues of the "free market". Textbooks and curricula were often influenced or directly produced by these entities, embedding pro-business perspectives within educational content. These materials frequently downplayed or ignored the negative aspects of capitalism, such as economic inequality and environmental degradation, while portraying government intervention in the economy as inherently problematic. They also sought to influence teachers and scholars by offering grants, fellowships, and other incentives. By funding academic research and rewarding educators who promoted these ideas, even when they contradicted the facts, businesses ensured that pro-market ideology gained legitimacy within academic circles.

Public-private partnerships became another avenue through which businesses influenced education. Corporations sponsored educational programs and initiatives that aligned with their interests, further embedding their perspectives in the educational system. These partnerships were often framed as benevolent efforts to improve education but served the dual purpose of promoting corporate agendas.

This was an extensive and multifaceted campaign by American business interests to influence educational content and public perception in favor of free market capitalism. Through strategic investments in schools, universities, and educational materials, as well as the cultivation of influential academic and teaching figures, businesses have succeeded in embedding a pro-market ideology deeply within American society. This propaganda campaign contributed to skepticism and opposition towards government regulation and intervention, regardless of the potential benefits such actions might offer. This has had lasting implications for economic policies and the role of government, often to the detriment of addressing broader societal issues such as inequality and environmental sustainability.

The cumulative effect of these efforts has been a widespread acceptance of free market capitalism as the optimal economic system in the United States, which has led to the entrenchment of policies that favor business interests at the expense of broader societal well-being.

Free Market Fundamentalism reached new heights in the modern political era under U.S. President Ronald Reagan and British Prime

Democracy for sale

Minister Margaret Thatcher, both advocating staunchly pro-business, anti-government policies. Thatcher was very influenced by Hayek, her famous phrase "There-Is-No-Alternative", encapsulates this whole argument that there is no alternative; that it's either communist dictatorship or unregulated capitalism.

Looking back at the history of capitalism, you can see that it has changed significantly from the days of Adam Smith. "The capitalism of small shop owners imagined at the time was very different from the managerial and monopolistic capitalism of the nineteenth century, and that of the manufacturing-based capitalism of mid-20th century America, which is extremely different from the globally financed capitalism of today. Later in the book we'll explore how capitalism has been confused and conflated with democracy and that of communism and socialism with totalitarianism.

*Sources: The Big Myth: How American business taught us to loathe government and love the free market By Naomi Oreskes and Erik M Conway, The Guardian, The Washington Post.

"The larger the group, the more toxic, the more of your beauty as an individual you have to surrender for the sake of group thought. And when you suspend your individual beauty you also give up a lot of your humanity. You will do things in the name of a group that you would never do on your own. Injuring, hurting, killing, are all part of it, because you've lost your identity, because you now owe your allegiance to this thing that's bigger than you are and that controls you."

George Carlin

What is a Corporation?
Are Corporations Really People?

The notion that corporations are people has been a contentious topic in legal, economic, and philosophical debates for over a century. Rooted in the concept of corporate personhood, this idea grants corporations some of the same legal rights and responsibilities as individuals. However, arguing that corporations are fundamentally the same as human beings oversimplifies the complex nature of both entities and overlooks critical distinctions that have profound implications for society.

Corporate personhood, a novel legal theory, promoted by, you guessed it, corporations, emerged from the desire to facilitate business interests and protect individual stakeholders from risk. In the 19th century, the U.S. Supreme Court shot down this idea in Santa Clara County v. Southern Pacific Railroad (1886) but is often misinterpreted as recognizing corporations as people under the Fourteenth Amendment. The law allows corporations to enter contracts, sue and be sued, own property, and enjoy certain constitutional protections. These measures were intended to promote economic growth and stability by providing a clear framework for corporate activity.

These are some of the Legal and Practical Distinctions:
1. Rights and Responsibilities: Unlike human beings, corporations do not possess intrinsic rights but rather a set of privileges conferred by law (corporate charter). These privileges are designed to serve specific economic and social purposes, such as enabling collective

business ventures and protecting investments. Human rights, conversely, are inherent and recognized universally as fundamental to dignity and liberty.

2. Moral Agency and Accountability: Corporations lack the moral agency that characterizes human beings. While individuals within a corporation can make ethical or unethical decisions, the corporation itself operates on legal and economic imperatives. Holding a corporation morally accountable in the same way as an individual blurs the lines of responsibility and dilutes the concept of personal accountability.

3. Lifespan and Continuity: A corporation can exist indefinitely, far beyond the lifespan of any individual human. This perpetual existence allows corporations to accumulate power and resources in ways that are unattainable for individuals. It also means that corporations can outlast any single person's ability to control or influence them, leading to potential issues with long-term accountability and governance.

Economic and Social Implications:

1. Power and Influence: Corporations wield immense power in modern economies, often surpassing that of individual citizens and even some governments. Their ability to lobby, influence legislation, and impact public policy raises concerns about democratic governance and equity. When corporations are treated as people, their disproportionate power can distort the political and economic landscape, marginalizing the voices of actual human beings. The enforcement of Anti-Trust laws have become rare and corporate

consolidation has allowed for the rise of "multi-national" corporations that are richer than many nations and have all but eliminated competition. Have we learned nothing from the "Gilded Age"?

2. Wealth Accumulation and Inequality: The resources and capital that corporations can amass contribute significantly to economic inequality. Unlike human beings, corporations can continuously grow and expand their wealth, leading to a concentration of economic power that exacerbates disparities in income and opportunity. This dynamic undermines the social contract and challenges the notion of a fair and just society. The founding fathers instituted the "Estate Tax" to prohibit inherited wealth from accumulating and challenging the elected government. The "conservative" side of our politics have successfully chipped away at this by falsely labeling it a "death" tax. Every person dies, but only the wealthiest are subject to the Estate tax.

3. Environmental and Social Responsibility: Corporate personhood complicates efforts to hold corporations accountable for environmental degradation and social harm. While individuals within the corporation rarely face penalties, the entity itself can continue its operations, sometimes with minimal repercussions. Often the penalties are considered just a cost of doing business and regulatory capture ensures that laws that would actually deter bad behavior never comes to pass. This separation of individual and collective accountability impedes genuine progress toward sustainability and ethical business practices. With increased destruction due to climate

change there are serious social and economic repercussions for the "slap on the wrist" policies toward corporate polluters.

Ethical and Philosophical Considerations

1. Intrinsic Value: Humans possess intrinsic value based on their capacity for consciousness, emotional experience, and moral reasoning. Corporations, however, are artificial constructs designed to serve specific functions. Equating the two devalues human life and experience by suggesting that an entity created for economic purposes can hold equivalent status to a human being. The prime directive of corporate executives is the increase shareholder value which often supersedes human decency and may reduce the value of human life to a dollar amount.

2. Moral Obligation: The ethical obligations of human beings stem from their inherent dignity and capacity for moral judgment. Corporations, lacking these qualities, cannot fulfill moral obligations in the same way. Assigning human-like status to corporations shifts moral and ethical considerations away from individual human experiences and towards abstract entities, which can dilute the moral fabric of society. We see this clearly in industries such as weapons manufacturing, oil and gas, as well as the health care industry. The morality of "profit" take precedent over human safety and decency.

3. Community and Social Bonds: Human beings are social creatures, forming communities and relationships that provide emotional and social support. Corporations, by contrast, are primarily transactional entities driven by profit motives, and function operationally as dictatorship. Confusing the two undermines the importance of social

bonds and community well-being, which are essential for a healthy society. Which may explain why they have been so insistence on referring to us as consumers rather than citizens.

Corporations are clearly not people. They are powerful, legally constructed entities that society grants to certain businesses to facilitate aspects of our economy but lack the intrinsic qualities that define human beings. Recognizing the distinction between corporations and people is crucial for ensuring that our legal, economic, and social systems remain just and equitable. By rejecting the idea of corporate personhood and reaffirming the unique value of human beings, we can build a society that better balances economic progress with the well-being of all its members and honors the spirit of our founding fathers.

Understanding Corporate Charters

This section is a bit dry but it serves to point out that corporations only live on paper, they are not people.

A corporate charter, also known as the articles of incorporation or certificate of incorporation, is a legal document that establishes a corporation as a separate legal entity from its owners. This chapter delves into the intricacies of corporate charters, their significance, the process of creating one, and the essential components they typically contain.

1. Definition and Purpose of a Corporate Charter
A corporate charter is essentially the birth certificate of a corporation. It is filed with a state government, usually the Secretary of State, and marks the legal inception of the corporation. The charter serves several critical purposes:
Legal Recognition: It grants the corporation a legal identity, allowing it to enter into contracts, sue and be sued, own assets, and conduct business.
Regulatory Compliance: It ensures that the corporation complies with state laws governing corporate entities.
Framework for Operation: It outlines the basic structure and governance of the corporation, including the roles and responsibilities of directors and officers.

2. The Process of Creating a Corporate Charter
Creating a corporate charter involves several steps, which may vary slightly depending on the jurisdiction. However, the general process includes:
Choosing a State: Corporations can choose to incorporate in any state. Many opt for Delaware due to its business-friendly laws and well-established legal precedents.
Drafting the Charter: The corporation's founders or their legal representatives draft the charter, including all required information.
Filing with the State: The completed charter is submitted to the appropriate state office, usually along with a filing fee.
State Review and Approval: The state reviews the charter to ensure it meets all legal requirements. Once approved, the corporation is officially recognized as a legal entity.

3. Essential Components of a Corporate Charter

While the specifics can vary by state, most corporate charters contain the following key elements:

a. Corporate Name

The name of the corporation must be unique and comply with state naming requirements, which often include the inclusion of a corporate designation such as "Inc." or "Corporation."

b. Purpose

The charter outlines the general nature of the business. Some states allow a broad statement such as "to engage in any lawful business," while others require a more specific description.

c. Duration

Corporations are typically formed to exist perpetually unless otherwise specified. The charter can include a finite duration if desired.

d. Registered Agent and Office

The charter must designate a registered agent who will receive legal documents on behalf of the corporation. It also specifies the address of the registered office.

e. Incorporators

These are the individuals or entities responsible for the formation of the corporation. Their names and addresses are included in the charter.

f. Stock Information

If the corporation is authorized to issue stock, the charter will detail the types and number of shares, along with any rights and preferences associated with them.

g. Initial Directors

The names and addresses of the initial board of directors may be included, although some states allow this information to be provided in a separate document called the bylaws.

4. Amendments to the Corporate Charter

Over time, a corporation may need to amend its charter to reflect changes such as a new business name, alterations in the number of authorized shares, or modifications to its business purpose. The process for amending a charter typically involves:

Board Approval: The board of directors must approve the proposed amendment.

Shareholder Approval: In many cases, shareholders must also vote to approve the amendment.

Filing with the State: The approved amendment is filed with the state, often with an additional fee.

5. Significance of the Corporate Charter

The corporate charter is a foundational document that serves several critical functions:

Legal Identity: It establishes the corporation as a separate legal entity from its owners, protecting their personal assets from business liabilities.

Operational Framework: It provides a basic governance structure and operational guidelines, ensuring clarity and organization from the outset.

Investor Assurance: By formally documenting the corporation's structure and purpose, the charter provides assurance to investors about the legitimacy and stability of the business.

A corporate charter is much more than a bureaucratic requirement; it is a vital document that lays the groundwork for a corporation's existence and operation. Understanding its components and the process of creating and amending it is essential for anyone involved in forming or managing a corporation. By ensuring compliance with legal requirements and clearly defining the corporation's purpose and structure, a well-crafted charter can significantly contribute to the long-term success and stability of the business.

As you may have noticed, there has been a drastic change in the rules governing corporations from our country's founding.

PART 2:

Governance vs. Economics

Capitalism, Socialism, Communism - Oh my!

People talk a lot these days about the various -isms: *Communism, Socialism, Capitalism*. But there's often little explanation of what these terms actually mean. For decades, they have been used either as a "boogeyman" or as a symbol of ultimate freedom. Let's unpack the facts and debunk some myths.

Economics vs. Government Structure:

Communism, Socialism, and Capitalism are economic systems, not forms of government. However, they are often conflated with political structures, leading to widespread confusion.

Here are some common forms of governance:
- **Democracy** – A Government Voted for by the people.
- **Dictatorship** – Rule by a single leader or small group with absolute power.
- **Oligarchy** – Rule by a few, often the wealthy elite.
- **Parliamentary System** – The legislature (parliament) selects the government.

- **Republic** – A state where power is held by the people and their elected representatives, typically with a president instead of a monarch.
- **Theocracy** – Rule based on religious authority.
- **Totalitarianism** – Centralized control by an autocratic leader or ruling hierarchy.
- **Monarchy** – Rule by a single sovereign (e.g., king or queen), which can be absolute or constitutional.
- **Anarchy** – The absence of government.

When we hear "Communism," we often think of Russia or China. "Socialism" brings up Venezuela and Cuba, but also Scandinavian countries like Denmark and Sweden. And the U.S.? Many assume we are purely capitalist—but the reality is more complex.

The U.S. is structured as a **Constitutionally Governed Democratic Republic**. Russia and China claim to be democratic but are clearly authoritarian. When it comes to their economies, however, their structures are not entirely different from our own.

The Misconception of Economic Systems

Communism is frequently conflated with socialism and then contrasted with democracy and capitalism. However, as discussed in previous chapters, this misrepresentation was historically used to promote pro-business policies.

The confusion partly arises because the term "Communism" has evolved over time. Originally, it referred to an economic theory advocating for "the communal sharing of all resources equally among a group of people." In practice, this system has only existed in small-scale indigenous communities. By this definition, neither Russia nor China were ever truly communist.

Similarly, socialism is often wrongly linked to centralized government planning, as seen in the USSR. This portrayal overlooks how socialism functions in many modern democracies, where it is used to provide essential services without a profit motive.

Here's a simplified breakdown of economic systems:

Communism – The government controls most resources and distributes them equally. This has never been achieved on a large scale, most likely, due to structural challenges and human greed.

Capitalism – Most resources are privately owned. However, pure capitalism doesn't exist because large-scale infrastructure (roads, bridges, etc.) requires public investment, and unchecked capitalism leads to wealth concentration and anti-democratic power structures. (Our founding fathers were skeptical of this because, the more money someone has, the more power they wield.)

Socialism – Exists in various forms between the two. Socialism can be expressed in the level of social spending on the needs of citizens which is seen in most advanced nations today.

How the U.S. Compares to Other Nations

The U.S. leans toward the capitalist end of the spectrum but incorporates significant socialist policies:
National Military, Social Security, Medicare, Fire & police departments, Food assistance programs, and, of course, Corporate welfare subsidies.

By comparison:
Canada is similar to the U.S. but includes universal healthcare.
Britain (UK) & Japan have stronger public services.
Germany, Sweden, Finland, and Denmark have extensive social programs and are consistently ranked among the world's happiest countries.

A **society** is defined as a large group of people living together in an organized way, sharing responsibilities and making collective decisions. By this definition, the U.S. has long been a **Democratic Socialist country**—but with fewer social benefits than other wealthy nations.

Where Do Countries Fall on the Spectrum?

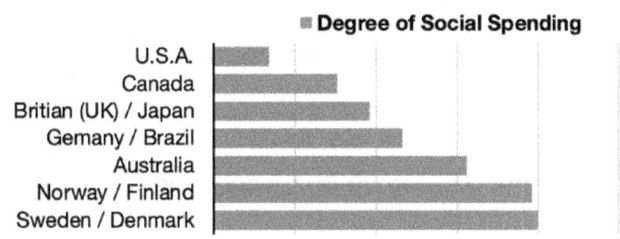

Degree of Spending = Degree of Socialism

Rethinking the Fear of Socialism

Despite paying a significant amount in taxes, Americans receive fewer public benefits than citizens in other developed nations. Countries with tax rates between 38%-55% use collective cooperation and economies of scale to provide universal healthcare, affordable education, maternity care, and elder care. Meanwhile, billionaires and corporations in the U.S. often pay little to no taxes while benefiting from our public infrastructure and receiving billions in subsidies.

So when critics claim that universal healthcare, affordable college, or a living wage would mark the "end of America," they may be victims of a long-standing propaganda campaign—or they may be among those benefiting from an uneven, highly profitable system. Every business uses *"economy of scale"* to drive down costs on goods and services, but the corporate cronies in congress have forbidden the government from doing the same, costing taxpayers much more for medicine, healthcare, transportation and education than any other industrialized country. If corporate billionaires could truly provide a better quality of life for hardworking Americans while saving money, why do they continually demand subsidies? And if capitalism is so efficient, why must we keep bailing out corporations from crises of their own making?

Perhaps it's time to rethink what we fear—and what we aspire to.

The Rise and Fall of Neoliberalism

Neoliberalism, once the dominant force in global economic policy, is now a term often used pejoratively. For about forty years, it was the leading doctrine guiding American and international economic strategies. Neoliberalism is an economic ideology that promotes free market policies, deregulation, privatization, and globalization. While its proponents argue that it promotes economic growth and development, there are several compelling arguments against neoliberalism that suggest it can lead to negative social, economic, and political outcomes. Recent events and intellectual shifts suggest that neoliberalism may be in decline. This chapter explores the evolution of neoliberalism, its impact on global economies, and the factors contributing to its (hopefully) potential fall.

Neoliberalism emerged in the mid-20th century as a response to the perceived failures of state intervention and Keynesian economics. Prominent figures like Milton Friedman and Friedrich Hayek championed the idea that free markets, deregulation, and privatization would lead to economic efficiency and growth. This ideology gained traction in the 1980s under leaders like Ronald Reagan in the United States and Margaret Thatcher in the United

Kingdom, who implemented policies aimed at reducing the role of government in the economy.

During the 1990s and early 2000s, neoliberalism reached its zenith. The Washington Consensus, a set of ten economic policy prescriptions promoting free-market reforms, became the standard framework for international financial institutions like the IMF and the World Bank.
Many countries embraced neoliberal policies, believing that integration into the global market would spur development and reduce poverty.

In the United States, Bill Clinton's administration continued to endorse neoliberal principles, despite being a Democratic president. Policies such as welfare reform and financial deregulation reflected the prevailing belief that markets were more efficient at allocating resources than governments. This era saw significant economic shifts, including financial sector innovations and increased globalization.

These policies emphasized the primacy of the market in solving economic and social problems. Proponents argued that markets, free from government intervention, could allocate resources more efficiently than any centralized planning. This belief extended to various sectors, including finance, where deregulation was seen as a means to foster innovation and growth.

Despite its initial success, neoliberalism began revealing its significant flaws. Critics argued that it exacerbated income inequality, financial instability, and the erosion of social safety nets. The 2008 financial crisis marked a critical turning point, exposing the dangers of deregulated financial markets. The crisis led to massive economic downturns, highlighting the vulnerabilities created by neoliberal policies. Additionally, globalization—a cornerstone of neoliberalism—became increasingly viewed as a double-edged sword. While it facilitated economic growth and lifted millions out of poverty, it also resulted in job losses in developed nations, particularly in manufacturing sectors, and contributed to widening economic disparities.

Neoliberal policies have deepened inequality and economic insecurity. By prioritizing corporate and elite interests over those of ordinary citizens, neoliberalism has contributed to rising income and wealth disparities. Millions struggle to afford basic necessities like healthcare, education, and housing. A striking indicator of economic precarity is that nearly half of Americans cannot cover a $1,000 emergency expense without going into debt.

Moreover, neoliberalism undermines democratic institutions and governance. By promoting deregulation, privatization, and free trade agreements, it limits governments' ability to regulate corporate behavior, protect the environment, and provide social welfare. This weakens democratic processes and curtails citizens 'influence over public policy.

Corporate-centric policies result in environmental devastation and social dislocation. Corporations prioritize economic growth and profit maximization over social and environmental concerns, these policies lead to increased pollution, resource depletion, and climate change with increased oil leases, mining on public lands, and lax enforcement on corporate polluters as seen during the Trump administration. This has negative impacts on the health and well-being of everyone, especially marginalized communities, as well as leading to global dislocation, migration, and conflict.

Neoliberalism also fosters economic instability and crises. By championing deregulation and financialization, it has created volatile economic environments vulnerable to financial collapses. As we saw in 2008, giving the banking industry a "free hand" led to the worst financial crisis since the great depression. The crisis, the worst since the Great Depression, was a direct consequence of these policies. While millions suffered job losses, business failures, and financial hardship, as well as undermined the long-term sustainability and resilience of the economy, but the irony of this was that the very businesses that created the crisis ended up benefitting and making billions of dollars from bailouts and capitalizing on the real estate market that was decimated by their banking "innovations", leading to a massive transfer of wealth from the general public to financial institutions.

The COVID-19 pandemic and recent geopolitical events have further questioned the viability of neoliberalism. The pandemic exposed the fragility of global supply chains and the limitations of market-driven healthcare systems. Governments worldwide were forced to intervene extensively, providing support to businesses and individuals, which ran counter to neoliberal principles of minimal state intervention.

Additionally, shifting geopolitical dynamics signal a departure from neoliberal orthodoxy. The rise of China as a global economic power and events such as Russia's invasion of Ukraine have underscored the strategic risks of economic dependence on foreign corporations. These developments have spurred a renewed interest in rebuilding a national industrial policy, energy independence, and economic liberalism, signaling a departure from neoliberal orthodoxy.

Criticism of neoliberalism spans economic, social, and political dimensions. Its role in exacerbating inequality, undermining democracy, degrading the environment, and fostering financial instability underscores its deep flaws. At its core, neoliberalism is a financial strategy designed to enrich corporate elites at the expense of societal well-being and economic sustainability.

Louis Menand, in his New Yorker article, "The Price is Right," discusses the intellectual and political transformations that have contributed to the waning influence of neoliberalism. He argues that the same market mechanisms that once promised prosperity are now widely recognized as drivers of inequality and instability.

Naomi Oreskes and Erik M. Conway, in their book "*The Big Myth: How American Business Taught Us to Loathe Government and Love the Free Market*" explore how decades of pro-business propaganda have entrenched neoliberal ideas in American culture. They contend that this propaganda has convinced many Americans that neoliberal economics and political freedoms are inseparable, which has complicated efforts to address market failures and public health crises like the COVID-19 pandemic.

The decline of neoliberalism does not imply a clear path forward. The global economy is at a crossroads, grappling with the challenges of inequality, climate change, and geopolitical instability. Whether a post-neoliberal world will emerge, and what it will look like, remains uncertain. What is clear is that the once-dominant ideology of neoliberalism is under intense scrutiny, and its future may be in doubt.

This last chapter emphasized the complex interplay of economic policies, political ideologies, and global events that have shaped our financial trajectory. As we move forward, understanding these dynamics will be crucial in navigating the challenges of the 21st century.

Personal Responsibility but Corporate Welfare

A common refrain from conservative advocates of neoliberalism is that individuals should be self-reliant—pull themselves up by their bootstraps. Yet, these same advocates readily distribute public funds to corporations in the form of subsidies, bailouts, and tax breaks. This contradiction exposes the hypocrisy at the heart of neoliberal ideology: while ordinary citizens are expected to navigate economic hardships alone, corporations receive extensive government support. This corporate welfare system underscores the fundamental inequities of neoliberalism and its failure to create a truly fair and sustainable economy.

TAXES, Uh! - What are they Good For?

Let face it, nobody enjoys paying taxes, we all want to keep what we earn and most of us feel a little violated when we look at our paychecks and see what's been taken by our government. There is a growing sense in the country, especially for the working class, of "what has the government done for me lately?" I'll try to shed some light on that later but for now here's some of the ways that "We the People" spend our money or I should say how politicians spend our money.

This chart breaks down how the federal government allocates its budget. This includes major categories like defense, healthcare, education and more.

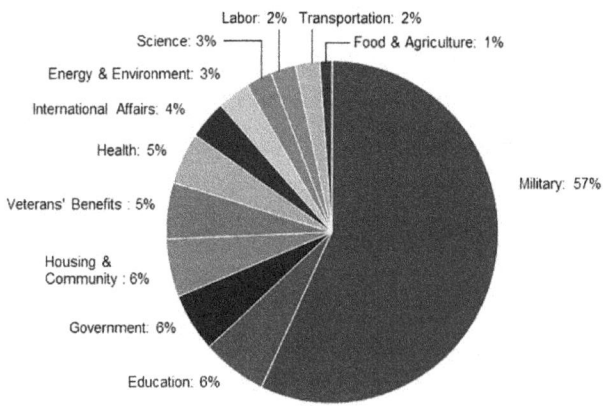

Social Security and Medicare: (social insurance programs)

In fiscal year 2023 we spent $2.4T dollars which was offset by $1.6T in payroll taxes for a total of $800 billion. The discrepancy may be due to pandemic spending, the "baby boomers' hitting retirement age as well as the cap on payroll taxes that largely excludes the wealthy.

Other HealthCare such as Medicaid, CHIP, Etc.

Medicaid, which gives money to the states to provide healthcare for the poorest Americans, cost $616 Billion. Because these funds are administered by individual states, the outcome can vary widely as some of the "conservative" states have a poor track record of delivering services to the needy. We'll discuss fraud and abuse later in the chapter.

Spending on Veterans

In 2023, the federal budget allocated $302 billion to veteran's programs:
Income security programs: $151 billion, including $148 billion for compensation for service-connected disabilities. Mandatory spending: $170 billion and Discretionary spending: $131 billion. VA Medical Care: $119 billion, VA Home Loan Programs: $284 million, Cost of War Toxic Exposures Fund (TEF): $24.5 billion, Armed Forces Retirement Home: $77 million, Court of Appeals for Veterans Claims: $47 million.

Defense:

In FY23 the defense budget was $805 Billion but the DoD's share of available funding was $1.52 trillion, including special allocations for wars. The U.S. spends more each year on the military than the next 10 largest countries combined and is the single largest item in the budget.

Education:

For FY24 the budget was $224 Billion divided into 10 categories, which is only 11% of total education spending when factoring in state education budgets.

There a plenty of worthy things that we should be spending our tax dollars on, but corporate welfare for highly profitable companies is not one of them. In later chapters we'll explore how corporations not only avoid paying taxes but manage to get billions of our tax dollars in subsidies.

Government and Corporations: A Love story.

I find it interesting that "free market" advocates argue the perils of Socialism, yet, at the same time lobbing the government for corporate welfare and handouts. While there are legitimate areas that the government may want to invest to spur innovation or foster change, most of those subsidies go to already highly profitable corporations.

Major oil companies receive significant federal subsidies, which can be categorized into direct subsidies, tax breaks, and other financial benefits. Estimates vary, but here's a broad overview:

1. Direct Subsidies: These are grants or other financial assistance directly from the government. These are generally smaller compared to tax breaks and indirect subsidies.

2. Tax Breaks and Credits: These are more substantial and include various deductions and credits that reduce the overall tax liability of oil companies. Key examples include the following:

   - Percentage Depletion Allowance: Allows companies to deduct a percentage of the revenue from oil and gas wells.
   - Domestic Manufacturing Deduction: Originally intended for all manufacturers, this deduction has been used by oil companies to reduce their taxable income.
   - Intangible Drilling Costs: Allows companies to deduct most costs associated with drilling, which can be 60-80% of the total drilling cost.

3. Other Financial Benefits: These include low-cost leases for drilling on public lands and waters, as well as government-funded research and development.

According to estimates by environmental and economic think tanks, the value of these subsidies and tax breaks can range widely:

- Direct and indirect federal subsidies: Reports suggest the U.S. government provides about $20 billion annually to fossil fuel companies in direct and indirect subsidies. This figure includes the cost of tax breaks and other financial incentives.

- Global Context: When considering state and local subsidies, as well as global figures, the numbers are even higher.

Organizations like the International Monetary Fund (IMF) have estimated that fossil fuel subsidies worldwide amount to over $5 trillion when accounting for externalities like environmental damage and health costs. These subsidies are a topic of significant debate, with many advocating for their reduction or elimination to promote cleaner energy alternatives and reduce greenhouse gas emissions.

Sources:
1. [The International Monetary Fund (IMF)](https://www.imf.org)
2. [The Environmental and Energy Study Institute (EESI)](https://www.eesi.org)

Pharmaceutical companies often derive substantial benefits from publicly funded research in several key ways:

Access to Foundational Research
Publicly funded institutions, such as universities and government research laboratories, conduct fundamental research that lays the groundwork for drug discovery. This research is often too risky or long-term for private companies. By leveraging these foundational studies, pharmaceutical companies exploit public research for private gain.

Reduced Research and Development Costs
Drug companies often rely on publicly funded research. The initial stages of drug discovery, including basic science and early-stage research, are typically the most expensive and time-consuming.

Public funding allows pharmaceutical companies to focus their resources on later-stage development and commercialization.

Access to Cutting-Edge Technology and Knowledge

Publicly funded research institutions often pioneer new technologies and methodologies. Which are then exploited for massive profit returning only a fraction back to the public coffers.

Reduced Financial Risk

Drug development is inherently risky, when promising treatments emerge from publicly funded research, pharmaceutical companies can reap the profits, knowing that most of the scientific and financial risks have been mitigated.

Examples of Successful Drugs from Publicly Funded Research

Many blockbuster drugs have their origins in publicly funded research. For instance, the development of the HIV/AIDS drug AZT was significantly supported by research funded by the NIH. Similarly, the cancer drug Taxol (paclitaxel) was discovered and developed through a partnership involving the NIH and various academic institutions and The Moderna mRNA Vaccine was developed through the NIH and other publicly fund organizations.

The parasitic relationship between pharmaceutical companies and publicly funded research underscores the importance of continued investment in public science. Pharmaceutical companies reap substantial benefits from this situation, society benefits from the development of innovative treatments but at high cost. One of the darker aspects of development of pharmaceuticals is that the tend to be focused on the treatment of, rather than curing diseases because that provides more long term profit potential. Ensuring that publicly funded research benefits the general public and not just Big Pharma is a critical challenge for policymakers who unfortunately receive large amounts of campaign donations from the industry.

Other top corporate recipients of federal subsidies in the U.S. span various industries, primarily in energy, automotive, and aerospace sectors. According to reports from *Good Jobs First* and other sources, these companies have received significant federal grants and tax credits since 2000.

1. Iberdrola: A Spanish energy company, Iberdrola is the largest single recipient of federal grants and tax credits, having received nearly $2.2 billion, primarily for investments in U.S. power generation facilities.

2. NextEra Energy: This American energy company has received approximately $1.9 billion in federal subsidies.

3. NRG Energy: Another significant player in the energy sector, NRG Energy has secured about $1.7 billion in federal support.

4. Southern Company: This major American gas and electric utility holding company has received around $1.5 billion in subsidies.

5. Summit Power and SCS Energy: These companies have each received over $1.2 billion for their contributions to energy projects.

In addition to these top recipients, companies like Duke Energy, General Electric, Exelon, and others have also received substantial federal support, each receiving hundreds of millions of dollars in grants and tax credits.

Furthermore, Boeing has been a major beneficiary of state and local subsidies, totaling $13 billion, and has also been a significant recipient of federal subsidies. Other notable companies benefiting from both state and federal subsidies include General Motors, Ford Motor, and General Electric, and Tesla.

These subsidies are typically aimed at encouraging investment in specific sectors such as renewable energy, automotive innovation, and aerospace development. So if the "free market" works so well why are we subsidizing already profitable companies and should we really have to pay companies to do the right thing?

Some examples of other federal corporate welfare programs.

Market Access Program. This program hands out about $200 million annually to help pay for the marketing costs of certain farm products. Some of the recipients include the Brewers Association, the Pet Food Institute, Sunkist Growers, Welch's Food, and the Wine Institute. I wonder why food prices are still so high.

Advanced Technology Program. This program, which costs more than $100 million annually, gives grants to companies for technology research. Some of these are worthy investment but much of the money goes to things such as The Advanced Pharmaceutical Manufacturing (APM), Wind Power Electrical programs that the companies will profit from for decades, leaving the public to foot the bill.

Foreign Military Financing. U.S. taxpayers fund the purchases of weapons by foreign governments through this program, which costs more than $4 billion annually.

Export-Import Bank. This agency helps finance the foreign purchase of U.S. goods, and it has been involved in numerous scandals. For example, it backed the risky overseas ventures of Enron Corporation and it has provided $243 million in loans to bogus Mexican companies, including drug cartels. Again this is a round about way of giving our tax dollars to corporations.

Additionally the Government provides loan guarantees that cover $1.3 trillion dollars primarily to corporations. When these companies go bust, we pay the bill.

As these examples illustrate, corporate welfare comes in many flavors. All in all, the federal government spends an estimated $92 billion annually on corporate welfare. Imagine what that money could do if it were invested in education.

PART 3:

Government - It's a Family Affair

"Liberty may be endangered by the abuse of liberty, but also by the abuse of power."
James Madison

How the Trump Family Cashed In: A Masterclass in Rigging the System.

Ah, the art of the deal—only this time, the deal is democracy itself. The Trump family's financial escapades have been under the microscope for years, with watchdog groups, such as Citizens for Responsibility and Ethics in Washington (CREW), Public Citizen, and journalists tirelessly exposing their alleged habit of turning public office into a private ATM. From shady business dealings to eyebrow-raising international transactions, the Trumps have seemingly treated the presidency like a golden business opportunity—one where the customers (a.k.a. taxpayers) don't get a refund.

Of course, let's not pretend this is a Trump-exclusive phenomenon. Corruption in politics is as American as apple pie. Take Democratic Sen. Robert Menendez, for example—currently starring in his own bribery scandal. And thanks to some creative legal acrobatics by the Supreme Court, prosecuting political corruption is harder than ever.

Democracy for sale

But for now, let's use the 45th president as our case study in how to blur the lines between public service and personal enrichment.

When Donald Trump took office in January 2017, he did not fully divest from his business empire, the Trump Organization. Instead, he transferred control to his sons, Donald Trump Jr. and Eric Trump, while retaining ownership. This arrangement led to numerous conflicts of interest as the Trump Organization continued to operate and expand its business ventures domestically and internationally.

According to CREW, the Trump Organization has benefited from a continuous flow of money from political events, foreign governments, and lobbyists held at Trump properties. For example, they reported that the Trump International Hotel in Washington, D.C., became a favored spot for political gatherings and meetings, leading to significant revenue from entities that might seek to influence U.S. policy. The Trump Hotel management greatly increased fees for those politicos visiting the hotel funneling even more money into the family's coffers.

Emoluments Clauses Violations are one of the primary legal frameworks for scrutinizing the Trump family's financial dealings is the U.S..
The Constitution mentions emoluments in three provisions, each sometimes referred to as the "Emoluments Clause":
- **The Foreign Emoluments Clause** (art. I, § 9, cl. 8): "[N]o Person holding any Office of Profit or Trust under [the United States], shall, without the Consent of the Congress, accept of any present,

Emolument, Office, or Title, of any kind whatever, from any King, Prince, or foreign State."

- **The Domestic Emoluments Clause** (a.k.a. the Presidential Emoluments Clause) (art. II, § 1, cl. 7): "The President shall, at stated Times, receive for his Services, a Compensation which shall neither be increased nor diminished during the Period for which he shall have been elected, and he shall not receive within that Period any other Emolument from the United States, or any of them."

- **The Ineligibility Clause** (art. I, § 6, cl. 2): "No Senator or Representative shall, during the Time for which he was elected, be appointed to any civil Office under the Authority of the United States, which shall have been created, or the Emoluments whereof shall have been increased during such time; and no Person holding any Office under the United States, shall be a Member of either House during his Continuance in Office."

These clauses are designed to prevent the president from receiving gifts or payments from foreign governments without congressional approval. Public Citizen has highlighted numerous instances where foreign governments and officials spent large sums at Trump properties, potentially violating these clauses.

For instance, the Saudi government booked entire floors at the Trump International Hotel in New York shortly after Trump's election. These stays generated hundreds of thousands of dollars in revenue for the Trump Organization. Public Citizen argues that such transactions create a direct financial benefit from foreign entities, raising concerns about undue influence on the president's policies.

Democracy for sale

Saudi Arabia was the first official visit for president Trump and they received benefits during his administration including weapons sales.

The Trump family has also been accused of using political events and campaign funds to enrich their businesses. According to a report by CREW, the Trump campaign and Republican National Committee spent millions at Trump-owned properties. This spending includes booking venues, catering services, and lodging, all of which funnel money back into the Trump Organization .

In addition, Public Citizen's analysis of Federal Election Commission records revealed that the Trump campaign and affiliated political committees spent over $20 million at Trump properties during the 2020 election cycle. This practice not only raised ethical questions but also created a significant financial benefit for the Trump family .

Beyond domestic dealings, the Trump Organization has pursued numerous international projects that have raised questions about potential conflicts of interest. During Trump's presidency, the organization expanded its licensing deals in countries such as Indonesia, the Philippines, and Turkey. These deals involve the Trump name being used on hotels, resorts, and residential projects, generating substantial revenue through licensing fees and property sales. For example, a report by The New York Times detailed how the Trump Organization secured a lucrative licensing deal for a luxury resort in Bali, Indonesia. The timing and nature of these deals have led to speculation about whether they were influenced by Trump's political position and whether foreign entities sought favor by engaging in business with his company .

Another avenue through which the Trump family has been accused of profiting is through government spending at Trump-owned properties. During Trump's presidency, his frequent visits to properties like Mar-a-Lago in Florida and the Trump National Golf Club in Bedminster, New Jersey, resulted in significant taxpayer-funded expenditures. These visits required extensive security and logistical arrangements, leading to millions of dollars being spent at Trump businesses . CREW has documented these expenditures, highlighting how government spending on Trump properties raises concerns about the use of public funds for private gain. For instance, the Secret Service and other government agencies spent substantial sums on lodging and other expenses at Trump properties during his visits, effectively transferring taxpayer money to the Trump Organization.

The Trump family's financial dealings during Donald Trump's presidency have been a subject of intense scrutiny and criticism. Watchdog organizations like CREW and Public Citizen, along with various news outlets, have documented numerous instances where the Trumps have allegedly leveraged the presidency for personal financial gain. From conflicts of interest and potential Emoluments Clause violations to the use of campaign funds and government spending at Trump properties, these practices have raised significant ethical and legal concerns. The full extent and legality of these actions remain a matter of public and judicial debate, highlighting the need for robust mechanisms to prevent and address corruption at the highest levels of government.

Trump's Inauguration: A study in buying influence.

The Pulitzer Prize-winning investigative journalist, David Cay Johnston, has written extensively on the intersection of money, politics, and power, most recently in his trio of books on Donald Trump. A prime example of buying influence is the inauguration of Donald Trump as the 45th President of the United States, which has been scrutinized for the potential buying of influence.

The inauguration held on January 20, 2017, marked a significant moment in American political history, not only for its contentious nature but also for the unprecedented financial contributions it attracted. According to David Cay Johnston, this event was emblematic of a larger pattern of money-driven politics that has characterized much of Trump's career and presidency. Trump's inauguration raised a staggering $107 million, nearly double the amount raised for President Obama's 2009 inauguration. This record-breaking sum raised eyebrows and questions about the motivations behind such generous contributions. Unlike past inaugurations, where a significant portion of the funds came from individuals, Trump's inauguration saw an influx of large donations from corporations and wealthy individuals. This raised concerns about whether these donors were seeking to buy influence in the new administration. Among the notable donors were billionaires and corporate entities with vested interests in the administration's policy decisions. Sheldon Adelson, a casino magnate, donated $5 million, the largest single contribution ever made to a presidential inauguration. Adelson's business interests and his strong pro-Israel stance aligned well with Trump's subsequent policy decisions, including the controversial move of the U.S. embassy to Jerusalem.

Similarly, other donors had clear business interests. For example, AT&T donated $2 million amid its efforts to secure approval for a merger with Time Warner. Boeing, another significant donor, had substantial defense contracts with the government. These contributions suggest a strategic investment aimed at securing favorable policy outcomes from the new administration.

Regulatory and Policy Paybacks? Johnston posits that the large donations to Trump's inauguration were not merely ceremonial contributions but strategic investments intended to yield substantial returns. This assertion is supported by the subsequent policy decisions that appeared to favor the interests of major donors. For instance, shortly after the inauguration, the Trump administration moved to ease regulations on industries that were well-represented among the donors. The rollback of environmental regulations, changes in tax policies, and efforts to dismantle the Affordable Care Act all had significant implications for corporate donors.

One of the critical issues highlighted by Johnston is the lack of transparency and accountability surrounding the inauguration funds. Unlike campaign contributions, which are subject to stringent reporting requirements and limits, inauguration donations are less regulated. This loophole allowed for a significant influx of money with minimal disclosure about how the funds were spent. Reports of extravagant spending on inaugural events further fueled suspicions about the potential misuse of funds. Additionally, several donors used limited liability companies (LLCs) to make contributions, obscuring the true sources of the money. This practice made it difficult to trace the origins of the funds and to identify potential conflicts of interest or quid pro quo arrangements.

The potential for buying influence through inauguration donations raises serious legal and ethical concerns. While the donations themselves may not be illegal, the implications of such financial influence on policy decisions can undermine public trust in the democratic process. Johnston argues that this influx of money can lead to a form of legalized corruption, where policy decisions are effectively auctioned off to the highest bidder.

In the case of Trump's inauguration, ongoing investigations have sought to uncover whether any laws were broken in the fundraising and spending process. The scrutiny has extended to possible foreign influence, with reports suggesting that foreign nationals may have used intermediaries to contribute to the inauguration in hopes of gaining access and influence.

David Cay Johnston's examination of Trump's inauguration highlights the broader issue of money in politics and the potential for buying influence. The record-breaking fundraising, the strategic interests of major donors, and the lack of transparency all point to a system where financial contributions can significantly shape policy outcomes. This case serves as a stark reminder of the need for stronger regulations and greater transparency to protect the integrity of the democratic process. As Johnston's work illustrates, the health of democracy depends on the vigilance and accountability of its institutions and the active participation of its citizens in demanding ethical governance.

Trump 2.0: Monetizing the Presidency (Again!)

If you thought Donald Trump's first term was a masterclass in self-enrichment, his second term is essentially a graduate seminar. After all, why just be the leader of the free world when you can also be the CEO of a never-ending, grift-fueled empire? From meme coin scams to hawking overpriced Bibles, Trump's latest run in the Oval Office looks less like a presidency and more like a QVC special with nuclear codes.

The Gospel According to Grift

It started with the God Bless Trump Bible, because nothing says "faith" like a $60 book endorsed by a man who probably considers "Two Corinthians" an actual person. Sold as a "patriotic keepsake," this divine cash grab is just one more way Trump turns his followers ' devotion into dollars. If Jesus flipped the money changers 'tables, Trump would've charged them a licensing fee first.

Crypto Chaos: The MAGA Meme Coin

But why stop at exploiting religion when you can also swindle your fans with a cryptocurrency that crashes faster than his casinos? Enter the Trump-branded meme coin, promising to "make crypto great again." What could go wrong? (Spoiler: everything.) While MAGA enthusiasts eagerly bought in, Trump & Co. cashed out— because, as history shows, the only sure bet with Trump businesses is that someone else is left holding the bag.

The Emoluments Clause? Never Heard of It.

Remember when ethics experts screamed about Trump violating the Emoluments Clause by raking in foreign money during his first term?

Well, now it's a full-on business model. Foreign dignitaries still flock to his hotels and golf courses, and his resorts mysteriously end up hosting government events. At this point, the Constitution might as well be printed on the back of a Mar-a-Lago cocktail napkin.

The Presidency as a Personal Brand

While past presidents focused on policy, Trump treats the White House like a revolving-door marketing gig. Whether it's slapping his name on sketchy products, peddling fear to boost his media empire, or convincing his base to bankroll his never-ending legal troubles, the message is clear: in Trump's America, patriotism isn't about democracy—it's about buying in.

References
1. Citizens for Responsibility and Ethics in Washington (CREW). "Trump's businesses raked in millions from political groups and federal agencies." Accessed May 26, 2024. [crew.org](https://www.citizensforethics.org).
2. Public Citizen. "Presidency for Sale: Trump's Failure to Divest and the Resulting Conflicts of Interest." Accessed May 26, 2024. [citizen.org](https://www.citizen.org).
3. Public Citizen. "Foreign Governments Spent Millions at Trump Properties." Accessed May 26, 2024. [citizen.org](https://www.citizen.org).
4. CREW. "Political Spending at Trump Properties." Accessed May 26, 2024. [crew.org](https://www.citizensforethics.org).
5. Public Citizen. "Trump Campaign Spent $20 Million at Trump Properties." Accessed May 26, 2024. [citizen.org](https://www.citizen.org).
6. The New York Times. "Trump's Business Empire and Foreign Dealings." Accessed May 26, 2024. [nytimes.com](https://www.nytimes.com).
7. The New York Times. "Trump Hotel and Licensing Deals." Accessed May 26, 2024. [nytimes.com](https://www.nytimes.com).
8. CREW. "Taxpayer Spending at Trump Properties." Accessed May 26, 2024. [crew.org](https://www.citizensforethics.org).
9. The Washington Post. "Government Spending at Trump Properties During Presidency." Accessed May 26, 2024. [washingtonpost.com](https://www.washingtonpost.com).
10. CREW. "Secret Service Spending at Trump Properties." Accessed May 26, 2024. [crew.org](https://www.citizensforethics.org).

Insider Trading:
How to Make Big Bucks in Congress.

Insider trading refers to the practice of buying or selling a security by someone who has access to material, non-public information about the security. While this practice is illegal for corporate insiders, a growing body of evidence suggests that members of Congress have engaged in similar activities with relatively few repercussions. This potential for financial gain by elected officials at the expense of public trust raises significant ethical and legal questions.

Legislative Privilege and Financial Transparency: Members of Congress are not subject to the same insider trading laws as corporate executives. This discrepancy is rooted in a legal gray area: while insider trading laws prohibit the use of non-public information for private gain, Congress members have access to extensive non-public information through their legislative activities.

The Stop Trading on Congressional Knowledge (STOCK) Act was enacted in 2012 with the intention of combating insider trading among members of Congress, their staff, and other federal employees. This legislation aimed to increase transparency and accountability by prohibiting the use of non-public information for private profit and requiring timely public disclosure of stock trades and other financial transactions. Despite these intentions, the effectiveness of the STOCK Act has been questioned, particularly in light of stock trading activities by members of Congress just before the coronavirus pandemic.

The STOCK Act included several key provisions designed to curb insider trading and increase transparency:

1. Disclosure Requirements: The Act required members of Congress, their staff, and other federal employees to disclose any stock trades of over $1,000 within 45 days.

2. Public Access to Financial Disclosures: These financial disclosures were to be made available online for public access, thereby increasing transparency and allowing the public to scrutinize the trades.

3. Ban on Insider Trading: The Act explicitly makes it illegal for members of Congress and their staff to trade stocks based on non-public information they obtain through their positions, stating that they were not exempt from securities laws that prohibit trading on non-public information.

4. Creation of a Database: The Act mandated the creation of an electronic database to house the disclosures, making it easier to track and analyze trading activity.

5. Ethics Training: Mandatory ethics training for all Congressional staff and certain federal employees to ensure compliance with the new regulations.

Despite these provisions, the STOCK Act has faced significant criticism regarding its effectiveness. Critics argue that the Act has several loopholes and enforcement issues that undermine its ability to prevent insider trading:

Numerous investigative reports have highlighted suspicious trading activities by Congress members. A 2020 report by the New York Times found that at least 27 senators made significant stock transactions after receiving briefings on the emerging coronavirus pandemic, well before the public fully understood the gravity of the situation.

1. Delayed Reporting: Although the Act requires trades to be reported within 45 days, this window still allows members to profit from non-public information before the public becomes aware of their trades.

2. Lack of Enforcement: There have been few significant penalties or prosecutions under the STOCK Act, leading to questions about its deterrent effect.

3. Complex Financial Instruments: Members of Congress can still engage in complex financial transactions, such as options and futures trading, that are harder to track and regulate.

The coronavirus pandemic highlighted the potential shortcomings of the STOCK Act. In early 2020, several members of Congress faced scrutiny for their stock trades made just before the market turmoil caused by the pandemic but none of them faced consequences. Here are the are just a few of them:

Democracy for sale

1. Senator Richard Burr: Senator Burr, who was the chair of the Senate Intelligence Committee at the time, sold a significant portion of his stock holdings in February 2020, just before the market crash. He had access to classified information about the potential impact of the virus.

2. Senator Kelly Loeffler: Senator Loeffler and her husband, the CEO of the New York Stock Exchange, made substantial stock transactions in the same period. Loeffler defended the trades, claiming they were made by third-party advisors.

3. Senator Dianne Feinstein: Senator Feinstein's husband sold stocks worth millions before the market downturn. Feinstein claimed she had no involvement in her husband's trades.

4. Senator James Inhofe: Senator Inhofe sold stocks worth hundreds of thousands of dollars in late January and early February 2020. He stated that his financial decisions were handled by a third-party advisor.

The Department of Justice (DOJ) opened investigations into several senators' trades, but many of these investigations were eventually closed without charges. For example, the DOJ ended its investigation into Senator Burr without filing charges in January 2021.

The controversy reignited calls for stronger regulations and reforms to prevent insider trading in Congress. Proposals included shortening the reporting window for trades, increasing penalties for violations, and establishing more robust oversight mechanisms.

These trades raised concerns about whether the STOCK Act effectively prevents the use of non-public information for personal gain. Several points of analysis emerge:

The timing of these trades reinforced the belief that members of Congress might prioritize personal financial gain over public service. The complexity of financial markets and the sophistication of trading strategies make it difficult to prove insider trading, even with the STOCK Act in place. These bring up a clear need for stricter regulations, such as mandatory blind trusts for members of Congress or outright bans on stock trading while in office.

The 2012 STOCK Act represented a significant step towards addressing insider trading in Congress, but its effectiveness has been limited by loopholes, enforcement challenges, and the sophisticated nature of financial markets. The stock trades made by members of Congress just before the coronavirus pandemic underscore the need for further reforms to ensure that public officials cannot exploit their positions for personal financial gain. Continued scrutiny and legislative action will be essential to restore public trust and enhance the accountability of elected officials.

References
- [The New York Times](https://www.nytimes.com/2020/03/19/us/politics/senator-richard-burr-stock-sales.html)
- [NPR](https://www.npr.org/2020/03/20/818192804/republican-senator-faces-calls-to-resign-over-stock-sales-ahead-of-market-plunge)
- [Business Insider](https://www.businessinsider.com/stock-act-violations-congress-members-trades-2021-12)

The Revolving Door:
Government, to Corporate Lobbying, and back again.

The concept of the "revolving door" between government and corporate lobbying is one of the most pernicious and insidious dynamics affecting modern democracies. This metaphorical door swings freely as individuals move between roles in public service and high-paying positions in the private sector, particularly within industries they once regulated. This not only undermines the integrity of democratic institutions but also skews public policy in favor of corporate interests, often at the expense of the common good. Let's examine the mechanics of the revolving door, its impact on governance, and the broader consequences for society. Be careful, if you try to follow all the many people who pass through that revolving door, you may get whiplash.

The revolving door is characterized by the seamless transition of individuals between public sector roles—such as legislators, regulators, and aides—and private sector positions, especially in lobbying firms or corporations with substantial stakes in governmental decisions. This cycle perpetuates a corrupted relationship where knowledge, influence, and access are traded for cushy jobs and sweetheart legislation for their corporate masters.

Public service used as a vehicle to get into the Private Sector. Public service doesn't make you rich but it does open the door to lobbying. Former government officials leverage their knowledge and connections to secure lucrative positions in the private sector. Their understanding of the process and access to former colleagues provide corporations with a strategic advantage in navigating regulatory and legislative landscape.

Conversely, individuals from the corporate sector often take up positions in government, bringing with them a predisposition towards the interests of their former employers. Often pitching themselves as "experts and reformers" but with an eye on the bottom line... Theirs. This leads to regulatory capture, where regulatory agencies serve the interests of the industries they are supposed to regulate rather than the public. This has far-reaching implications for governance and public trust in our democratic institutions.

When regulators and lawmakers are heavily influenced by the industries they oversee, policies are often tailored to benefit those industries, where agencies prioritize corporate interests over public safety, environmental protection, and fair market practices. This is especially obvious in the energy and the financial sector.

The perception that government officials are influenced by their past or future private sector employers erodes public trust. Citizens lose faith in the impartiality and integrity of public institutions when decisions appear to be driven by corporate interests rather than the common good. Sometimes, the spouses of regulators or congressional members are employed by the very companies they are charged with regulating and despite laws that requires them to recuse themselves, they often don't. Is it any wonder that congresses approval rating is in the toilet?

The prioritization of corporate interests often exacerbates economic inequality and social injustice. Policies that favor big businesses can lead to the neglect of critical social issues such as healthcare, education, and social welfare, disproportionately affecting the most vulnerable populations.

Examples: The financial crisis of 2008 highlighted the devastating impact of the revolving door in the financial sector. Key policymakers and regulators who had strong ties to Wall Street were implicated in the crafting of regulations that ultimately failed to prevent the crisis. Post-crisis, many of these individuals returned to lucrative positions in the same industry they had once overseen, raising questions about the adequacy and impartiality of financial regulation.

Prior to the 2008 financial crisis, Tim Geithner was the President of the Federal Reserve Bank of New York, a position he held from 2003 to 2009. In this role, Geithner was at the center of the U.S. financial system, responsible for overseeing some of the largest financial institutions in the country. Geithner, along with other key figures in the Bush administration, favored a hands-off regulatory approach to Wall Street. The Federal Reserve Bank of New York, under Geithner's leadership, did not take action to curb risky practices like excessive leverage and the growth of the shadow banking system, which played a significant role in the financial collapse.

In early 2009, he was appointed Secretary of the Treasury under President Barack Obama. In this capacity, he became one of the central figures in the government's response to the crisis. Geithner was instrumental in the decision to bail out major financial institutions, including AIG and Citigroup. These bailouts used taxpayer money to rescue companies that had engaged in risky behavior, but they were sold to the public as necessary to prevent a complete collapse of the financial system. He also oversaw the implementation of the Troubled Asset Relief Program (TARP), a $700 billion initiative designed to stabilize the financial system by purchasing toxic assets from banks and providing capital injections. In layman's terms, they gambled but the American people got stuck with the bill. Adding to the catastrophic consequences of the crisis, in the aftermath, these companies foreclosed on millions of family homes.

The Pharmaceutical Industry, as we mentioned previously, already derives massive benefit from public research dollars, but the revolving door between the Food and Drug Administration (FDA) and the pharmaceutical industry is especially insidious. Former FDA officials often take up positions in pharmaceutical companies, where they lobby for favorable drug approval processes and minimal regulation. This rightly raises concerns about drug safety and the prioritizing corporate profits over public health. The Journal of the American Medical Association (JAMA): In a 2016 analysis estimated that medical errors, including adverse drug reactions (ADRs), could be the third leading cause of death in the U.S., potentially contributing to over 250,000 deaths per year.

Defense and Military is notorious for the revolving door. High-ranking military officials and defense department personnel frequently transition to positions within defense contractors. The implications for defense policies and military spending are enormous, leading to an increase in defense contracts and expenditures that has ballooned the "defense" budget, greatly benefitting private companies at the expense of other much needed social spending such as veteran's benefits and education.

The revolving door has a disastrous effects on the country, compromising not only good governance but also the broader socio-economic fabric. Public policies that are heavily influenced by corporate interests tend to overlook critical issues such as environmental sustainability, consumer protection, and social welfare. This can result in inadequate responses to crises and a lack of progress on essential public goods. This can lead to an attitude of "never let a crisis go to waste" and looking for the profit opportunity. When government policies align with corporate interests it often leads to economic disparities. Tax breaks, subsidies, and deregulation favoring large corporations stifles competition, hurt small businesses, and exacerbate wealth inequality.

The perception of corruption also weakens our democratic institutions. When citizens believe that their voices are drowned out by corporate lobbying, political apathy and disillusionment grow, reducing civic engagement and weakening democratic governance. People often say that politicians should have to wear patches of the companies who they actually work for.

When regulatory agencies prioritize industry interests, public health and safety can be compromised. The failure to adequately regulate industries such as pharmaceuticals, food production, and environmental pollutants poses significant risks to public health and safety.

Addressing the influence of corporate lobbying is one of the most challenging obstacles to solving some of our most daunting problems such as climate chance or another public health crisis. Law makers are reluctant to pass tough laws because they see it as a way they can profit after they leave office and this behavior rarely makes headlines as it is seen as "just the way business is done" in Washington. If we are going to restore the integrity of public institutions we will need stringent restrictions on the transition between public service and private sector. This includes mandatory cooling-off periods and stricter lobbying disclosure requirements. Enhancing transparency including robust disclosure of lobbying activities and potential conflicts of interest and holding public officials accountable for their post-government employment. Imagine if politicians were required to record every conversation regarding policy making or future job opportunities and requiring the recording to be made public. This would certainly make it more difficult to cut back-room deals that that lead to the revolving door.

Reducing the influence of money in politics through campaign finance reform is crucial. Limiting corporate contributions to political campaigns and increasing public funding for elections can level the playing field and reduce corporate influence.

Ensuring that regulatory agencies are adequately funded and staffed with individuals committed to public service, rather than industry interests, is essential. This includes protecting agencies from political interference and ensuring their independence.

Only by closing the revolving door can we hope to restore public trust and ensure that government serves the interests of all citizens, rather than a privileged few.

We have examined some of the ways that corporations use lobbying, insider trading or outright fraud to line their pockets but there's a whole world of cheating going on and much of it resides in a legal grey area.

The World is full of Cheaters:
Taxes? What Taxes?

It's all too common for large U.S. corporations to pay no U.S. income taxes despite making billions of dollars in profits. In fact, one study of corporate securities filings found 55 of America's largest companies paid no income taxes in 2020 despite making large profits, while getting $3.5 billion in aggregate tax rebates. Nearly half of those companies paid no U.S. income taxes for three successive years. Among those not paying income taxes for at least three years were very profitable blue chips Nike, FedEx, and Salesforce, and many other companies with household names.

For instance, Apple avoided millions of dollars in taxes in California and 20 other states. Apple currently holds about $252 billion in profits offshore, where it can avoid paying U.S. taxes, something central to its corporate strategy. That's over 90% of the company's total cash on hand. This profit is subject to the corporate income tax as soon as it's "repatriated" back to the U.S. but that's why it's still off-shore. The shameful thing about Apple's ability to structure its business to avoid United States taxes was not that it did it, but that its legal. Off-shoring money is central to our next section.

Papers, Papers Everywhere:
The Panama and Paradise Papers and other revelations.

When the billionaire class use schemes to avoid paying taxes it puts the burden on the working and middle classes. The people who can least afford it are hit the hardest while those who benefit most from our laws, courts and infrastructure craft elaborate ways to hide their money and pay very little, if anything. Tax evasion and avoidance are pressing global issues, with substantial implications for economic inequality and public finance. Tax enforcement for wealthy individuals is a very different game compared to tax enforcement for everyone else. In 2007, a whistleblower named Bradley Birkenfeld shocked the world when he revealed that the Swiss bank UBS had been helping thousands of wealthy Americans conceal their wealth from US authorities and evade taxes. Two other major journalistic exposés, the Panama Papers and the Paradise Papers, shed significant light on how the wealthy and powerful use offshore tax havens to hide their income and avoid taxes. These investigations revealed the mechanisms and scale of tax evasion and avoidance, involving numerous prominent individuals and corporations.

The Panama Papers, released in April 2016, were a groundbreaking leak of 11.5 million documents from the Panamanian law firm Mossack Fonseca. The documents, dating back to the 1970s, exposed the offshore financial activities of over 214,000 entities and high-profile clients from around the world.

The leak involved 2.6 terabytes of data, revealing how Mossack Fonseca facilitated the creation of shell companies and trusts in offshore jurisdictions, enabling clients to conceal their wealth. The documents implicated numerous politicians, celebrities, and business leaders. Notable names included the Prime Minister of Iceland, Sigmundur Davíð Gunnlaugsson, Pakistani Prime Minister Nawaz Sharif, and close associates of Russian President Vladimir Putin. The papers detailed various methods used to hide income and assets, such as the use of nominee directors and shareholders, complex ownership structures, and bogus loans. These mechanisms made it difficult for tax authorities to trace the true ownership of assets. The revelations led to political fallout in several countries, with resignations and investigations initiated against those implicated. It also spurred calls for greater transparency and reforms in the global financial system.

The Paradise Papers, released in November 2017, were another significant look into the elite cheaters, this time involving 13.4 million documents primarily from the offshore law firm Appleby, as well as from corporate services provider Estera. The documents spanned nearly 70 years, from 1950 to 2016.

The leak exposed the offshore investments of over 120 politicians and world leaders, including Queen Elizabeth II, U.S. Secretary of Commerce Wilbur Ross, and members of the Trump administration. It also involved major corporations like Apple, Nike, and Uber. The documents detailed sophisticated tax avoidance schemes used by corporations and wealthy individuals, including profit shifting, redomiciling, and the use of tax havens like Bermuda, the Cayman Islands, and the Isle of Man. The Paradise Papers highlighted the pervasive use of offshore jurisdictions to exploit legal loopholes, reduce tax liabilities, and maintain financial secrecy. This secrecy made it challenging for tax authorities to enforce compliance and recover lost revenues. The revelations intensified public outrage over tax avoidance and evasion, leading to renewed pressure on governments to address these issues. In response, several countries implemented measures to increase transparency, such as beneficial ownership registries and stricter regulations on tax havens.

Both the Panama Papers and the Paradise Papers provided a detailed look at the tools and techniques used to evade taxes. Let's look at just a few:

Shell Companies: These are entities that exist only on paper, with no real business operations. They are often used to obscure the true ownership of assets and income.

Nominee Directors and Shareholders: Offshore service providers often supply individuals who act as directors or shareholders on behalf of the true owners, adding another layer of anonymity.

Complex Ownership Structures: By creating a web of interconnected companies and trusts across multiple jurisdictions, it becomes difficult for tax authorities to trace the flow of money and identify the real beneficiaries.

Tax Havens: Jurisdictions with low or zero taxes and strong financial secrecy laws are attractive destinations for those seeking to hide their wealth. These havens often have minimal reporting requirements and limited cooperation with international tax authorities. Making them a haven for Oligarchs, Organized Crime and Tech Billionaires.

According to the Congressional Budget Report (CBR) On average, very little tax is paid on the foreign source income of U.S. firms. Ample evidence of a significant amount of profit shifting exists. Evidence also indicates a significant increase in corporate profit shifting over the past several years. Recent estimates suggest losses that may approach, or even exceed, $100 billion per year.

These leaked documents had significant implications for global tax policy and enforcement: Tax authorities worldwide have increased their scrutiny of offshore activities and are collaborating more closely to tackle tax evasion and avoidance. Several countries have introduced or strengthened laws to improve transparency and close loopholes that facilitate offshore tax evasion. This includes the implementation of stricter anti-money laundering and other regulations. The leaks raised public awareness about the scale of tax evasion and its impact on economic inequality. This has fueled demands for more equitable tax systems and greater accountability for those who exploit offshore structures. There has been a push for greater international cooperation to combat tax evasion, including initiatives like the OECD's Common Reporting Standard (CRS) and the Base Erosion and Profit Shifting (BEPS) project, which aim to enhance information sharing and prevent profit shifting. While these are steps in the right direction some of the very people responsible for writing and enforcing tax laws are the very people benefiting from these schemes.

The Panama Papers and the Paradise Papers exposed the extensive and intricate methods used by the wealthy to hide their income and avoid taxes. These revelations underscored the need for greater transparency, stricter regulations, and international cooperation, but there also needs to be real consequences for those who use offshore tax evasion and avoidance and place the tax burden on "We the People". While significant progress has been made, greater ongoing efforts are essential to ensure a fairer and more transparent global financial system.

Part 4:

The Billionaire Class

"I believe there are more instances of the abridgment of freedom of the people by gradual and silent encroachments by those in power than by violent and sudden usurpation."
James Madison

"Winners Take All"
Doing good without doing much.

One of the most reliable products churned out by massive corporations—aside from record profits and morally flexible press releases—is billionaires. These are people with more money than they could ever spend, yet they still feel compelled to lecture the rest of us on the virtues of *hard work* and *bootstraps*, as if they got where they are by sheer grit rather than stock buybacks and tax loopholes.

In his eye-opening book *Winners Take All: The Elite Charade of Changing the World*, Anand Giridharadas dismantles the feel-good myth that billionaires and their philanthropic pet projects are here to save us. A former *New York Times* columnist and Aspen Institute fellow, Giridharadas unpacks how the ultra-wealthy use philanthropy as a PR stunt—keeping just enough people hopeful (and quiet) while ensuring the system stays rigged in their favor.

Through slick TED Talks and "win-win solutions" (translation: solutions that never inconvenience the wealthy), these elites present themselves as benevolent problem-solvers while conveniently overlooking the fact that they're often the ones who created the problems in the first place. Giridharadas makes several cutting observations that deserve serious attention—especially if you're tired of billionaires treating social justice like a branding exercise.

1. The Illusion of Philanthropy
The wealthy elite's philanthropic activities are often more about maintaining the status quo than creating genuine social change. Many philanthropic endeavors are designed to provide a veneer of benevolence while avoiding any real challenge to the systemic inequalities that benefit the elites. These activities allow the rich to feel good about themselves and portray themselves as heroes, without addressing the root causes of the issues they claim to solve.

2. Market-Based Solutions and the "Win-Win" Ideology
where initiatives are designed to be profitable for businesses while also purportedly solving social problems. He argues that such solutions are inherently flawed because they prioritize profit over genuine social impact and contends that true social change often requires sacrifices and redistributive measures that may not be profitable or comfortable for the wealthy.

3. The Role of the Elite in Perpetuating Inequality
The global elite, through their control of philanthropic organizations, think tanks, and policy-making institutions, perpetuate a system that benefits them. He explores the paradox of the same people who are responsible for creating many social problems being the ones who are most celebrated for their efforts to solve them. He calls into

question the effectiveness and sincerity of these efforts, suggesting that they are often more about self-preservation than altruism.

Giridharadas uses the Aspen Institute as a case study to illustrate his points. The Aspen Institute, which hosts gatherings of influential leaders and thinkers, is portrayed as a microcosm of the elite-driven approach to social change. Through his experiences at Aspen, Giridharadas exposes how these gatherings often serve to reinforce elite perspectives and marginalize dissenting voices that call for more systematic changes.

The book also focuses on the rise of social entrepreneurship and the influence of Silicon Valley. Giridharadas critiques figures like Sheryl Sandberg and companies like Uber for promoting the idea that business acumen and technological innovation can solve societal problems. He argues that this mindset overlooks the necessity of structural changes and government intervention to address issues like inequality and poverty. As with Uber, many of the "disrupters" only exacerbate the inequalities in our society and exploit working class who find it more difficult to make ends meet.

Some potential counterarguments from defenders of philanthropy might contend that market-based solutions can be part of a broader strategy to address social issues and that any positive impact, no matter how small, is valuable. Giridharadas acknowledges these points but maintains that without addressing the underlying systems of power and privilege, these efforts will always fall short.

"Winners Take All" asks us to rethink the relationship between wealth, power, and social change and urges readers to consider how true progress requires not just benevolent acts by the elite but fundamental changes to the systems that perpetuate inequality. He advocates for more democratic and inclusive approaches to solving social problems, where the voices of those most affected by these issues are prioritized over the interests of the wealthy. The book serves as a provocative and insightful critique of modern philanthropy, calling for a deeper and more honest examination of what it truly means to make a positive difference in the world. That is the perfect Segway into our next chapter on how those benevolent philanthropists find creative ways to avoid contributing to the common good... You know, taxes.

How the Wealthy Use Charities as Tax Shelters

How sweet it is when you have enough money that you can avoid paying taxes and look like you're doing good at the same time. The wealthy use charitable organizations not just as a means of philanthropy, but also as a strategic tool to reduce their tax burden. This process involves creating, donating to, or utilizing charitable foundations and trusts in ways that can provide significant tax advantages that both deprive the government of funds that could otherwise go to public projects and are beyond the reach of average tax payers.

Private Foundations are a popular vehicle for the wealthy to channel their philanthropic efforts. These foundations offer several tax benefits:

1. Income Tax Deductions: Donors can receive immediate tax deductions for the contributions they make to their private foundation. This deduction can be up to 30% of the donor's adjusted gross income (AGI) for cash donations and 20% of AGI for appreciated assets, such as stocks or real estate.

2. Avoiding Capital Gains Tax: When appreciated assets are donated to a private foundation, the donor avoids paying capital gains tax on the appreciation. This is particularly beneficial for donors who hold assets that have significantly increased in value.

3. Estate Tax Benefits: Assets transferred to a private foundation can also reduce the donor's taxable estate, potentially saving significant estate taxes.

<u>Donor-Advised Funds</u> (DAFs) are another popular tool used by the wealthy to manage their "charitable giving" while reaping tax benefits:

1. Immediate Tax Deduction: When donors contribute to a DAF, they receive an immediate tax deduction, even if the funds are not disbursed to operating charities right away.

2. Flexibility: Donors retain advisory privileges over the disbursement of the funds, allowing them to recommend grants to specific charities over time. This provides flexibility in managing the timing of their charitable impact.

3. Investment Growth: Funds in a DAF can be invested, potentially growing tax-free, which can increase the amount available for charitable purposes over time.

Charitable Remainder Trusts (CRTs) provide a way for wealthy individuals to receive income during their lifetime while making a future charitable donation:

1. Income Stream: A CRT provides the donor (or other beneficiaries) with a stream of income for a specified period or for life.
2. Tax Benefits: Donors receive a partial income tax deduction based on the present value of the future charitable gift. They also avoid capital gains taxes on the appreciated assets transferred to the trust.
3. Estate Tax Reduction: The assets in the CRT are removed from the donor's estate, potentially reducing estate taxes.

Administration Costs. While charitable organizations are designed to benefit specific causes or communities and a "social good", a significant portion of the donations they receive can be spent on administrative costs. This diminishes the funds available for the intended beneficiaries and can be funneled back to the donor, their family or chosen benefactor.

Administrative costs in charities can include expenses related to:

1. Salaries and Benefits: Compensation for staff, including executives, fundraisers, and other employees.
2. Fundraising Expenses: Costs associated with soliciting donations, such as marketing, events, and donor relations.
3. Operational Expenses: Rent, utilities, office supplies, and other day-to-day operational costs.
4. Compliance and Legal Fees: Costs related to maintaining legal compliance and managing any legal issues that arise.

There can be little scrutiny of these expenses and has been shone in some high profile cases. United Way in 1995, the CEO, William Aramony was convicted of 25 felony counts, including fraud and conspiracy, for diverting $1.2 million of the charity's money to benefit himself and his friends. The Wounded Warrior Project: Faced criticism when reports emerged that a significant portion of donations was spent on lavish conferences and travel rather than on veterans' services. Cancer Fund of America was also accused of spending only a small fraction of its donations on actual cancer patients, with the majority going to salaries, fundraising, and other administrative costs. Other charities fly under the radar of the media and the regulators where some of the worst spend as little as 4% on actual charitable activities.

The wealthy often utilize charitable organizations and structures such as private foundations, DAFs, and CRTs to gain tax advantages while fulfilling their "philanthropic" goals. However, these charitable efforts may not be anything more than clever tax cheating schemes, which divert tax funds away from critical government services. The "market" will not correct for these types of fraud and abuses and its up to our law makers to ensure that "charities" are not used as tax dodges and that funds are used effectively, and for the public good.

Hidden Wealth:
How the Ultra Rich are Robbing the American People... Legally

In recent years, the vast disparity between the ultra-wealthy and the rest of the American population has garnered significant attention. A groundbreaking 2021 ProPublica article, titled "The Secret IRS Files," revealed the extent to which America's richest individuals exploit legal loopholes, complex financial strategies, and sometimes outright fraud to minimize their tax obligations. This chapter delves into the methods these wealthy individuals use to cheat on taxes and the broader implications for American society.

The Millionaire's Guide to Evading Taxes:

One of the most common methods the ultra-wealthy use to avoid paying their fair share of taxes is exploiting legal loopholes in the tax code. These loopholes are often the result of years of lobbying and influence over policymakers. For instance, capital gains are taxed at a significantly lower rate than ordinary income, which benefits those whose income primarily comes from investments. This means that billionaires like Warren Buffett and Jeff Bezos can pay a lower effective tax rate than a middle-class worker.

Another notable loophole is the "carried interest" provision, which allows hedge fund managers and private equity partners to pay capital gains taxes on their earnings instead of the higher ordinary income tax rate. This results in billions of dollars in lost tax revenue that could otherwise be used to fund essential public services.

The Art of Depreciation - Depreciation is a non-cash expense that allows property owners to deduct a portion of the cost of their assets over time. While depreciation is meant to account for the wear and tear on physical assets, it is often manipulated by the ultra-wealthy to reduce taxable income significantly. Real estate moguls, for example, can depreciate their properties over several years, even as those properties increase in value.

Donald Trump, the former / future president and real estate tycoon, famously claimed massive depreciation deductions to reduce his tax liabilities to almost nothing in some years. According to the ProPublica report, Trump was able to write off millions of dollars in losses, despite maintaining a lavish lifestyle and profitable business operations.

Offshore tax havens are jurisdictions with low or no taxes, which provide financial secrecy and attract wealth from around the globe. (As discussed earlier) The ultra-wealthy use these havens to hide their assets and income from the IRS. By moving money offshore, they can evade taxes that would otherwise be owed in the United States.

Trusts and shell companies are often used by the ultra-wealthy to obscure ownership and evade taxes. Trusts can be structured in ways that allow wealth to be passed down through generations without incurring significant estate taxes. For example, a "dynasty trust" can theoretically last forever, shielding assets from estate taxes indefinitely.

Shell companies, on the other hand, only exist on paper and do not conduct any real business activities. Often used to hide assets, launder money, and avoid taxes. The ProPublica article highlighted how individuals like Sheldon Adelson, a casino magnate, used such entities to shift money around and minimize tax liabilities.

While charitable contributions are generally seen as a positive, they can also be used as a tax avoidance strategy. Donations to private foundations, which are often controlled by the donors themselves, can be deducted from taxable income allowing the ultra-wealthy to retain control over their money while reducing their tax bill.

The ProPublica investigation revealed how individuals like Bill Gates and Mark Zuckerberg have used private foundations to shelter billions of dollars from taxes. While these foundations do engage in philanthropic activities, the tax benefits they confer to their wealthy benefactors cannot be ignored.

The tax avoidance strategies employed by the ultra-wealthy have profound implications for American society. The lost tax revenue, estimated to be in the hundreds of billions of dollars annually, could be used to address critical issues such as healthcare, education, infrastructure, and social services. Instead, this burden is increasingly shifted onto middle and lower-income Americans, exacerbating economic inequality. Moreover, the perception that the tax system is rigged in favor of the rich erodes trust in democratic institutions and the rule of law. When the public sees that the wealthy can buy influence and manipulate the system to their advantage, it undermines the social contract and fuels cynicism and disillusionment. This can be a critical step towards fascism when an aspiring dictator exploits these sentiments to gain power.

The revelations from the "The Secret IRS Files" provide a sobering look at how the ultra-wealthy cheat on taxes and rob the American people. Addressing these issues requires comprehensive tax reform, greater transparency, and a renewed commitment to equity and justice in the financial realm but it also takes the average American to wake up and stop falling for the old "bait and switch" where they want us to blame the "other guy" for the lack of good schools, affordable healthcare and such, and start following the money.

The Ultra-Wealthy's $8.5 Trillion of Untaxed Income

According to an analysis by American for Tax Fairness of new Federal Reserve data on household income and wealth (January 3, 2024), America's billionaires and centi-millionaires (those with at least $100 million of wealth) collectively held at least $8.5 trillion of "unrealized capital gains" in 2022. These profits from unsold investments constitute the largest source of income for the super-rich. This staggering accumulation of "quiet" income may never be taxed unless special taxes on the ultra-wealthy now under consideration in Congress are enacted.

The data show that more than one in every six dollars (18%) of the nation's unrealized gains is held by these roughly 64,000 ultra-wealthy households, who make up less than 0.05% of the population. That is nearly triple the share that billionaires and centi-millionaires held when the Federal Reserve started tracking unrealized gains in 1989. This tiny handful of the super-rich hold as much unrealized capital gains as the entire bottom 84% of American society (110 million households). Under current law, these gains in the value of stocks, bonds, businesses, real estate and other assets are not taxed unless the gain is "realized" through a sale.

But the ultra-wealthy don't need to sell to benefit: they can live off low-cost loans secured against their growing fortunes. And once inherited, such gains disappear completely for tax purposes. There are proposed reforms that would tax the unrealized gains of the nation's wealthiest households. These plans would raise hundreds of billions of dollars in tax revenue exclusively from the nation's very richest households, revenue that could be used to lower costs and improve services for the rest of America.

The Fed data comes from its Survey of Consumer Finances (SCF). Conducted every three years since 1983, the SCF is a unique study of Americans 'income and wealth, broken down by demographic and other characteristics. For 40 years policymakers and researchers have relied on the SCF for timely and detailed information on the economic status of American households.

The Right's War on the IRS

In recent years, the dynamics of tax evasion and the political machinations surrounding the Internal Revenue Service (IRS) have taken center stage in the United States. The increasing sophistication of tax evasion strategies among the wealthy, coupled with a concerted political effort to undermine the IRS, has created a complex landscape of financial manipulation and regulatory resistance. This chapter delves into the intricate tactics employed by millionaires to minimize their tax liabilities and examines the ideological battle waged by the Right against the IRS.

The Landscape of Tax Evasion

Tax evasion, distinct from tax avoidance, involves illegal methods to avoid paying taxes, such as underreporting income, inflating deductions, and hiding money offshore. Over the past few decades, the wealthy have perfected these techniques, often with the help of high-priced accountants and legal advisors.

As discussed previously, the ultra-rich use offshore accounts, Shell Companies and Foundations to set up complex trust structures that help them shield income and assets from taxes. Multinational corporations such as Apple, use transfer pricing to shift profits to subsidiaries in low-tax jurisdictions. By manipulating the prices of goods and services exchanged between controlled entities, they can significantly reduce taxable income. Real Estate Investors are provided numerous tax benefits, including deductions for depreciation and interest, as well as the ability to defer capital gains taxes through mechanisms like 1031 exchanges.

The Ideological Battleground

The IRS, as the enforcement arm of the U.S. tax system, has long been a target for political attacks. However, the hostility has intensified in recent years, particularly from the Right, which views the agency as an overreaching bureaucratic entity. This ideological battle manifests on several fronts:

One of the most effective strategies employed by the Right has been to reduce the IRS's budget. Since 2010, the agency has faced significant funding cuts, leading to a decrease in enforcement capabilities. Reduced budgets mean fewer audits and less oversight, making it easier for high income tax evaders to slip through the cracks while the auditor are forced to focus on lower income citizens.

Conservative lawmakers have introduced and supported legislation aimed at curbing the IRS's powers. This includes efforts to limit the agency's ability to access certain financial records, impose penalties, and expand reporting requirements.

The Right has also engaged in public perception campaigns, painting the IRS as a villain. High-profile cases of IRS missteps, such as the controversy over the alleged targeting of conservative groups seeking tax-exempt status, have been used to bolster arguments for reigning in the agency.

Tax reforms advocated by the Right often include provisions that benefit the wealthy, such as lowering top marginal tax rates, reducing capital gains taxes, and increasing estate tax exemptions. These reforms can indirectly support tax evasion by making it less financially detrimental.

The Right frequently supports legal challenges to IRS regulations and actions. By contesting the legality of certain IRS rules and enforcement mechanisms in court, they can create a more favorable legal environment for tax evasion especially when these cases are brought before the extreme business friendly courts such as the 5th circuit.

The dual forces of sophisticated tax evasion strategies and political attacks on the IRS have serious consequences for the U.S. economy and society: The U.S. Treasury loses hundreds of billions of dollars annually due to tax evasion. Tax evasion exacerbates income and wealth inequality. When the wealthy successfully evade taxes, the burden shifts to middle and lower-income taxpayers, undermining the progressive nature of the tax system. Public trust in the tax system and government institutions has eroded, this has lead to a decrease in voluntary compliance and a weakened social contract.

The battle over taxes and the role of the IRS is far from over. As the wealthy continue to devise new ways to minimize their tax liabilities and political forces seek to reshape the agency's powers, the landscape of tax enforcement will remain a contentious and evolving field. The future of this battle will significantly influence the economic and social fabric of the United States.

* History of Corporations in America - Source - "Corporations Are Not People," Attorney Jeffrey Clements

Carrying Water for the Rich:

The "Carried Interest Loophole" is a provision in the U.S. tax code that allows private equity and hedge fund managers to pay significantly lower tax rates on their earnings than other high-income individuals. This loophole enables them to treat much of their income as "capital gains" rather than "ordinary income," resulting in a maximum tax rate of about 20% instead of the top income tax rate of around 37%. Here's a breakdown of how it works and why it is often criticized as unfair:

In the private equity world, fund managers are compensated through both a management fee (often around 2% of assets under management) and "carried interest," which is typically 20% of any profits generated above a certain threshold. This 20% is where the carried interest loophole comes in. Instead of being taxed as regular income, carried interest is classified as a capital gain since the managers are technically sharing in the "ownership" of investments. This categorization allows the income to qualify for the lower capital gains tax rate.

For most people, high earnings are taxed as regular income. However, fund managers can have substantial portions of their income taxed at lower rates. This arrangement effectively rewards a particular group of high-income earners with an advantageous tax rate not available to other workers who earn similar (or even far lower) amounts.

Because the government loses tax revenue by allowing this lower rate on carried interest, that lost revenue is typically made up elsewhere, often by the taxes paid by regular income earners. The carried interest loophole thus contributes to broader income inequality and shifts a greater tax burden onto individuals who earn less and don't benefit from such special tax treatment.

Carried interest can encourage fund managers to prioritize quick, profitable exits from investments over long-term, sustainable growth. This mentality can hurt companies and employees, as the emphasis often falls on extracting maximum short-term profit rather than creating value that might take longer to realize.

Proponents of the loophole argue that carried interest should be taxed as capital gains because it involves investment risk. However, critics argue that fund managers typically don't put their own money at risk; instead, they are paid to manage someone else's money. This bogus argument that they should be rewarded like other capital gains investors who risk their own funds is just an excuse for avoiding paying their fair share.

While the carried interest loophole is legal, its critics view it as a "tax cheat" because it enables high-income individuals to exploit a specific provision to avoid paying their fair share. Efforts to close the loophole have repeatedly stalled, partly because of strong lobbying from the finance industry. In this sense, the loophole reflects how certain wealthier groups have influenced tax policy to benefit themselves disproportionately at the expense of broader public interest, often perpetuating tax advantages that only reinforce the gap between ordinary taxpayers and the wealthiest individuals.

Greed-flation:
Why US Corporations Are Raising Prices Despite Surging Profits.

In recent years, Americans have been grappling with ever increasing prices, at the market, at the gas pump and for just about every aspect of life. This phenomenon is what has been coined "greedflation." A term that describes the practice where corporations exploit economic conditions to inflate prices far beyond their increased costs, leading to substantial profit surges.

During the COVID-19 pandemic, supply chain disruptions, increased labor costs, and heightened demand were commonly cited reasons for rising prices. However, an analysis by the Groundwork Collaborative reveals that these factors alone do not account for the sustained price increases. Instead, corporations leveraged these crises to hike prices disproportionately, boosting their profit margins substantially. From 2021 to 2023, corporate profits drove 53% of price increases, a stark contrast to the pre-pandemic era where profits accounted for just 11% of price growth.

The diaper industry is great example of Greedflation. Procter & Gamble and Kimberly-Clark, which dominate 70% of the U.S. diaper market, have significantly increased prices, citing rising costs of materials like wood pulp. However, even as wood pulp prices decreased by 25% over the past year, diaper prices remained high. This pricing strategy resulted in substantial profit increases, with P&G alone reporting an $800 million windfall.

Similarly, companies like PepsiCo and General Mills have openly discussed their strategies to maintain high prices despite decreasing input costs. PepsiCo, for example, increased consumer prices by 15% while planning to enhance profit margins further as costs stabilized.

The persistence of high prices despite easing supply chain issues and stabilized costs points to a deliberate strategy by corporations to maximize profits at the expense of consumers. This practice exacerbates economic inequality and places additional financial strain on American families who struggle to afford basic necessities. This is the equivalent of corporate Shock Doctrine, as described in Naomi Klien's "The Shock Doctrine", where corporations exploit any disruption, real or imagined to raise prices on the American public. Due to extreme consolidation in many sectors of the American economic landscape, there are few counterweights to combat this problem.

Economic analysts and advocates argue that such corporate behavior necessitates regulatory intervention. They propose measures such as revisiting corporate tax policies and implementing stricter price-gouging regulations to curb excessive profiteering and ensure a more equitable economic environment. With the increased consolidation in the markets, there is no functional competition which has led to just a few large providers of goods. When life's necessities are controlled by these few largely unregulated corporations, the "market solution" is a myth perpetuated by the very people who have created virtual monopolies on the necessary goods and services.

There is a growing call for policymakers to address greedflation through legislative means. Proposals include revising the corporate tax code and enforcing stricter regulations on price increases that cannot be justified by rising business costs. These measures aim to protect consumers from exploitative practices and promote a fairer distribution of economic gains. As the debate over greedflation intensifies, it is clear that a forceful, multifaceted approach involving regulatory oversight, corporate accountability, and corporate divestment (breaking up large companies) to ensure consumers are protected is essential in fostering a more balanced economy free from price gouging.

Greedflation highlights a critical issue in the current economic landscape, where corporations prioritize profit maximization over consumer welfare. Corporations love monopolies and hate competition, consolidation gives them purchasing power and control over pricing leading to lower quality and higher prices. Addressing this challenge will require concerted efforts from policymakers, regulatory bodies, and the public to ensure that economic growth benefits all segments of society, not just the corporate elite.

For more detailed analysis, refer to articles by Julia Conley on Common Dreams and other related reports on the impact of corporate profits on inflation and "Prices, Profits, and Power": An Analysis of 2021 Firm-Level Markups by Mike Konczal Niko Lusiani of the Roosevelt Institute, June 2022.

How Oil Corporations Work Together to Keep Prices Painfully High:

If you've ever wondered why filling up your gas tank feels like donating a kidney, you're not alone. Consumers worldwide are stuck watching oil prices soar, dragging up the cost of gasoline, heating, and just about everything else that depends on petroleum (which is, well... *everything*). But don't be fooled—this isn't just some natural fluctuation in supply and demand. No, this is a carefully orchestrated performance by oil corporations who have perfected the art of squeezing every last penny out of the public while blaming *anything but themselves*.

Of course, the oil market is *complicated*—or at least that's what industry execs would have you believe. They love to point fingers at geopolitical crises, refinery maintenance schedules, and even the weather to explain why prices remain high. But lurking behind all that noise is the real reason: major oil corporations and oil-producing nations colluding to keep prices at maximum pain levels while padding their bottom lines.

Take the **Organization of the Petroleum Exporting Countries (OPEC)** — a group of 13 oil-producing nations that claim to "stabilize" the market but mostly just stabilize their own profits. Sure, they openly manipulate production levels to influence prices, but the real fun happens in the shadows. According to a 2022 *Reuters* investigation, OPEC members, non-OPEC oil producers (like Russia), and major oil corporations have been holding *secret* meetings to discuss — you guessed it — production cuts and price controls. These supposedly innocent "market stabilization" talks are really just a polite way of saying, *"How can we make consumers suffer while maximizing shareholder value?"*

And let's not forget, when prices are high, oil companies get to flaunt record-breaking profits while ordinary people are left choosing between filling their gas tank or buying groceries. But hey, they'll tell you it's just the free market at work — nothing to see here!

The International Consortium of Investigative Journalists (ICIJ) uncovered documents showing that several major oil companies, including ExxonMobil, Shell, and BP, deliberately reduced production or delayed new projects to create artificial scarcity in the market . This practice, often falsely justified as a response to environmental regulations or market conditions, serves to keep prices elevated, benefiting the companies' bottom lines at the expense of consumers.

Geopolitical events significantly impact oil prices, and major oil corporations have not hesitated to leverage their influence over governments and international policies to create favorable conditions for price hikes. A report by The Guardian in 2023 highlighted how oil companies lobbied for sanctions against oil-rich nations like Venezuela and Iran, which constrained global oil supply and drove up prices . Furthermore, these corporations have been found to fund think tanks and political campaigns that support policies conducive to maintaining high oil prices.

The collusion among oil corporations and their manipulation of market dynamics have far-reaching consequences for consumers and the global economy. Elevated oil prices contribute to higher transportation and production costs, which are passed down to consumers in the form of increased prices for goods and services. This example of "Greedflation," hits working class Americans the hardest, it exacerbates inflationary pressures, erodes purchasing power and economic stability.

The 2022 surge in oil prices offers a stark illustration of the impact of collusion on consumers. Investigative reporting by ProPublica uncovered that while consumers faced record-high gasoline prices, oil companies reported unprecedented profits . For instance, ExxonMobil and Chevron posted quarterly profits exceeding $10 billion each during the peak of the price surge. Despite the public outcry and political pressure, these companies continued to prioritize shareholder returns over price relief for consumers.

The repercussions of sustained high oil prices extend beyond economic metrics. They contribute to greater economic inequality, disproportionately affecting low- and middle-income households who spend a larger share of their income on energy costs. This inequality often leads to social unrest, as seen in the widespread protests in Europe and Latin America in response to rising fuel prices . Governments, in turn, face increased pressure to implement subsidies or price controls, which can strain public finances and lead to long-term economic challenges.

Addressing the issue of Greedflation and collusion in the oil industry requires robust regulatory frameworks and international cooperation. However, the pervasive influence of oil corporations poses significant challenges to effective regulation. One critical step is the strengthening and enforcement of antitrust laws to prevent monopolistic practices and price-fixing agreements. The U.S. Federal Trade Commission (FTC) and the European Commission have launched investigations into potential anticompetitive behaviors in the oil industry, but these efforts need to be more aggressive and comprehensive.

Increasing transparency in the oil market is essential to curbing collusive practices. Governments and international organizations must mandate greater disclosure of production levels, pricing strategies, and lobbying activities by oil corporations. Initiatives like the Extractive Industries Transparency Initiative (EITI) aim to enhance transparency, but broader participation and stricter compliance are necessary. The proper thing to do would be to regulate these industries like "utilities", meaning that they are limited in how they conduct business. After all they are granted license to pump a natural resource that rightly belongs to the people and their profit should be reflected in the public good they provide.

Ultimately, reducing the global economy's dependence on oil is crucial to mitigating the impact of climate change. Investments in renewable energy sources and the promotion of energy efficiency can provide sustainable alternatives to fossil fuels. Policies that incentivize the adoption of electric vehicles, solar power, and wind energy can help decrease the market power of oil corporations and foster a more competitive energy landscape .

The collusion of oil corporations to keep prices high, poses significant challenges to consumers and the global economy. Through secretive agreements, manipulation of supply and demand, and influence over geopolitical events, these corporations have managed to maintain their profitability at the expense of broader economic stability while also endangering the environmental future of the planet. Addressing this issue requires a multifaceted approach, including stronger regulatory measures, increased transparency, and a shift towards alternative energy sources. Only by tackling the root causes of this collusion can we hope to achieve a more equitable and sustainable energy future.

References:
1. Reuters Investigative Report on OPEC and Non-OPEC Collusion, 2022.
2. ICIJ Report on Oil Companies' Manipulation of Supply, 2023.
3. The Guardian's Analysis of Oil Companies' Influence on Geopolitical Events, 2023.
4. ProPublica Investigation into Oil Price Surge and Corporate Profits, 2022.
5. Report on Social Unrest Due to High Fuel Prices, 2023.
6. FTC and European Commission Antitrust Investigations in the Oil Industry, 2023.
7. Extractive Industries Transparency Initiative (EITI) Reports, 2023.
8. Policies and Investments in Renewable Energy Sources, 2024.

Big Ag's Big Scam:

Subsidized Poison, Stressed-Out Farmers, and the Taxpayer pick up the Tab.

Welcome to the wild world of Big Ag, where giant corporations play the heroes of "feeding the world" while quietly turning your tax dollars into their personal buffet fund. It's a tale as American as apple pie—if the apples weren't coated in subsidized pesticides.

The Corporate Welfare Program You Didn't Sign Up For:
Let's start with farm subsidies. In theory, they're meant to help struggling farmers weather droughts, floods, and market crashes. In practice, most of that cash lands in the pockets of agribusiness giants like Monsanto (now Bayer) and Cargill, not the small farmers. These mega-corps rake in billions while the little guy is stuck scrounging in the dirt just to make some green.

Your hard-earned money funds this scheme, supporting monoculture crops like corn and soy that do wonders for corporate profit margins but wreak havoc on soil health. And let's not forget how those crops often get turned into less-than-nutritious goodies like high-fructose corn syrup. So, not only are you paying for it—you're eating it too!

Poisoning the Well (and the Field):
Speaking of what's on your plate, let's talk pesticides. Big Ag's playbook includes liberal doses of chemicals to maximize yield, leaving small farmers in a bind. Want to go organic? Good luck

competing when your neighbor's GMO crops drown yours in drift sprays of glyphosate.

And it's not just the environment that takes a hit. Small towns near industrial farms face contaminated water supplies, while farmworkers are exposed to health risks Big Ag would rather you didn't think about. Who knew "amber waves of grain" could double as a toxic wasteland?

Small Farmers: The Underdogs in an Unfair Fight

The mom-and-pop farms that built this country? They're being squeezed out faster than toothpaste from a tube. Big Ag monopolizes supply chains, forcing small farmers into contracts that make loan sharks look generous. Want to sell your corn? Sure, but only if you use our patented seeds, our fertilizer, and, oh yeah, sign here to lock in prices that barely cover costs.

Meanwhile, Big Ag lobbies for trade policies and tax breaks that make it nearly impossible for small farmers to compete. Imagine trying to run a lemonade stand when the guy down the street is getting free lemons from Uncle Sam.

So, What's the Fix?

Reforming the system means demanding transparency in subsidies, holding Big Ag accountable for environmental damage, and leveling the playing field for small farmers. Maybe it's time we reimagine the farm bill as a "food bill" that prioritizes public health, sustainability, and fairness.

Until then, every trip to the grocery store is a reminder: you're not just buying groceries—you're funding Big Ag's bottom line.

Supersizing Profits, Supersizing Waistlines:

It all started innocently enough: a juicy burger, a pile of fries, and a frosty milkshake. But somewhere along the way, fast food chains—most notably the golden arches themselves, McDonald's, decided to turn dinner into a supersized spectacle. And in the name of profits, they've helped fuel an obesity crisis that's as hard to ignore as that second helping of fries.

The Recipe for Disaster:
McDonald's didn't invent fast food, but it perfected it. The secret? Efficiency, consistency, and, most importantly, making everything irresistible and dirt cheap. But there's a catch: creating food that's affordable, addictive, and convenient often means sacrificing health. Sugary sodas, fat-laden fries, and sodium-packed patties became the norm—not because they're good for you, but because they're good for the bottom line.

Fast food companies turned portion sizes into a competitive sport. The "supersize" craze of the 1990s wasn't just about giving you more bang for your buck; it was about getting you hooked on the dopamine rush that comes from eating more salt, sugar, and fat than your body knows what to do with. (Spoiler: It stores it. Around your belly.)

Marketing Meets Biology:

The genius of McDonald's lies in its ability to make unhealthy eating feel like a celebration. Who can resist the allure of Happy Meals, complete with toys that lure kids into a lifetime of brand loyalty? They made fries fun, burgers cool, and soda the drink of choice. They didn't just sell food—they sold a lifestyle.

The problem? Our biology didn't get the memo. Humans are hardwired to crave calorie-dense foods—a survival mechanism from the days when dinner might not show up for another week. But McDonald's made it so dinner was always five minutes away. Cheap calories, zero effort. Our waistlines never stood a chance.

The Cost of Cheap Eats:

For McDonald's, the strategy was a gold mine. But for the public? A health crisis. By prioritizing profit over nutrition, fast food chains have contributed to skyrocketing rates of obesity, diabetes, and heart disease. The long-term costs are staggering—not just for individuals but for healthcare systems worldwide.

And let's not forget the food deserts, where McDonald's arches often outnumber grocery stores. For many communities, it's easier to grab a Big Mac than find fresh produce. Convenience isn't just an option; it's a trap.

Can't We Have It All?

The irony? McDonald's has the resources to do better. They've flirted with healthier options over the years—salads, fruit, even the occasional veggie burger. But let's be real: no one goes to McDonald's for kale. The healthier menu items often feel like an afterthought, a token gesture rather than a genuine shift.

Still, the tide is turning. Public awareness about the health impact of fast food is growing, and so are demands for accountability. People want convenience without sacrificing their health—or their future.

A Happy Meal for Change:

McDonald's may have helped create the obesity crisis, but they could also play a role in solving it. Imagine if the same marketing savvy used to sell fries was applied to promoting healthier, more sustainable options. It's a big ask, sure—but if anyone knows how to make a big impact, it's the company that brought you the Big Mac.

Until then, let's just say that the next time Ronald McDonald offers to supersize your meal, it might be worth thinking twice. Or at least asking if kale chips are on the menu yet.

Corporate Consolidation:
The Road to Market Manipulation and Price Gouging.

Fewer choices, higher prices. Even when it appears we have a choice between brands, they are often owned by the same parent corporation. Corporate consolidation, characterized by mergers and acquisitions that reduce the number of competitors in the marketplace, has become a defining feature of the modern economy. While proponents argue that such consolidation can lead to efficiencies and economies of scale, a growing body of investigative reporting and economic research reveals a darker side. As market power becomes concentrated in the hands of a few large corporations, instances of market manipulation and price gouging become more prevalent, adversely affecting consumers and the economy at large. The drive for greater and greater profit will inevitably lead to not only price increases, reduction of labor, either by automation or off-shoring jobs, but also to dubious business practices and tax cheating schemes.

Over the past few decades, industries ranging from healthcare to technology have witnessed significant consolidation. According to a report by the Institute for Local Self-Reliance, the number of independent pharmacies in the United States dropped by nearly 9% between 2010 and 2019, largely due to the aggressive expansion of major chains like CVS and Walgreens . Similarly, the airline industry has seen a dramatic reduction in competition, with four major airlines—American, Delta, United, and Southwest—controlling approximately 80% of the domestic market.

One of the most insidious effects of corporate consolidation is the ability of dominant firms to manipulate markets. In the pharmaceutical industry, for instance, large firms have been found to engage in practices that restrict competition and inflate prices. A 2018 investigation by ProPublica revealed how insulin prices in the United States tripled over a decade, a result of behind-the-scenes agreements among the few companies that dominate the insulin market . These companies exploited their market power to set high prices, knowing that patients reliant on insulin had no alternative but to pay.

In the tech sector, giants like Amazon, Apple, Google, and Meta (Facebook) have been scrutinized for using their platforms to favor their products over those of competitors. The House Judiciary Committee's 2020 antitrust report highlighted how Amazon manipulated its search algorithms to prioritize its products, thereby disadvantaging smaller sellers and stifling competition . Such practices not only undermine market fairness but also limit consumer choices.

Price gouging, the practice of raising prices to exorbitant levels, is another pernicious outcome of reduced competition. The COVID-19 pandemic provided stark examples of how consolidated markets can exploit crises. A report by the New York Times detailed how meatpacking giants like Tyson Foods, JBS, and Cargill raised prices significantly during the pandemic, citing increased costs and disruptions. However, subsequent investigations revealed that these companies were also reaping record profits, suggesting that the price hikes were not justified by increased costs.

In the healthcare sector, hospital mergers have led to similar outcomes. Research by the National Bureau of Economic Research found that hospital prices increased by 12% following mergers in concentrated markets . Patients, often with no alternative providers, are left to bear the burden of these inflated costs, leading to higher insurance premiums and out-of-pocket expenses as well as rationing care for those who can't afford the increased costs.

These are but a fraction of the industries that have seen substantial consolidation over the last few decades. These are some others that effect most Americans.

The Telecom Industry:
The merger of major telecommunications companies has resulted in fewer choices and higher prices for consumers. The consolidation of companies like AT&T and Time Warner has been criticized for leading to reduced competition and increased prices for cable and internet services. Investigative reports have pointed out how these mergers often come with promises of improved services and lower prices, which rarely materialize post-merger. These companies often operate as a monopoly in areas that have only one "reasonable" option for service.

The Agricultural Sector:
Monsanto's acquisition by Bayer is a prominent example of how consolidation in the agricultural sector leads to market manipulation. The combined entity controls a significant portion of the seed and pesticide market, allowing it to set higher prices and limit the availability of alternative products. ADM (Archer Daniels Midland Co),

Cargill, BASF and a few other large companies, some with revenues of 165 billion annually, control most of the agriculture market. Reports have highlighted the detrimental impact on farmers, who face higher input costs and reduced options. These companies also receive massive subsidies from the American tax payers and use their money and influence to perpetuate their control and profit. The result is small and minority farmers struggle to stay solvent while these mega-corporations reap huge profits.

The Airline Industry:

Consolidation in the airline industry has also been a focal point of investigative journalism. Mergers between major airlines have resulted in fewer choices for consumers and higher fares. Reports indicate that the promised benefits of efficiency and improved service often do not materialize, with consumers facing higher prices and frequent service issues. Air travel has become essential in American life and many small cities have seen a reduction or elimination of airline service. Cheyenne, Wyo. became one of dozens of small American cities to lose commercial air service—in its case, for the first time in 90 years.

As the airline industry continues its decades-long consolidation, more cities like Cheyenne are faced with the choice of either losing air service or coming up with millions of dollars in compensation, called "minimum revenue guarantees," so that multibillion-dollar airlines will deign to serve their relatively smaller communities. The trend has grown over the course of the pandemic: in the last few years, several medium-sized metro areas like Lincoln, Neb.; Pocatello, Idaho; and Tulsa, Okla., have had to use federal COVID-19 relief funds to pay airlines minimum revenue guarantees. These funds should have gone to improving their health care system and getting their children back in school but when faced with a choice of loosing air service, it's really a devil's bargain.

The ripple effects of market manipulation and price gouging extend beyond individual consumers. When large corporations inflate prices, they effectively extract more money from the economy, reducing the disposable income available for other goods and services. This can slow economic growth and exacerbate income inequality. Furthermore, smaller businesses, unable to compete with the pricing strategies of consolidated giants, often struggle to survive, leading to reduced innovation and fewer job opportunities and cities are often forced to reduce services and increase taxes to pay these higher prices effecting all the citizens of our country.

Recognizing the detrimental effects of corporate consolidation, policymakers and activists are calling for stricter antitrust enforcement and regulatory reforms. The Biden administration has signaled a more aggressive stance on antitrust issues, appointing advocates for stronger competition policies to key positions within the Federal Trade Commission and the Department of Justice . Additionally, legislative proposals such as the Ending Platform Monopolies Act aim to curb the market power of tech giants by imposing structural separations and prohibiting self-preferencing practices. These are steps in the right direction but the lobbying power and the "conservative" wing of our government have blocked many of these efforts or conservative judges have stepped in to invalidate government effort to reign in corporate excesses.

The consolidation of corporate power has far-reaching implications not only for market dynamics, but for democracy itself. Investigations have shed light on the mechanisms through which dominant firms manipulate markets and engage in price gouging and political interference, revealing a need for robust antitrust enforcement and regulatory oversight. As policymakers grapple with these challenges, the goal must be to restore competitive markets that work for consumers and the broader economy.

References

1. Institute for Local Self-Reliance. (2020). *Pharmacy Closures and Their Impacts on the Community*. Retrieved from [ilsr.org](https://ilsr.org/pharmacy-closures/)

2. U.S. Department of Transportation. (2020). *Airline Competition in the U.S.* Retrieved from [transportation.gov](https://www.transportation.gov/airline-competition)

3. ProPublica. (2018). *Insulin's High Cost Leads to Lethal Rationing*. Retrieved from [propublica.org](https://www.propublica.org/article/insulin-prices-unaffordable)

4. House Judiciary Committee. (2020). *Investigation of Competition in Digital Markets*. Retrieved from [judiciary.house.gov](https://judiciary.house.gov/issues/competition-in-digital-markets)

5. The New York Times. (2020). *Meatpacking Giants Lied About Price Hikes During Pandemic*. Retrieved from [nytimes.com](https://www.nytimes.com/meatpacking-pandemic-prices)

6. National Bureau of Economic Research. (2019). *The Price Effects of Cross-Market Hospital Mergers*. Retrieved from [nber.org](https://www.nber.org/papers/w26380)

7. The White House. (2021). *Executive Order on Promoting Competition in the American Economy*. Retrieved from [whitehouse.gov](https://www.whitehouse.gov/competition)

8. Congress.gov. (2021). *Ending Platform Monopolies Act*. Retrieved from [congress.gov](https://www.congress.gov/bill/117th-congress/house-bill/3825)

PART 5:

The military-corporate complex.

"*A standing military force, with an overgrown Executive, will not long be safe companions to liberty".*
James Madison - On the dangers of a standing military

The Black Hole Where They Throw Our Money:

As Americans we have a deep respect for our soldiers and rightly so, these men and women put themselves on he front lines whenever our politicians decide they're needed. Even when our leaders make decisions based on ideological rhetoric rather than any real threat to the U.S.. They have played fast and loose with what constitutes provocation for war. Since WWII the United States has been involved in numerous military conflicts, most notably the Korean War, the Vietnam War, the Persian Gulf War, the War in Afghanistan, and the Iraq War, plus numerous other minor conflicts all over the globe. The justifications for these wars have been found to be "thin" at best and at worst outright lies.

One thing has been pretty clear through it all, that caring for the veterans of these ill-advised military adventures has not been a priority for either party. Both major parties love to wave the flag and repeat "thank you for your service" any chance they get, and the Republicans are quick to target the Veterans Administration when looking to cut spending, but the military budget grows every year.

The DoD budget of $820 billion dollars (FY2023), some 13% of the federal budget, is larger than the next 10 largest countries combined. The bloated military budget, which is the vast majority of federal discretionary spending, breaks down like this.

$318 billion for Operation and Maintenance, which covers operations such as training and planning, maintenance of equipment, and most of the military healthcare system (separate from the Dept. of Veterans Affairs).

The next largest expense is military personnel, covering pay and retirement benefits for service members at a cost of $184 billion dollars.

Several smaller categories include Procurement of Weapons and Systems costs $142 billion, $122 billion for Research and Development of Weapons and Equipment. The military also spent over $10 billion on the construction and management of military facilities and $1 billion on family housing.

We are talking about hundreds of billions each year to develop, maintain and procure weapons and a large part of that goes to military contractors.

Military Contractors - Keep the Money Flowing:

The relationship between military contractors and politicians is a system that often ensures continuous funding for defense projects, even when the equipment in question is neither needed nor wanted by the military. This intricate interplay involves various strategies and mechanisms, including lobbying, political contributions, and leveraging local economic dependencies. This section delves into the dynamics of this relationship, examining how military contractors influence political decisions to secure ongoing financial support.

Lobbying is a primary tool used by military contractors to influence legislation and secure funding for their projects. Defense companies maintain large lobbying arms, staffed with former military personnel and government officials who possess extensive knowledge of the defense procurement process and the inner workings of government. These lobbyists engage with lawmakers to advocate for continued or increased defense spending on specific projects.

This involves direct interaction with legislators and their staff to persuade them to support defense contracts. Lobbyists provide detailed information, technical reports, and arguments to justify the necessity of ongoing projects.

Military contractors often mobilize employees, subcontractors, and suppliers to contact their representatives, emphasizing the local economic benefits of defense contracts and the potential job losses if funding is cut.

"Astroturf Campaigns" are orchestrated efforts that appear to be spontaneous grassroots movements but are actually coordinated by lobbyists. They aim to create the illusion of widespread public support for defense projects.

Military contractors are significant contributors to political campaigns, using political action committees (PACs) and direct donations to gain favor with lawmakers. By financially supporting candidates who advocate for robust defense spending, contractors ensure a political climate conducive to their interests. Defense companies typically contribute to both major political parties to hedge their bets and maintain influence regardless of which party holds power. Contributions are often directed towards key members of defense-related committees in Congress, such as the Armed Services and Appropriations Committees, which have significant control over defense budgets.

The revolving door between government and the defense industry allows former military officers and government officials to take high-paying jobs with defense contractors after their public service careers, while individuals from the defense industry join government positions, influencing policy from within. Individuals transitioning from government to industry bring with them insider knowledge and connections, which can be leveraged to secure contracts and influence procurement decisions. Those moving from industry to government positions can shape defense policies and budgets in ways that benefit their former employers.

Defense contracts often have significant economic implications for local communities. Contractors strategically distribute production and maintenance facilities across multiple congressional districts to build a broad base of political support. Lawmakers, motivated by the economic interests of their constituents, are thus inclined to support continued funding for these projects.

Defense contracts create and sustain jobs in local communities, making them politically sensitive issues. Politicians are reluctant to cut funding for projects that provide substantial employment in their districts. Beyond direct employment, defense spending stimulates local economies through secondary and tertiary economic activities, further increasing political pressure to maintain funding.

The F-35 program is a prime example of how military contractors and politicians interact to maintain funding. Despite numerous delays, cost overruns, and technical issues, the program continues to receive substantial financial support. This is partly due to the widespread distribution of subcontractors and suppliers across various states and congressional districts, creating a strong incentive for lawmakers to advocate for its continuation.

The production of Abrams tanks offers another illustration. The U.S. Army has, at times, indicated that it does not need additional tanks, yet production continues due to political pressure. The main contractor, General Dynamics, has leveraged its economic impact on local communities and its relationships with key lawmakers to sustain funding.

The relationship between military contractors and politicians is characterized by a symbiotic dynamic where financial influence, lobbying efforts, and economic dependencies ensure a continuous flow of defense funding. Despite instances where the military does not require the equipment being produced, this system remains resilient due to the interlocking interests of contractors, lawmakers, and local economies. Understanding this relationship is crucial for comprehending the broader dynamics of defense spending and procurement in the United States.

A side note: It's estimated that 100 billion dollars could end poverty in the US, or power every household in the United States with solar energy, or hire one million elementary school teachers amid a teacher shortage. It would provide free tuition for 2 out of 3 public college students in the U.S., or send every household in the U.S. a $700 check to help offset inflation or hire 890,000 Registered Nurses to address staffing shortages or cover medical care for 7 million veterans or line the pockets of a few high powered CEOs.

The Military Money Machine and the $400 Toilet Seat:
Cost-Plus Arrangements.

Military contracting is a lucrative industry, with significant financial stakes for companies involved in defense procurement. A substantial portion of this wealth is derived from cost-plus arrangements, a type of contract where the government agrees to reimburse contractors for allowable costs incurred during a project, plus an additional fee for profit. While this contracting method promises "flexibility and responsiveness" in defense projects, it also creates opportunities for contractors to maximize profits at the expense of taxpayers.

Cost-plus contracts, also known as cost-reimbursement contracts, are agreements where the contractor is paid for all legitimate costs incurred during the performance of the contract, plus a fee representing profit. These contracts are categorized into several types:

1. Cost-Plus-Fixed-Fee (CPFF): The contractor is reimbursed for allowable costs and receives a fixed fee determined at the outset.

2. Cost-Plus-Incentive-Fee (CPIF): The contractor is reimbursed for costs and receives a fee that can vary based on performance in meeting specified targets.

3. Cost-Plus-Award-Fee (CPAF): Similar to CPIF, but with the fee determined subjectively based on the government's evaluation of the contractor's performance.

While incentive and award fees are meant to promote efficiency and quality, they can sometimes be manipulated. Contractors might negotiate favorable terms that ensure they receive these fees with minimal effort. Additionally, the subjective nature of award fees can lead to situations where contractors receive bonuses despite mediocre performance.

Cost-plus contracts are advantageous in scenarios where project scope is uncertain, technical complexity is high, or rapid changes are expected. They ensure that contractors are not discouraged from undertaking high-risk or innovative projects due to financial uncertainties. Additionally, they provide the government with a mechanism to start projects quickly without having to negotiate fixed costs upfront.

While cost-plus contracts offer flexibility, they also create a potential for financial exploitation. Contractors have financial incentives to inflate costs or prioritize higher-cost solutions to increase their overall profit, which is calculated as a percentage of the total costs. Since their reimbursement is directly tied to the costs incurred, there is an inherent incentive to maximize those costs within the bounds of what is allowable.

These include:

Overestimating Labor Costs:
Contractors might overestimate the number of hours required or the skill level needed, thereby increasing the total cost.

Marking Up Materials:
Charging higher prices for materials than what was actually paid or using more expensive suppliers unnecessarily.

Administrative Overhead:
Increasing indirect costs such as administrative support, management, and other overheads.

Lack of Cost Control:
Cost-plus contracts do not incentivize contractors to control or reduce costs effectively. Since all allowable costs are reimbursed, there is little motivation to find efficiencies or cost-saving measures. This lack of cost control can lead to massively Inflated Costs.

Over-billing and Fraud:

In some cases, contractors might engage in outright fraud by over-billing for work not performed, inflating hours, or charging for higher-grade materials and services than what was actually used. While such actions are illegal, oversight and enforcement can be inconsistent, allowing some contractors to exploit the system.

Cost Overruns:

Where the contractors don't exercise stringent cost controls, padding their profits with higher overall project expenses. Gold-Plating, where Contractors might opt for higher-cost materials or technologies that exceed project requirements, driving up costs unnecessarily or extended timelines where contractors draw out the time to complete projects, leading to schedule delays and increased costs.

Numerous examples highlight the potential for abuse in cost-plus contracting. One of the most infamous cases is the *F-35 Joint Strike Fighter program*, where cost overruns and delays have drastically increased the program's total cost. Initially projected to cost around $200 billion, estimates now exceed $1.7 trillion over its lifecycle. These overruns have been blamed on various factors, including technical challenges, but also reflect the dynamics of cost-plus contracting.

Another example is the logistics contracts awarded to companies like Halliburton and its subsidiary KBR (formerly Kellogg Brown & Root), during the Iraq War. Reports and investigations revealed significant overcharging and cost inflation on various projects, including building bases and providing logistical support. These contracts were largely cost-plus, leading to substantial profits for the companies involved. For instance, KBR was accused of charging $45 for a case of soda and $100 to wash a bag of laundry. These companies had ties to then Vice President Dick Cheney, he was Halliburton's former CEO and maintained significant financial interest in the company at the same time it was awarded highly lucrative contracts by his administration.

In response to the potential for abuse, several regulatory and oversight mechanisms have been put in place:

1. Defense Contract Audit Agency (DCAA): The DCAA audits and oversees defense contracts to ensure that costs are allowable and reasonable.

2. Federal Acquisition Regulation (FAR): FAR provides comprehensive guidelines for government procurement, including cost principles and administrative requirements for cost-reimbursement contracts.

3. Inspector General (IG) Reports: IG offices regularly conduct investigations and audits of defense contracts to identify and rectify issues of waste, fraud, and abuse.

Despite these oversight mechanisms, critics argue that cost-plus contracts still pose significant risks of financial mismanagement. Some of us will remember the $400 toilet seats that shocked the public and kickstarted the calls for an audit.

Calls for reform include suggestions to increase the use of fixed-price contracts, where appropriate, to ensure better cost control and accountability. Stricter Oversight and Auditing, Performance-Based Contracting and a Cap on Fees. Additionally, enhancing the transparency and rigor of oversight mechanisms can help mitigate the risks associated with cost-plus arrangements.

The use of cost-plus contracts can lead to significant financial burdens on taxpayers. When contractors are incentivized to increase costs, the overall expenditure on defense projects can balloon, leading to higher national debt or reallocation of funds from other critical areas.

Ironically, the lack of cost control can also lead to suboptimal outcomes in terms of quality and efficiency. Projects may be completed with unnecessary features or at a slower pace, ultimately impacting the readiness and capability of the armed forces.

The Federal Trash Can:
Waste and Abuse in the Military Budget.

The United States military budget is the largest in the world, consistently accounting for a major portion of the federal budget. However, the allocation and expenditure of these funds have often come under scrutiny due to instances of waste, fraud, and abuse. The inability of the Department of Defense (DoD) to pass a comprehensive audit, the misplacement of substantial funds, and specific case studies like Iraq, highlight systemic issues in financial management and accountability within the military.

The Department of Defense has historically struggled to pass a comprehensive financial audit. Despite efforts spanning decades, the DoD remains the only federal agency unable to account for all of its assets and expenditures satisfactorily. The Government Accountability Office (GAO) and various watchdog organizations have repeatedly pointed out deficiencies in the DoD's financial management systems. These include outdated accounting systems, lack of proper documentation, and poor internal controls.

The first full-scope audit of the DoD, completed in 2018, revealed numerous deficiencies. These included unsupported accounting adjustments, poor record-keeping, and a lack of internal controls. Subsequent audits have similarly identified significant issues, reflecting deep-seated structural problems within the department's financial management systems. The significance of this failure cannot be overstated. The inability to pass an audit makes it difficult to ensure that taxpayer dollars are being spent appropriately.

One of the most alarming instances of financial mismanagement within the DoD came to light in the early 2000s when it was revealed that the Pentagon could not account for approximately $1 trillion in transactions. This revelation was part of a broader pattern of fiscal disarray, including undocumented adjustments and untraceable transactions. The DoD's then-Chief Financial Officer admitted that the department had lost track of massive amounts of money, further emphasizing the need for comprehensive oversight and reform.

The issue of misplaced funds is indicative of deeper systemic problems. The complexity of military operations, coupled with a lack of rigorous financial controls, creates an environment where funds can easily be misallocated or lost. This situation not only leads to significant waste but also opens the door to inevitable fraud and corruption.

Iraq: A Case Study in Legal Corruption. The U.S. military's involvement in Iraq provides a stark example of how legal corruption can manifest in large-scale military operations. The Iraq War, initiated in 2003, saw an unprecedented flow of money into the country for reconstruction efforts, military contracts, and various operational expenses. However, much of this expenditure has been marred by waste, fraud, and abuse.

One of the critical factors contributing to financial debacle in Iraq was the extensive use of private contractors. Companies like Halliburton and its subsidiary, KBR, were awarded no-bid contracts worth billions of dollars. These contracts were criticized for their lack of transparency and oversight. Reports of overcharging, substandard work, and outright fraud were rampant. For instance, KBR was found to have billed the government for services that were either not rendered or grossly overpriced, such as charging $45 for a case of soda. There were numerous cases where if a vehicle had a flat tire or needed other minor repairs, they would scrap it and requisition a new one, leading to massive expense to the tax payers and a thriving black market in military surplus. Then there were the pallets of US currency shipped to Iraq. Beginning in the very earliest days of the war in Iraq, the New York Federal Reserve shipped billions of dollars in physical cash to Baghdad to pay for the reopening of the government and restoration of basic services. By one account, the New York Fed shipped about $40 billion in cash between 2003 and

2008. In just the first two years, the shipments included more than 281 million individual bills weighing a total of 363 tons. Soon after the money arrived it evaporated and there is still no accounting for hundreds of millions of dollars.

The lack of accountability in contracting processes facilitated an environment where corruption could thrive. The complex web of subcontractors and the sheer scale of operations made it difficult to monitor and control spending effectively. This scenario underscores the need for stringent oversight mechanisms to prevent financial abuses in future military engagements. Maybe a better idea would be to return our military to a more self-sustaining organization and use far fewer contractors.

Billions of dollars allocated for the reconstruction of Iraq were either wasted or unaccounted for. The Special Inspector General for Iraq Reconstruction (SIGIR) reported numerous instances of mismanagement, including projects that were never completed and facilities that were unusable due to poor construction. For example, the construction of a police academy in Baghdad, which cost $75 million, resulted in a facility that was unsafe and unsanitary.

These failures highlight not just inefficiency but also the impact of corruption on reconstruction efforts. The misallocation of funds and resources meant that many Iraqis did not see any benefits of the massive expenditure, further destabilizing the region and undermining U.S. objectives.

When President Bush sent the former Henry Kissinger staffer and neoconservative "terror expert" Paul Bremer to Baghdad in the summer of 2003, he boldly declared that Iraq was "open for business." Bremer swiftly set about applying Milton Friedman's radical economic formula in the Arab world, this would come in the form of privatization, complete free trade, a 15% flat tax and a dramatically downsized government. It didn't take long for the relief the Iraqi's felt about life without Saddam Hussein to become collective rage at the US policies.

A US ally in the region declared Iraqis were "sick and tired of being the subjects of experiments. There have been enough shocks to the system, so we don't need this shock therapy in the economy." This radical economic agenda, combined with the disastrous de-Baathification policy, resulted in tens of thousands of state workers as well as some 250,000 Iraqi soldiers losing their jobs overnight, and the "Bremer agenda" would give rise to a widespread Iraqi resistance to the occupation, costing tens of thousands of lives and the almost total destruction of Iraq. All at the expense of the American tax payer.

The financial mismanagement and corruption in Iraq had significant consequences for both military operations and local populations. For U.S. forces, the failed economic policies, the lack of accountability and inefficiency translated into an operational boondoggle, as funds that could have been used for critical support and resources were wasted. For Iraqi civilians, the failure of reconstruction efforts exacerbated the hardships caused by the war, contributing to ongoing instability and resentment towards the U.S.

The issues of waste and abuse in the military budget, exemplified by the inability to pass an audit, the misplacement of funds, and the legal corruption seen in Iraq, underscore the need for reform within the Department of Defense. Addressing these challenges is not only a matter of financial prudence but also critical for maintaining public trust and ensuring that defense spending genuinely enhances national security. Implementing robust oversight mechanisms and modernizing financial management systems are essential steps towards addressing these persistent challenges. Fostering a culture of fiscal responsibility within the military is vital and we also need to hold the people responsible for the mismanagement, fraud and abuse accountable, with real consequences including jail time.

The issues of waste and abuse in the military budget, exemplified by the Pentagon's audit failures and financial mismanagement, highlight the urgent need for reform. When we fund the military at this level, we are sacrificing resources that could go schools, infrastructure, housing or healthcare. So it's about time we had a reckoning with the bloated, corrupt military budget.

For an eye-opening account of not only the waste and abuse of taxpayer dollars but also the human rights abuses that took place in Iraq and Afghanistan, I suggest the excellent work by journalist Jeremy Scahill in his book *Blackwater - The Rise of the World's Most Powerful Mercenary Army.*

Part 6:

Public Money, Private Profit

The Great American Sell-Off: How Privatization Screws the Public:

Take a look around—if it hasn't been privatized yet, give it a minute. Schools, roads, libraries, courts, prisons, and even *the law itself* are being handed over to private companies by state and local governments that have fallen for the myth that the private sector is magically more efficient at running public services. Spoiler alert: it's not. What actually happens is taxpayers end up paying more for worse service while corporations laugh all the way to the bank.

Just ask the people of **Chicago**, who got the privilege of witnessing one of the worst privatization deals in history. The city leased out its parking meters to a private company, which promptly hiked prices and locked in a deal so bad that Chicagoans will be paying for it **until 2084**. What a win for efficiency! The truth is, when we privatize essential services, we're not making them more efficient—we're just handing over public assets to companies that turn around and sell them *back to us* at a premium. It's the corporate equivalent of stealing your wallet and then offering to *rent* it back to you.

This madness isn't accidental. There's been a long-running effort— mostly from the right—to smear public services as "Big Government" boogeymen. They even rebranded public schools as "government schools" to make them sound sinister, as if kids are being taught in some Orwellian dystopia instead of, you know, *a classroom*. This is why we desperately need a **pro-public culture**—one that unapologetically demands that what belongs to the people stays in the hands of the people.

So let's break down exactly why privatization is one of the worst scams the American people keep falling for—and why it's time to stop selling off our future to the highest bidder.

Selling America by the Pound:

The Privatization of government services, a process advocated by many conservatives, involves transferring the management and delivery of services traditionally provided by the public sector to private companies. Proponents argue that this can lead to increased efficiency, cost savings, and improved service quality due to competition and profit-driven incentives. However, results show that privatization often results in the transfer of wealth from public to private hands, benefiting private corporations at the expense of the public. This is a look into the various ways that corporations are extracting more and more money from the American citizens and degrading our infrastructure and eroding our civic power.

The Privatization of Everything:
How the Plunder of Public Goods Transformed America.

Let's start this chapter with the a book written by Donald Cohen and Allen Mikaelian, "The Privatization of Everything". The authors delve into the widespread trend of privatizing public goods and services in

America, examining the impact this has had on society and offering insights on how to counter this movement.

"When you move a service to the market, the market excludes. But the only way for us to create a healthy nation is to make sure everybody's healthy. The only way for us to clean the air and solve climate change is for all of us, collectively, as individuals, as businesses, as government, doing things together. Government is the instrument for making this happen. But it's also important to understand that the market is made up of real people, institutions, and companies. Private companies sell things, right? Oil companies sell gasoline and everything else that comes from the extraction and production of oil. Apple sells iPhones. They care about sales volume, production, distribution, market share, and profit. Do private entities sell things to people who don't have money? No. When hospitals are private, rural hospitals close because there's no money there. If markets exclude it's because that's what they do, the public needs to *include*. Also, the private sector doesn't share information with competitors.

Take privatized education, in the form of charter schools. Charter schools were supposed to be innovative laboratories, sharing new ideas about how to teach that could benefit all schools. But in today's market model, schools compete against one another, and they don't share. Teachers who work for charter schools must often sign nondisclosure agreements that protect the charter school's trade secrets: lesson plans, curriculum, teaching methods, and ideas. That works exactly against what we want to happen in education.

"Markets are legit things. Public goods are legit things. But markets are the wrong instrument for delivering what should be universally accessible public goods."

Quoted from Donald Cohen interview.

The book traces the history of privatization in America, highlighting how it gained momentum in the late 20th century. It explains how neoliberal policies and ideologies promoted the idea that private companies could manage public services more efficiently than government entities. It also discusses the consequences of privatizing essential public services such as education, healthcare, water, transportation, and prisons. They demonstrate that privatization often leads to higher costs, reduced access, and lower quality of services. The authors provide numerous examples to illustrate how privatization has failed to deliver on its promises. The book emphasizes that privatization exacerbates economic and social inequalities. By turning public goods into profit-driven enterprises, it often benefits wealthy investors at the expense of ordinary citizens. The authors contend that privatization undermines the principles of equity and fairness that public goods are supposed to uphold. Cohen and Mikaelian explore the role of corporate lobbying and political influence in driving the privatization agenda. They argue that powerful corporations and interest groups have shaped policies to favor privatization, often through campaign contributions and lobbying efforts. Despite the pervasive influence of privatization, the book highlights instances of community resistance and successful efforts to reclaim public goods. The authors showcase grassroots movements and policy initiatives that have challenged privatization and promoted the reinvestment in public services.

The authors argue passionately for the importance of preserving and strengthening public goods and services and offer strategies for fighting back against privatization. They advocate for stronger regulations, increased public investment, and greater transparency in government contracts and stress the importance of public engagement and community activism in reclaiming public goods.

"The Privatization of Everything" serves as both a warning about the dangers of unchecked privatization and a call to action for citizens to reclaim control over essential public resources.

Key Mechanisms of Wealth Transfer through privatization:

Governments may outsource services such as waste management, public transportation, or prison operations to private companies. These companies often aim to cut costs to maximize profit, which can lead to reduced wages and benefits for workers, lower quality of services, and increased fees for users. The savings generated through cost-cutting are then transferred to the company's executives and shareholders rather than being reinvested in public services or returned to taxpayers.

Public-Private Partnerships (PPPs): involve collaboration between government and private sector companies to fund, build, and operate projects like infrastructure, schools, or hospitals. While PPPs are touted as a means to leverage private investment for public goods, they often include long-term contracts that guarantee private profits, sometimes at the cost of higher expenses for the public sector. Over time, these costs are borne by taxpayers, transferring public wealth to private investors.

Privatization of Public Assets: Selling public assets, such as utilities, transportation networks, or natural resources, to private companies can provide a short-term influx of cash to government budgets. However, these sales often result in private monopolies or oligopolies controlling essential services. This can lead to higher prices for consumers and reduced accountability. The long-term revenues generated from these assets, which would have funded public services, now enrich private owners.

Voucher Systems and Charter Schools: In education, voucher systems and the expansion of charter schools divert public funds to private institutions. Vouchers allow parents to use public money for private school tuition, while charter schools are publicly funded but privately operated. Critics argue that these systems drain resources from traditional public schools, leading to a two-tiered education system that benefits private entities while public schools face budget shortfalls and declining quality. It also benefits those wealthy individuals with a cash infusion who would been sending the children to private schools anyway.

Healthcare: Privatizing aspects of healthcare, such as hospitals, health insurance, or services like ambulance operations, shifts control and profits to private companies. This can lead to increased healthcare costs for patients and reduced access to care, especially for low-income individuals. Public funds that once supported universal healthcare services are redirected to private insurers and providers, leading to a wealth transfer from taxpayers to the private sector.

Some of the problems with the corporate privatization movement: Privatization often exacerbates economic inequality. High profits and executive compensation in privatized sectors contrast sharply with wage stagnation or job losses for workers. Moreover, access to essential services like education, healthcare, and utilities can become more unequal, disproportionately affecting low-income and marginalized communities.

Private companies are primarily accountable to shareholders, not the public. This often leads to a lack of transparency, reduced public oversight, and decisions driven by profit rather than public interest. In sectors like prisons or healthcare, this can have severe consequences for service quality and ethical standards. More on this later.

While privatization can provide short-term financial relief for local governments, it often leads to higher long-term costs. Public sectors may lose revenue-generating assets, and the government may face increased expenses due to contractual obligations or the need to address service failures by private providers.

The commodification of services that were once considered public goods can undermine their availability and quality. Education, healthcare, and infrastructure are vital for social well-being and economic stability, and their privatization leads to a focus on profitability over accessibility and equity.

The conservative push for privatization of government services is rooted in the purported belief in "free-market" principles and the perceived inefficiencies of the public sector. However, the process often results in a significant transfer of wealth from the public to private hands. Leading to increased inequality, reduced accountability, and higher long-term costs for society. While privatization can offer benefits in specific contexts, it is crucial to consider these broader impacts and ensure that essential services remain accessible, equitable, and accountable to the public.

Water, Water Everywhere...

The Privatization of Pennsylvania's Sewer System.

BREAKING NEWS! - *Sewer rates soar as private companies buy up local water systems!*

For residents in several Pennsylvania communities, flushing the toilet has suddenly gotten much more expensive. Private water companies have bought up wastewater systems from local governments and rates hikes have begun to smell like crap.

Over the past few years, the privatization of Pennsylvania's sewer systems has sparked significant debate among residents, policymakers, and economists. While the primary goal of privatization often includes improved efficiency and infrastructure investment, the reality for many Pennsylvanians has been a sharp increase in sewer service costs. This trend raises questions about the benefits and drawbacks of transferring public utilities to private ownership.

Privatization of sewer systems in Pennsylvania began as a strategy to address aging infrastructure and budgetary constraints faced by municipalities. By selling or leasing these utilities to private companies, local governments aimed to secure immediate financial relief and long-term investments in modernization. Companies like Aqua America and Pennsylvania American Water have been prominent players in acquiring these assets, promising better service and compliance with environmental regulations.

The private water industry has lobbied hard in state capitols, while also pushing Congress to provide them with federal funding that has historically been reserved for local governments.

Despite these promises, the financial burden on consumers has increased substantially. Numerous communities have reported that their sewer bills have doubled or even tripled following privatization. For example, in the Borough of Limerick, residents experienced a significant rate hike shortly after their sewer system was sold to a private entity. This pattern has been observed across various municipalities, leading to widespread public outcry.

What factors contribute to these price increases: Research published last year (2023) surveyed the United States '500 largest water systems and found that private ownership was the most significant variable in driving up utility bills — even more than aging infrastructure, water supply and local regulations.

Private companies are driven by profit, which often leads to higher rates as they seek returns on their investments, also when private companies acquire public utilities, they often incur substantial debt. These costs are frequently passed on to consumers through increased rates. While infrastructure improvements are necessary, the costs associated with these upgrades are typically reflected in the rates charged to customers.

Regulating private utilities presents another layer of complexity. The Pennsylvania Public Utility Commission (PUC) oversees rate changes and service quality, but critics argue that the commission often approves significant rate increases proposed by private companies. The regulatory framework may lack sufficient rigor to protect consumers from excessive price hikes, thus weakening public trust in the government's commitment to protect consumers.

The impact of rising sewer prices extends beyond individual households. Higher utility bills disproportionately affect low-income families. Additionally, businesses facing increased operational costs may pass these expenses onto consumers or reduce their workforce, indirectly impacting the local economy.

Public response to sewer privatization has been overwhelmingly negative, with numerous communities organizing to resist further privatization efforts. Some municipalities are exploring the possibility of reversing privatization deals, though this process is legally and financially challenging.

"Providing water is really expensive as it is," she said. *"If you then add making a profit as part of the cost of the service, it just makes it really unaffordable."*

In Pennsylvania, Food and Water Watch said that more than 30 water systems — primarily sewer — have been sold off since the passage of the 2016 law. Another dozen or so local governments are currently considering offers, according to Jennie Shade, senior director of government relations with the Pennsylvania Municipal Authorities Association, which represents the special purpose districts that oversee public services and is seeking to protect local oversight.

Since the beginning of the year, 31 water or wastewater systems nationwide have been purchased by private companies or have a pending sale proposal. All but three are in states with *"fair market value"* laws on the books.

Shade's group estimates that completed acquisitions are costing ratepayers $70 million to $85 million annually in higher water bills, and pending sales could double that amount.

"We're seeing buyer's remorse in a lot of communities," she said. "Pennsylvania has become ground zero for the commoditization of our precious public water supply."

In conclusion, while the privatization of Pennsylvania's sewer systems was intended to address fiscal and infrastructural challenges, it has resulted in significant price increases for consumers. This outcome highlights the need for careful consideration of the long-term implications of privatizing essential public services and underscores the importance of robust regulatory frameworks to safeguard public interests.

*Water Policy, the journal of the international think tank "World Water Counci"l.

Flush with Cash - The Importance of Utilities:

Utilities are essential services that we all rely on daily – electricity, gas, water, sewage, and waste management. These services can either be government-owned (public) or owned by private companies (private). Deciding whether utilities should be public or privatized is a complex debate with reasonable arguments on both sides. I will attempt to provide an overview of the key differences, pros, and cons of public and private utilities.

Public utilities are owned and operated by local, state, or federal governments on behalf of citizens and customers in that area. Public utilities include: Municipal water, sewage, and sanitation services, Public electricity providers, Government-run public transit systems, State-owned telecommunication companies. Public utilities have to balance serving the public interest while remaining financially sustainable. Since they are not profit-driven, any revenue earned is invested back into maintaining infrastructure and operations. This is often driven by politics, as elected representatives want to be seen as fiscally responsible at the same time maintaining public services without raising taxes.

Private utilities are owned and operated by private companies that include: Investor-owned electricity companies / telecommunication providers / Privately-owned oil, gas, and pipelines / Waste management companies. Private utilities aim to make a profit for their shareholders while delivering a public service. Most private utilities operate as regulated monopolies in their service areas, but these regulations vary depending localities and the contracts signed by local officials. Often this eliminates "market forces" like competition and maintenance and improvements costs are generally passed on to the public.

There are five main variables that differentiate private and public utilities:

1. Ownership & Motives

Publicly owned utilities serve the public interest rather than pursue profits. In contrast, private utilities are owned by investors and aim to maximize shareholder returns.

2. Regulation & Pricing

Public utilities are regulated by government-appointed commissions that oversee pricing and service standards. Private utilities are also regulated but usually have more flexibility in rate-setting.

3. Service Areas

Most public utilities only serve customers within municipal boundaries. Investor-owned utilities often have defined regional monopolies with little overlap or competition for customers. This can make sense when a municipality is too small to create it's own service (i.e. trash collection).

4. Infrastructure Spending

Public utilities may find it easier to raise funds for long-term capital projects and maintain infrastructure proactively. Privately owned utilities answer to shareholders seeking returns, which impacts investment decisions. Because of the profit motive, companies often resist making investments in necessary maintenance or improvements.

5. Customer Service Focus

Public utilities focus more on providing service to its customers and addressing community needs. Private entities have profit motives that may override localized customer concerns. A common misconception is the private companies offer better customer service, this may be true because public services are often the victim of political machinations, but private companies are always looking for ways to increase shareholder value and service is one of the easiest ways to cut costs.

There are many arguments in favor of keeping essential utilities under public ownership and operation. Their focus on serving community needs rather than shareholder profits. Revenues are reinvested to improve infrastructure and maintain reliable service. The public retains more control over long-term planning and investments and because it's not driven by profit margins, shareholders or quarterly earnings this promotes increased service stability and universal access.

Some of the issues associated with public control is the susceptibility to political interference and bureaucratic stall. Due to budget constraints this may result in slower modernization and technology adoption and difficulty raising funds for major capital projects. With the decades-long war on public management and the demonization of taxes can make it difficult to communicate the needs and benefits when budgets are tight.

Overall, public ownership ensures community-focused management and operations compared to private corporations accountable to distributed shareholders. However, political corruption, bureaucratic red-tape and aversion to raising taxes can also impede an agile response to ever evolving customer and infrastructure needs.

There are some reasonable arguments to be made in favor of privatization but the negative impulses of businesses and the track record of focusing on profits often at the expense of the public interest suggest it may be a "devil's bargain". With limited transparency and accountability coupled with the motivation to maximize profits for shareholder returns can lead to neglected maintenance and higher rates to satisfy shareholder dividends. The profit motive results in uneven service and lack of access for less profitable markets. Privatization also concentrates control of essential services into corporate hands that don't necessarily serve community needs equitably. Sometimes it's the elected officials decisions that have negative impact on the public welfare. For instance, in Flint Michigan's water crisis began in 2014 when the the Republican Government switched its drinking water source from Lake Huron to the Flint River, which led to lead contamination in the water supply, sickening thousands of people and especially children. This ultimately resulted in tens of millions of dollars to repair the damage and compensate victims. That money came from the tax payers.

Moving forward, a balance must be struck between the need for infrastructure investment and the protection of consumers from excessive costs. Potential solutions include: Stronger Regulatory Oversight: Enhancing the PUC's ability to scrutinize and limit rate increases could help mitigate the financial impact on residents.

Public-Private Partnerships: These arrangements can offer a middle ground, allowing for private investment while maintaining public control over pricing and service standards.

Increased Transparency: Ensuring that privatization deals are transparent and involve public input can help align the interests of all stakeholders.

All this being said, the pros of public control outweigh the cons when it comes to delivering essential services to the public. Many of the drawbacks could be overcome with greater public involvement and a commitment by our political representatives to act in the best interest of our citizens, but alas…

Chicago Sold Its Parking Meters: … No Parking Anytime, Anywhere:

In 2008, then-Mayor Richard M. Daley of Chicago proposed selling the city's 36,000 parking meters to raise money for the city's budget deficit. The deal was made with brokers affiliated with Morgan Stanley to create Chicago Parking Meters LLC (CPM), who would lease the meters to the city for 75 years at $1.15 billion. The agreement includes the following provisions:

The city must pay CPM for lost revenue if it: 1- Cuts parking fees, 2 - Reduces the number of spaces, 3- Reduces the hours of operation.

The city must reimburse CPM for every parking space taken out of service when streets are closed for special events, sewer repairs, and other construction projects. They are also limited in how they can regulate parking hours, which takes away their ability to make common-sense decisions about everything from snow emergencies to more efficient ways to use the streets for mass transit.

The parking meter deal gets even worse for Chicago taxpayers.

Chicago parking meter revenues are nearly back to pre-pandemic levels. After dipping to $91.6 million in 2020, they climbed to $136.2 million last year. With 61 years to go on the 75-year lease, Chicago Parking Meters LLC has now recouped its entire $1.16 billion investment, plus $502.5 million more.

In a short time, the cost to park on the streets of Chicago quadrupled. Now Chicago residents are on the hook for lost revenues for closing the streets for everything from street cleaning to festivals. A company like Morgan Stanley wouldn't enter into a contract without the massive upside for profit and the people, not the politicians, will have to pay for it.

Selling the Crossroads of America:

Indiana really is the crossroads of America. The moniker refers to Indiana's capital, Indianapolis, the city's central location is at the junction of four major Interstate Highways: In 2006, under the orchestration of Gov. Mitch Daniels (R), the state struck a deal to lease the Indiana Toll Road (ITR) to the ITR Concession Company (ITRCC). The ITR is a 157-mile toll road that runs east-west across northern Indiana, connecting the Chicago Skyway to the Ohio Turnpike. The governor used the firm Goldman Sacks to lease the road for a period of 75 years to Australia-based Macquarie Group and Spain-based Cintra. The investors paid the state $3.8 billion upfront in exchange for the right to collect tolls. The investors are required to maintain and upgrade the road for the duration of the lease." It put billions into state coffers, and took the expense of running the tollways off of the State's budget. This may sound like a good deal? Except that in as short as 5 years, the tolls for this highway have jumped 203%, from $18 to the new July 2011 cost of $36.60, effectively doubling the cost of travel along those routes. This effectively has forced the citizens to either continue to pay ever increasing rates or find other routes, which of course many have. Interstate truckers can't afford the tolls so they turned to other state roads that were never meant for truck traffic, creating dangerous conditions for those living on these roads as well as greatly increasing congestion and commute times. Even if the state wanted to improve those roads to make them wider and safer, they can't, due to a non-compete clause in the contract. So for the next three generations the residents of Indiana will be forced to deal with much higher fees, increased congestion and unsafe roads all to fund massive profits for international companies.

Ohio residents need to worry too. The Governor of Ohio is looking to privatize the Ohio toll road for a large sum of money upfront, but, if the deal is structured as most of these privatization contracts seem to be, it will likely be a giant loser for the people of Ohio.

Prisons: Crime Is Good for Business:

For-profit prisons, also known as privatized prisons, has been a contentious topic for decades, with proponents arguing it saves money and increases efficiency, while opponents contend it leads to negative outcomes, such as higher incarceration rates and longer sentences. Evidence increasingly supports the latter view, indicating that privatized prisons contribute to a cycle of mass incarceration with profound social and economic consequences including increased racial disparities, higher costs for taxpayers, and reduced opportunities for rehabilitation.

Privatized prisons emerged in the United States during the 1980s, a period marked by a tough-on-crime political climate and skyrocketing incarceration rates. The first privately run prison opened in 1984, and since then, the industry has grown exponentially. By 2019, the number of inmates in private prisons in the U.S. had reached approximately 116,000, representing about 8% of the total prison population. Evidence suggests that privatized prisons contribute to increased inmate populations and longer sentences, driven by the profit motives of the corporations that run them.

Let's break down some of the ways they contribute to the increased incarceration of American citizens.

For-profit prisons have a financial incentive to keep their facilities filled to capacity. Contracts with government agencies often include clauses that guarantee a minimum occupancy rate known as "lockup quotas", sometimes as high as 90% or more. This creates incentives to increase the number of incarcerated individuals. Private prison companies, such as CoreCivic and GEO Group, benefit financially from higher incarceration rates. This profit motive can influence various aspects of the criminal justice system, from lobbying for stricter laws to influencing parole decisions.

Private prison companies spend substantial amounts of money on lobbying and political contributions to influence legislation and policy decisions that favor increased incarceration. They lobby for tougher sentencing laws, mandatory minimum sentences, and other measures that lead to higher incarceration rates. For example, in 2016, the GEO Group and CoreCivic contributed nearly $1 million to political campaigns and spent over $1.5 million on lobbying efforts . These efforts are often aimed at promoting policies that result in higher incarceration rates and longer sentences, such as tough-on-crime legislation and opposition to criminal justice reform measures.

In some areas, private prisons are major employers and economic drivers. Local economies can become dependent on the prison industry, creating local political pressure to maintain or increase incarceration levels to keep these economic benefits.

The influence of private prison companies has been linked to the implementation and maintenance of harsh sentencing laws, such as the three-strikes laws, mandatory minimum sentences, and stringent drug laws. Private prison companies have been known to draft and promote legislation through organizations like the American Legislative Exchange Council (ALEC). ALEC's "truth in sentencing" and "three strikes" model bills that have been adopted in several states, leading to longer sentences and reduced parole opportunities (more on ALEC later). These policies disproportionately increase the number of incarcerated individuals adversely impacting lower economic populations. According to the NAACP, African Americans are incarcerated at more than five times the rate of white Americans, and this disparity is magnified in states with significant private prison populations.

For-profit prisons are heavily involved in immigration detention. The expansion of immigration detention policies and the increase in detainee numbers have been influenced by private prison companies seeking to fill their facilities. Many reports have exposed the harsh and often inhumane treatment in these facilities. Companies have come under increased scrutiny for putting their profit above the welfare of the people they're charged with housing.

In order maintain and/or increase their profit, there is a push towards criminalizing minor offenses that would otherwise be handled through fines, community service, or other non-incarceration measures. This leads to a higher number of incarcerations for relatively minor crimes. For instance, inmates in private prisons may face more disciplinary actions and have fewer opportunities for early release compared to those in public facilities. A report by the American Civil Liberties Union (ACLU) found that inmates in private prisons often receive infractions for minor offenses at higher rates, which can extend their sentences and delay parole eligibility. A 2016 study published in the journal "Criminology & Public Policy" found that inmates in private prisons were less likely to be granted parole compared to those in public prisons. The study suggested that private prison officials may manipulate parole hearings to retain inmates longer and increase profits.

To maximize profits, private prisons often cut costs in ways that compromise inmate care and safety. This includes lower staff salaries, inadequate training, and insufficient healthcare, which can lead to higher rates of violence and recidivism, perpetuating the cycle of incarceration. There is little financial incentive for private prisons to focus on rehabilitation and reducing recidivism. Programs aimed at reducing reoffending rates, such as education and job training, are often underfunded or insufficiently provided in private prisons. Higher recidivism means more inmates and therefore more profit. So much for second chances.

In comparison to other countries, many prioritize rehabilitation over punishment. They invest more in social services, education, and healthcare, which helps to prevent crime and reduce recidivism. This contrasts with the U.S. model, where punitive measures and incarceration are more prominent.

A study by the Sentencing Project found that states with higher proportions of privatized prisons tend to have higher incarceration rates overall. For example, in 2019, New Mexico, which has a significant portion of its prison population in private facilities, had an incarceration rate of 719 per 100,000 residents, compared to the national average of 698 per 100,000 residents. A 2017 study by the Bureau of Justice Assistance found that inmates in private prisons served sentences that were, on average, 7% longer than those in public prisons, even when controlling for factors such as the severity of the offense and the inmate's criminal history.

Moreover, a report by In the Public Interest highlighted that private prison companies spend millions of dollars on lobbying efforts to shape policies that increase incarceration. Between 2010 and 2015, these companies spent more than $10 million lobbying Congress and state legislatures. This lobbying often focuses on maintaining mandatory minimum sentences, three-strikes laws, and other policies that contribute to higher incarceration rates.

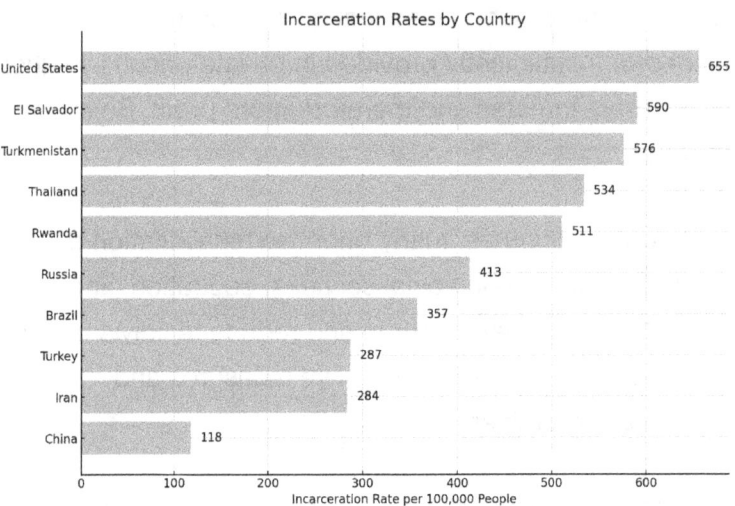

The legal systems in many other countries emphasize proportionality in sentencing, alternatives to incarceration, and restorative justice practices. These approaches help to maintain lower incarceration rates compared to the U.S.

The prevalence of private prisons is much higher in the U.S. than in many other countries. This difference in how the prison system is structured and financed contributes significantly to the disparity in incarceration rates.

For-profit prisons in the U.S. create and sustain high incarceration rates through economic incentives that promote tougher sentencing laws, increased criminalization, and higher recidivism rates. The profit model has significant implications for the criminal justice system. Evidence suggests that privatized prisons lead to higher incarceration rates and longer sentences, driven by financial incentives and legislative influence. These practices contribute to the perpetuation of mass incarceration, disproportionately affecting marginalized communities and placing a significant burden on state economies. Addressing these issues requires greater public awareness and comprehensive policy reforms aimed at eliminating our reliance on private prisons to ensuring a more equitable and just criminal justice system.

References

1. Sentencing Project. (2019). Trends in U.S. Corrections. Retrieved from [Sentencing Project](https://www.sentencingproject.org).
2. In the Public Interest. (2016). How Private Prison Companies Increase Incarceration. Retrieved from [In the Public Interest](https://www.inthepublicinterest.org).
3. University of Wisconsin-Madison. (2018). The Impact of Privatized Prisons on Sentencing. Retrieved from [University of Wisconsin-Madison].
4. American Civil Liberties Union. (2014). Warehoused and Forgotten: Immigrants Trapped in Our Shadow Private Prison System. Retrieved from [ACLU](https://www.aclu.org).
5. OpenSecrets. (2016). Private Prisons: Lobbying, Political Contributions, and Influence. Retrieved from [OpenSecrets](https://www.opensecrets.org).
6. American Legislative Exchange Council. (2019). Criminal Justice Reform. Retrieved from [ALEC](https://www.alec.org).
7. NAACP. (2020). Criminal Justice Fact Sheet. Retrieved from [NAACP](https://www.naacp.org).
8. Bureau of Justice Statistics. (2019). Recidivism Rates and Prison Rehabilitation Programs. Retrieved from [BJS](https://www.bjs.gov).

Lock Em' Up and Cash In:

The privatization of border security and immigration detention has turned into a significant profit center for the private prison industry, This trend is the result of the convergence of two key developments: the rise of for-profit incarceration and the intensification of immigration enforcement. The number of people held in Immigration and Customs Enforcement or ICE detention continues to grow, and private prison companies hold an increasingly tight grip on the mass immigration detention system.

The federal government's immigration detention system relies heavily on private prison corporations. Companies, like the GEO Group, CoreCivic, LaSalle Corrections, and the Management Training Corporation have pocketed billions from ICE detention contracts in the past two decades.

In 2019 as a candidate, President Biden promised to stop the use of private prison companies for immigration detention. In 2021, he announced that there should be "no private prisons, period," when addressing protesters. Even though the Biden administration issued an executive order in January 2021 directing the Department of Justice to phase out its contracts with private prison companies, it notably excluded ICE detention from the order. Since then, the number of immigrants detained by ICE — and revenues for private prison companies — have only increased.

The U.S. has significantly ramped up its immigration enforcement efforts over the last few decades, especially following the 9/11 attacks and the establishment of the Department of Homeland Security (DHS). Immigration and Customs Enforcement (ICE) and

Customs and Border Protection (CBP) increased border enforcement and detention of undocumented immigrants, resulting in a surge in the number of people held in detention facilities. From a little over 5,000 detainees in 1994, the average daily population in immigration detention grew to more than 50,000 by the late 2010s.

This boom in detention coincided with the increasing involvement of private prison companies in the immigration system. Private companies were well-positioned to respond to the surge in detainees, offering the government flexible capacity to house large numbers of individuals in a relatively short time. This paved the way for contracts worth hundreds of millions of dollars to build and operate immigration detention facilities.

How much would you pay for a basic motel room per night? $60, $80, $100 per night? For $100 per night I imaging it would be a pretty nice room with amenities, but tax payers are spending $150 or more per day to house undocumented immigrants in private prisons. Contracts with ICE make up a significant amount of revenue for private prison corporations. In 2022, the GEO Group made $1.05 billion in revenue from ICE contracts alone including $408 million from electronic monitoring of immigrants. CoreCivic similarly made $552.2 million in revenue from ICE detention contracts in 2022, representing 30 percent of its total revenue. Despite calls to decrease funding for ICE detention, Congress appropriated $2.9 billion dollars to hold 34,000 people in ICE detention for FY 2023.

Despite what former president Donald Trump says, immigrants pose a much lower risk of criminal behavior than native born Americans. A study by the National Institute for Justice examined data from the

Texas Department of Public Safety estimated the rate at which undocumented immigrants are arrested for committing crimes. The study found that undocumented immigrants are arrested at less than half the rate of native-born U.S. citizens for violent and drug crimes and a quarter the rate of native-born citizens for property crimes.

The laws used to criminally prosecute people for entering and reentering the United States without permission are known as Sections 1325 ("illegal entry") and 1326 ("illegal reentry") of Chapter 8 of the U.S. Code. These laws were passed in the late 1920s during the height of the eugenics movement, the not-science used to further the white supremacist ideology, and the racist intentions of the laws are still felt today. Justice Department data shows that roughly 94 percent of people prosecuted for unauthorized reentry in fiscal years 2020-21 were from Mexico, Honduras, Guatemala, and El Salvador, not Europe, Canada or Asia.

While the Trump administration weaponized these laws using them to block asylum seekers and separate families — such laws have been used in a discriminatory manner since their enactment and continue to cause harm today. While immigration violations are considered civil offenses, §§ 1325 and 1326 are misdemeanor and felony violations, respectively, under federal law, people who enter or reenter the United States without authorization are subject not only to civil immigration detention and deportation proceedings but also to criminal sanctions. In recent years, people charged with §§ 1325 and 1326 have been challenging the law based on the fact Congress enacted it for overtly racist purposes. Last year, in a landmark decision, a judge in the District of Nevada ruled that § 1326 is indeed unconstitutional. However, the government appealed this decision.

The for-profit prison industry plays an active role in shaping immigration policy through lobbying efforts. These companies have spent millions of dollars lobbying federal agencies and Congress, focusing on policies that directly affect their business models, including border security and immigration enforcement. One of the ways private prisons benefit is by advocating for stricter immigration laws and more aggressive enforcement practices that lead to higher detention rates, ensuring a steady flow of detainees.

A critical component of this profit model is the daily rate the government pays private companies per detainee. The more detainees held, the more revenue the private companies generate. Contracts often include guaranteed minimum occupancy rates, meaning that the government must pay for a certain number of beds, regardless of whether they are filled, further incentivizing private companies to maintain high detention numbers. The Heritage Foundation's Project 2025 and the Trump plan of mass deportation and detention of migrants would not only hurt communities, depriving them of a needed work force, but would be a massive transfer of wealth to the corporate prison industry and would likely plunge our economy into a deep recession.

Policy changes have a direct effect on the profitability of private prisons. For example, under the Trump administration, the "zero tolerance" policy and increased deportation efforts led to a sharp rise in the number of immigrants held in detention centers. Private prison companies reported record revenues during this period. In contrast, policy shifts aimed at reducing detention rates, such as the Biden administration's push to limit the use of private detention facilities, pose a threat to these companies' bottom lines.

Regardless of which party is in control of congress, private prisons have shown great resilience and adaptability by diversifying into other aspects of the immigration enforcement system, such as electronic monitoring services and the operation of halfway houses, allowing them to remain profitable even as immigration detention policies fluctuate.

While private prisons profit from border security and immigration enforcement policies, there is significant human cost. Aside from the inhumane "family separation" policy of the Trump administration, reports of overcrowding, poor living conditions, lack of medical care, and abuse, including rape of young girls by guards within private immigration detention centers have fueled calls for reform. Critics argue that the profit motive of these companies creates perverse incentives to cut costs on essential services, prioritizing financial gain over the well-being of detainees. Additionally, the very existence of a profit-driven detention system can encourage more aggressive immigration enforcement than may be necessary, prolonging the detention of individuals in substandard conditions. This profit-driven model raises ethical concerns, as it incentivizes policies that prioritize detention and incarceration, often at the expense of detainees' rights and well-being. The close ties between private prisons and government policy underscore the complexity of addressing immigration reform in a way that reduces reliance on detention while ensuring humane treatment for immigrants.

A note on the budgetary impact of undocumented migrants:

A study by the Institute on Taxation and Economic Policy found that undocumented immigrants paid $96.7 billion in federal, state, and local taxes in 2022. Most of that amount, $59.4 billion, was paid to the federal government while the remaining $37.3 billion was paid to state and local governments. More than a third of the tax dollars paid by undocumented immigrants go toward payroll taxes dedicated to funding programs that these workers are barred from accessing. Undocumented immigrants paid $25.7 billion in Social Security taxes, $6.4 billion in Medicare taxes, and $1.8 billion in unemployment insurance taxes in 2022.

The Great Disruptor Hustle:
How Uber, Airbnb, and Friends Privatized Profits and Socialized Costs

Disruptor companies like Uber and Airbnb arrived on the scene with grand promises: cheaper rides, more lodging options, and a brave new world of tech-enabled convenience. What they delivered was something a bit different: regulatory loopholes, artificially low prices bankrolled by billions in venture capital, and a strategy that depended on crushing existing industries before jacking up prices. And we let them do it.

The Business Model: Burn Cash, Bypass Rules, Crush Competition

Uber, founded in 2009, and Airbnb, founded in 2008, weren't just startups—they were economic wrecking balls. Rather than compete fairly, they externalized their costs onto workers, consumers, and the public while keeping the profits for themselves. A few highlights:

Labor Costs? Who Needs 'Em? Uber and Lyft classified drivers as independent contractors, conveniently avoiding employee benefits, healthcare costs, and labor protections. Drivers took on all the risk—car payments, insurance, maintenance—while Uber skimmed off a growing percentage of fares. (See: New York Times, ProPublica)

Hotels and Taxis Pay Fees and Taxes? Not Us! Airbnb dodged zoning laws, hotel taxes, and safety regulations by insisting it was just a platform, not a lodging company. The result? Rising rent prices, gutted local housing markets, and cities struggling to impose basic oversight. (See: The Atlantic, The Guardian)

Subsidize Until They Surrender: Both Uber and Airbnb ran on investor cash rather than profit. They lost billions of dollars annually, undercutting taxis and hotels with artificially low prices. Once the traditional industries were on life support, prices mysteriously crept up. (See: ProPublica, Financial Times)

From Cheap Rides to Sticker Shock

When Uber first hit the streets, it was cheap—absurdly cheap. That wasn't a fluke; it was a strategy. Investors were subsidizing rides so heavily that they often cost less than a bus ticket. Taxi medallions, once a golden ticket for drivers, plummeted in value. Cities spent decades building regulated transportation networks only to watch them crumble under Uber's blitzkrieg pricing. Then, once the taxi industry was a shadow of its former self, surge pricing and hefty fees became the new normal. (See: Wall Street Journal)

Airbnb played a similar game. At first, it was pitched as a way to rent out your spare room for extra cash. But soon, real estate investors saw the loophole and turned entire apartment buildings into illegal hotels, pushing up rental costs and depleting housing stock. Meanwhile, tourists flooded residential neighborhoods, and local governments scrambled to keep up. Once regulations tightened and competitors dwindled, Airbnb prices skyrocketed, often exceeding hotel rates. (See: Bloomberg)

Food Delivery: The Restaurant Squeeze

If Uber and Airbnb disrupted transportation and housing, food delivery companies like DoorDash, Uber Eats, and Grubhub took the same exploitative model and applied it to restaurants.

Here's how they did it:

Sky-High Fees: These platforms charge restaurants commissions as high as 30%, effectively eating into already thin profit margins. Many restaurants raise prices on delivery orders just to break even, while the apps keep pushing "free" delivery to customers—subsidized by the restaurants themselves. (See: Eater, Washington Post)

Hidden Costs: Many delivery apps sneak in extra charges, making it more expensive for customers while keeping restaurants hostage to their platforms. Some even list restaurants without permission, forcing them to either comply or lose control over their own branding. (See: New York Times)

Worker Exploitation: Just like Uber drivers, delivery workers are classified as independent contractors, meaning no benefits, no protections, and unpredictable wages. The only guaranteed winners? The delivery platforms. (See: ProPublica)

The Dangers of the Ride-Hailing Economy

Beyond financial exploitation, Uber's cost-cutting measures also led to safety concerns. Due to lax background checks, there have been numerous reports of violence, assault, and even rape in Uber and Lyft vehicles. Unlike traditional taxi companies, which require rigorous vetting and licensing, ride-hailing companies have repeatedly resisted stricter screening policies. A 2019 CNN investigation found that at least 103 Uber drivers in the U.S. had been accused of sexual assault or abuse. (See: CNN, Washington Post) Drivers, too, face risks. The gig economy structure means they receive little to no protection from violent passengers, with incidents of robbery and assault frequently making headlines. Yet, Uber's response has typically been reactive rather than proactive, offering PR-friendly "safety measures" while continuing to prioritize rapid driver onboarding over actual security. (See: ProPublica, New York Times)

The Inevitable Reckoning

Despite their best efforts to avoid regulation, both Uber and Airbnb eventually hit walls. Lawsuits, labor strikes, and housing crises forced city governments to push back. California's Prop 22, which Uber spent over $200 million to pass, temporarily let them keep drivers as contractors—until courts intervened. Cities like New York and Barcelona cracked down on Airbnb's unregulated sprawl. Investors, once enamored with the idea of perpetual losses for market dominance, started asking pesky questions like, "When will you turn a profit?"

Now, Uber and Airbnb are no longer cheap. Uber fares have soared, driver pay remains stagnant, and the dream of making a living from gig work is largely dead. Airbnb, once an affordable alternative to hotels, often charges more than luxury suites when you add cleaning fees and service charges.

The Playbook of Late-Stage Capitalism

The "disruptor" model wasn't about innovation—it was about brute force. By externalizing costs and internalizing profits, companies like Uber, Airbnb, and food delivery giants exploited regulatory gaps, scorched industries, and, once dominant, abandoned their promise of affordability. What was once a cheap and democratic alternative became just another overpriced, extractive service. But hey, at least we got an app for it.

So next time you book an Airbnb, hop in an Uber, or order delivery, remember: You're not just paying for a ride, a bed, or a meal. You're paying for the privilege of watching capitalism do exactly what it always does—privatize the gains and socialize the losses.

They Even Want to Own the Weather:

In the 1990s, at about the same time that forecasting got consistently good, private interests and free-market absolutists started insisting that the The National Weather Service (NWS) and related agencies were "competing" with private enterprise. As they had with schools and trash collection and myriad other public services, they accused the government of running a "monopoly" that prevented private business from entering the sector. Barry Myers, head of AccuWeather, led the charge. In his mind, the government has no business making forecasts. Perhaps in a life-threatening emergency government had a role, but even here. he claimed. "The National Weather Service does not need to have the final say on warnings." According to Myers, the prosaic daily forecasts were products to be sold, and "the customer and the private sector should be able to sort that out." His bottom line took things to extremes: "The government should get out of the forecasting business." President Trump nominated Barry Myers in 2017 to lead NOAA before Myers withdrew his nomination, citing health concerns.

A far-right initiative is set on privatizing the National Weather Service. The text of the nearly 1,000-page initiative, called Project 2025, authored by the conservative Heritage Foundation, in part, written by Trump's former chief financial officer of the Department of Commerce Thomas Gilman, among other extreme proposals, plans to commercialize the weather service, which would require Americans to pay for weather news from what has commonly been a free service. The Washington Post reported in 2019 that Gilman wrote. "Studies have found that the forecasts and warnings provided by the private companies are more reliable than those provided by the NWS,". "The NWS provides the data that private companies use and should focus on its data-gathering services. Because private companies rely on this data, the NWS should fully commercialize its forecasting operations." The private weather services get their data from The NWS / NOAA and then turn around and sell it to other companies and the public for a profit and so the government shouldn't give this essential service away.

Project 2025 calls for NOAA to be "dismantled and many of its functions eliminated." NOAA is made up of six agencies, including the Weather Service." By turning the weather service into something Americans should pay for, the authors suggest it would "ensure the taxpayer dollars are invested in the most cost-efficient technologies for high-quality research and weather data."

The move to privatize would grant these companies a virtual monopoly on weather forecasting, something that many Americans rely on when storms threaten their homes and communities. This is a prime example of private corporations attempting to extract public money for profit.

So, they want to take a publicly funded resource and turn around and sell it back to the public for a hefty profit even if it means that people who can't, or choose not to, buy their forecasts might not have the information to stay safe in an extreme weather event. Sure, that sounds right...

Your Opinion Literally Does Not Matter...
Unless You're an "Economic Elite."

In a world overflowing with political discussions, social movements, and the ubiquitous "voice of the people," one might assume that public opinion carries significant weight in shaping public policy. However, a disconcerting truth emerges when we scrutinize the mechanisms of power and influence in contemporary politics. Your opinion, and indeed the opinions of the vast majority, appear to hold almost no sway over the policies that govern your life. This assertion isn't merely a cynical musing but a conclusion supported by empirical research, most notably the Princeton study which starkly states: "The preferences of the average American appear to have only a minuscule, near-zero, statistically non-significant impact upon public policy."

The Princeton Study: A Harsh Reality

In 2014, political scientists Martin Gilens and Benjamin I. Page published a landmark study in the journal *Perspectives on Politics*. Their research, which meticulously analyzed nearly 1,800 policy initiatives over a 20-year period, sought to determine whose preferences were most likely to influence U.S. government policy. The findings were stark and unsettling: while the preferences of economic elites and organized interest groups had substantial impacts on policy, the preferences of the average American had virtually none.

Gilens and Page's study reveals a profound disconnect between public opinion and public policy. For the average citizen, participating in democratic processes like voting or public polling seems to be an exercise in futility. Despite the widespread belief in democratic representation, the empirical data suggest that policy decisions are overwhelmingly shaped by a narrow segment of the population: the affluent and the well-connected.

Represent.Us: Shedding Light on Systemic Corruption

The advocacy group Represent.Us has amplified the findings of the Princeton study to underscore the pervasive corruption within the American political system. Their storytelling approach translates complex academic research into accessible narratives that expose the mechanisms by which public opinion is sidelined.

Represent.Us highlights how systemic corruption—entrenched practices that prioritize the interests of wealthy donors and special interest groups over those of ordinary citizens—renders the average voter effectively powerless. Their work aims to mobilize citizens against this disenfranchisement by advocating for reforms such as anti-corruption laws, campaign finance reforms, and transparent lobbying practices.

Democracy in Name Only!

The implications of the Princeton Study, coupled with the advocacy of groups like Represent.Us, paint a bleak picture of contemporary democracy. If the majority's preferences do not influence policy, one must question the very nature of democratic governance. Are we living in a democracy or has the system been so co-opted by elite interests that it operates more as an oligarchy?

Our unique but antiquated form of democracy is by design somewhat anti-democratic. The Electoral Collage was a concession to the slave holding states who's population of white land owners, those allowed to vote at the time, was far fewer than the northern states because of the slave population. Coupled with the Senate which grants 2 senators to each state, regardless of population, i.e. California has approximately 39.5 million residents while North Dakota has less than 800 thousand, yet both have 2 senators. This creates uneven representation giving a minority virtual veto power over the majority.

This disenfranchisement is not merely academic but has real-world consequences. Voter apathy, declining trust in governmental institutions, and increasing political polarization are all symptomatic of a system where the average person's voice feels unheard. When citizens believe that their opinions do not matter, the very fabric of democratic engagement begins to fray.

The election of 2024 shined a spotlight on the imbalance of political power and influence. The richest man in the world gave upwards of 270 Million dollars to the Donald Trump campaign and was anointed the "Budget Zar", where, even before Donald Trump took office, he influenced the Republican congress to remove legislation that would have been unfavorable to his businesses. His net worth rose by 200 billion dollars after.

Acknowledging the problem is the first step towards seeking solutions. While the Princeton study offers a grim diagnosis, it also serves as a clarion call for change. To revitalize democracy, systemic reforms are imperative. Campaign finance reform, stricter lobbying regulations, and measures to increase political transparency are essential steps toward ensuring that the average American's voice is heard and valued.

Grassroots movements and civic engagement also play crucial roles. Organizations like Represent.Us, Citizens for Responsibility and Ethics in Washington (CREW), Public Citizen and other reform-minded groups are vital in this struggle, advocating for changes that can help restore the balance of power. Civic education and public awareness campaigns can empower individuals to demand more from their representatives and hold them accountable.

The realization that your opinion does not matter in the current political landscape is a sobering one. However, it also serves as a powerful motivator for change. By understanding the systemic issues at play and actively working towards reform, there is hope that the democratic ideals of representation and equality can be revitalized. The fight to make every voice count is not just a political struggle but a moral imperative, one that requires the collective effort of an informed and engaged citizenry.

Part 7:

The Courts

Justice is Blind... Deaf and Apparently Dumb too:

The Supreme Court: Where "Justice" Takes a Backseat to Bad Decisions

Since the founding of this great country, our courts have been the go-to place for resolving conflicts, with the Supreme Court sitting pretty at the top as the final arbiter of what's fair and just. Of course, the Court's rulings have been about as reliable as a broken compass—sometimes it gets it right, and other times, well, it sends us off a cliff.

Over the years, the Supreme Court has made decisions so bad they should come with a warning label. Some have been genuinely good (shocking, I know), but many others have been the kind of rulings that make you wonder if the justices were too busy checking their stock portfolios to notice the real issues at hand.

But don't worry—while we've had some landmark decisions that made a real impact on our lives, many of the Court's "gems" have only proven that being unelected doesn't mean you can't make some absolutely terrible decisions. So, let's take a walk down memory lane and revisit the Supreme Court's most embarrassing, nation-shaping failures.

1. *Dred Scott v. Sanford (1857)*: This one is hands-down the worst Supreme Court decision ever. Dred Scott held that African Americans, whether free men or slaves, could not be considered American citizens. The ruling undid the Missouri Compromise, barred laws that would free slaves, and all but guaranteed that there would be no political solution to slavery. The opinion even included a ridiculous "parade of horribles" that would appear if Scott were recognized as a citizen, unspeakable scenarios like African Americans being able to vacation, hold public meetings, and exercise their free speech rights.

The 13th and 14th Amendments to the Constitution overturned the 1857 Supreme Court decision in Dred Scott v. Sandford. The 13th Amendment outlawed slavery, and the 14th Amendment granted citizenship to all people born in the United States.

2. *The Civil Rights Cases of 1883*

These were five consolidated cases challenging the Civil Rights Act of 1875, which prohibited racial discrimination in public accommodations like hotels, restaurants, and transportation. In an 8-1 decision, the Supreme Court interpreted the Fourteenth Amendment so narrowly that it struck down the Act, arguing that it could not regulate private businesses. This decision effectively ushered in the Jim Crow era of legalized racial segregation.

It would take over 80 years for the Court to switch course, allowing for the government protection of civil rights in Heart of Atlanta Motel v. U.S. — this time under the Commerce Clause.

3. *Plessy v. Ferguson (1896)*: You've probably heard of the infamous concept of "separate but equal." This decision upheld racial segregation under the "separate but equal" doctrine. This flawed logic, despite supposedly guaranteeing equal facilities for both races, inherently implied Black inferiority and violated the 14th Amendment's Equal Protection Clause. Plessy's legacy is one of perpetuating Jim Crow laws, psychological harm to Black Americans, and impeding racial progress for decades.

Only in 1954 did Brown v. Board of Education finally overturn Plessy and dismantle its segregationist legacy, a stark reminder of the dangers of legalized discrimination and the ongoing fight for a truly just and equitable society.

4. *Lochner v. New York (1905)*: This case ignited a fiery debate for protecting employer interests over worker welfare, expanding judicial power through "substantive due process," and paving the way for the "Lochner era" of striking down progressive laws. Here, SCOTUS struck down a New York law limiting bakery work hours to 10 hours a day, finding an implicit "liberty of contract" in the Due Process Clause.

Though overruled, its legacy sparks ongoing discussions about balancing economic liberty with worker protection, interpreting fundamental rights, and the Court's cautious power to influence public policy in a changing society. There are cases similar to this currently with the conservative judges making striking similar decisions.

5. *Buck v. Bell (1927)*: "Eugenics" the Court declared in this terrible decision. In an 8-1 decision written by Justice Oliver Wendell Holmes, the Court upheld the forced sterilization of those with intellectual disabilities "for the protection and health of the state." Justice Holmes ruled that "society can prevent those who are manifestly unfit from continuing their kind" and ended the opinion by declaring that "three generations of imbeciles are enough."

Buck v. Bell was never overturned! Not formally, anyway. The decision did lose a lot of strength after Skinner v. Oklahoma, which shifted focus to individuals' fundamental right to procreate, undermining the eugenics argument and leading to the practice's decline. Though Buck v. Bell remains on the books, its authority is severely weakened and it's no longer considered good law.

6. **Korematsu v. United States (1944)**: Here, the Supreme Court upheld the internment of Japanese Americans during World War II, finding that the need to protect against espionage outweighed the individual rights of American citizens. In a cruel and ironic twist, this was also the first time the Court applied what is called "strict scrutiny" to racial discrimination by the U.S. government, belying the idea that strict scrutiny is "strict in theory, fatal in fact."

Technically, Korematsu was never overturned by SCOTUS. However, its legitimacy has been severely undermined and it is no longer considered good law for several reasons. In 1983, a federal court judge overturned Korematsu's original conviction, acknowledging government suppression of evidence and racial prejudice in the decision. In 2018, Chief Justice Roberts strongly rebuked the Korematsu decision in the Trump v. Hawaii case, calling it "gravely wrong" and stating it has "no place in law under the Constitution." Thus, thankfully, Korematsu has lost its practical authority and is highly unlikely to be used as precedent in future cases due to its discredited foundation and inconsistent history.

7. **Bowers v. Hardwick (1986)**: This decision upheld a discriminatory Georgia sodomy statute that criminalized sexually active gay and

lesbian relationships. As Justice Harry Blackmun noted in his dissent, the majority opinion displayed "an almost obsessive focus on homosexual activity."

The decision was inconsistent with precedent because it denied a fundamental right to privacy for consenting adults engaging in private sexual conduct, even though the Court had previously recognized privacy rights in cases like Griswold v. Connecticut (contraception) and Roe v. Wade (abortion). It invoked the slippery slope argument, suggesting that recognizing a right to homosexual sodomy would lead to the legalization of other "immoral" acts, which later proved unfounded. All this left many wondering where the line between permissible and non-permissible private acts could be drawn. The majority opinion also relied on outdated notions of morality and failed to provide a compelling legal basis for criminalizing private, consensual acts.

Fortunately, Bowers was overruled in 2003 by Lawrence v. Texas, which recognized a fundamental right to privacy for all consenting adults engaging in private sexual conduct, regardless of their sexual orientation. This was a major victory for LGBTQ+ rights and helped pave the way for future advancements, including marriage equality.

8. *Bush v. Gore (2000)*: Shaping the outcome of the 2000 presidential election, this remains one of the most controversial Supreme Court decisions in American history for several reasons. The razor-thin margin by which George Bush won, along with discrepancies in ballot counting in Florida and concerns about "hanging chads," raised allegations of voter disenfranchisement and fueled accusations of unfairness. SCOTUS's intervention in the election process was highly unusual and unprecedented, raising concerns about judicial overreach and undermining the public's confidence in the democratic process. Furthermore, the 5-4 decision along ideological lines, with conservative justices siding with Bush and liberal justices supporting Gore, ignited partisan tensions and accusations of political bias. This further amplified the controversy and deepened the public divide. The Republican majority stopped the recount, raising potential violations of the Fourteenth Amendment's Equal Protection Clause and arguing that different standards for counting votes across counties could unfairly disenfranchise voters. However, critics argued that stopping the recounts altogether disproportionately affected Gore's supporters in those counties. Sadly when the votes were counted, Al Gore had actually won.

The decision was never overturned, and its aftermath potentially set a precedent for future involvement of the Supreme Court in close elections. However, the Equal Protection holding in Bush v. Gore has never been cited as precedent, and the majority opinion specifically warned in the decision that "[o]ur consideration is limited to the present circumstances," discouraging future courts from relying on any legal holding in the decision.

9. *Citizens United v. FEC (2010)*: Another, more recent case about presidential elections, Citizens United is a household name to this day due to ongoing controversy. It held that political donations are speech protected by the First Amendment, opening the floodgates to unlimited personal and corporate donations to "super PACs." Critics argue this grants enormous influence to wealthy special interests and corporations, effectively drowning out the voices of everyday citizens and giving undue power to a select few. Supporters of the decision argue it's a victory for free speech, protecting the right of corporations and individuals to express their political views. They see limitations on campaign spending as censorship and believe increased money in politics doesn't inherently lead to corruption. Critics counter that free speech shouldn't translate to unfettered financial influence in elections, arguing it undermines democratic principles and fair representation. I think it's obvious that the later proved to be true.

List by Casey C. Sullivan, Esq. | Updated by Vaidehi Mehta, Esq. | updated on Jan 01, 2024

Key Legislation and Court Decisions:

The 1976 Supreme Court case *Buckley v. Valeo* was a turning point, establishing that spending money to influence elections is a form of constitutionally protected free speech. This decision laid the groundwork for the increased flow of money into politics. Further, the 2010 *Citizens United v. Federal Election Commission* ruling opened the floodgates, allowing corporations to spend unlimited amounts on political campaigns through independent expenditures.

The Supreme Court Rules Overwhelmingly for Corporations:

The role of the Supreme Court in shaping the socio-economic landscape of the United States cannot be overstated. Over the years, the Court's decisions have significantly influenced various aspects of American life, from civil rights to environmental policies. One area that has garnered considerable attention is the Court's rulings on issues involving corporations. Critics argue that the Supreme Court has increasingly favored corporate interests, often at the expense of individual rights and public welfare. Let's delve into the Court's jurisprudence concerning corporations, examine some landmark cases, plus the ideological leanings of the justices, and the broader implications of these rulings.

The Rise of Corporate Personhood:

The concept of corporate personhood, which grants corporations certain legal rights similar to those of individuals, has its roots in the early 19th century. However, it wasn't until the late 20th and early 21st centuries that the Supreme Court significantly expanded these rights. A pivotal moment came with the 2010 decision in *Citizens United v. Federal Election Commission.* As explained earlier, the Court held that corporate funding of independent political broadcasts in candidate elections cannot be limited under the First Amendment. This decision effectively allowed corporations to spend unlimited amounts of money to influence political campaigns, fundamentally altering the landscape of American politics.

The Aftermath:

The Citizens United decision was grounded in the belief that free speech, as protected by the First Amendment, applies equally to individuals and corporations. The majority opinion, authored by Justice Anthony Kennedy, argued that political speech is indispensable to a democracy, which is no less true because the speech comes from a corporation. Critics, however, contend that this ruling has given undue influence to wealthy corporations and special interest groups, undermining the democratic process.

Following the decision, there was a surge in the formation of Super PACs (Political Action Committees) that can raise and spend unlimited amounts of money on behalf of political candidates, as long as they do not coordinate directly with the campaigns. This has led to an unprecedented influx of corporate money in politics, raising concerns about the potential for corruption and the erosion of public trust in the electoral system.

The *Burwell v. Hobby Lobby* Decision:

Another significant ruling in favor of corporate interests came in 2014 with *Burwell v. Hobby Lobby Stores, Inc.* In a 5-4 decision, the Court held that closely held for-profit corporations can be exempt from regulations that violate their religious beliefs, specifically regarding the Affordable Care Act's mandate on contraception coverage. The Court's decision was based on the Religious Freedom Restoration Act (RFRA), which prohibits the government from substantially burdening a person's exercise of religion unless it is the least restrictive means of furthering a compelling governmental interest.

This ruling was controversial for several reasons. It marked the first time the Court recognized a for-profit corporation's claim to religious freedom, thereby extending the rights of individuals to corporate entities. Critics argue that this sets a dangerous precedent, potentially allowing corporations to opt out of various regulations on religious grounds, which could undermine employees' rights and public health objectives.

The Supreme Court's rulings on corporate matters are often influenced by the judicial philosophies of the justices. The conservative wing of the Court, which has been predominant in recent decades, tends to favor limited government intervention in the marketplace and robust protections for property rights and free speech. This ideological leaning often translates into rulings that prioritize corporate interests over regulatory measures intended to protect consumers, employees, and the environment. Going back to the influence of "free Market" ideology as described earlier has had a profound effect on the thinking of the most powerful people in our country.

Justices such as Antonin Scalia, Clarence Thomas, and more recently, Neil Gorsuch and Brett Kavanaugh, have consistently supported a broad interpretation of corporate rights. Their decisions reflect a commitment to originalism and textualism, which emphasize the original meaning of the Constitution and the precise wording of statutes. These judicial philosophies often align with pro-business positions, advocating for a "free market" with minimal regulatory constraints.

Case in point: The U.S. Supreme Court's ruling in *Loper Bright Enterprises v. Raimondo* dealt a severe blow to the ability of federal agencies to do their jobs, it ended the 40 year precedent of "Chevron deference." The Chevron doctrine stems from the Supreme Court's 1984 decision in Chevron v. Natural Resources Defense Council. The decision basically stated that if federal legislation is ambiguous or leaves an administrative gap, the courts must defer to the regulatory agency's interpretation if the interpretation is reasonable. The overturning of this important decision hamstrings agencies that are tasked with protecting the public from pollution, unsafe products, and dozens if not hundreds of other issues. Instead of deferring to the expertise of agencies on how to interpret ambiguous language in laws pertaining to their work, federal judges now have the power to decide what a law means for themselves. So, If the congress doesn't list every chemical, product or behavior in the legislation, then the "strict constructionists" will decide and we've seen who they side with.

The Supreme Court's tendency to rule in favor of corporations has far-reaching implications for American society. One of the most significant concerns is the potential for economic inequality to be exacerbated (at the time of this writing it is the most extreme in U.S. history). When corporations wield substantial influence over political and regulatory processes, they can shape policies that favor their interests, often at the expense of small businesses, workers, and consumers. This can lead to a concentration of wealth and power in the hands of a few large entities, undermining the principles of fair competition and equal opportunity.

Moreover, the expansion of corporate rights has eroded public trust in the judiciary and the democratic process. When the Court appears to consistently side with powerful corporate interests, it risks being perceived as an instrument of the elite rather than an impartial arbiter of justice. This has fueled public disillusionment and cynicism, weakening the foundations of democratic governance.

The Supreme Court's rulings have profound and wide ranging effects on American society and the balance between economic freedom and regulatory oversight. While the Court has consistently upheld the rights of corporations, these decisions have tilted the playing field towards the rich and powerful. As the Court continues to shape the legal landscape, its objectivity and legitimacy are coming into question with reports of lavish gifts and sweetheart jobs for family members, their rulings will undoubtedly have lasting impacts on the balance between corporate power and public welfare.

The Right-Wing's Decades-Long Project to Pack America's Courts:

For decades, a strategic and meticulously planned effort has been underway by right-wing activists, legal scholars, and political operatives to reshape the American judiciary. This campaign aims to tilt the courts towards conservative interpretations of the law, with far-reaching implications for the nation's legal landscape. This is a look into the origins, evolution, strategies, and impacts of the right-wing's project to pack America's courts.

The origins of the right-wing court-packing strategy can be traced back to the mid-20th century. Discontented with the rulings of the Warren and Burger Courts, particularly on issues such as civil rights, voting rights, and the separation of church and state, conservative activists began to recognize the judiciary's power in shaping American society. They understood that even though laws were enacted in Congress, they were validated and enforced by the courts.

A pivotal moment came with the establishment of the Federalist Society in 1982. Founded by a group of conservative law students and professors, the organization aimed to counter what they saw as the liberal dominance in law schools and the judiciary. The Federalist Society provided a forum for conservative legal thought and became a crucial network for grooming and promoting conservative judges.

Many elite law schools, traditionally leaning liberal, became battlegrounds for conservative legal ideas through the efforts of student chapters of the Federalist Society and similar groups. In these environments, young law students are exposed to conservative judicial philosophies, particularly "originalism" (championed by figures like Justice Antonin Scalia) and "judicial restraint".

Scholarships and fellowships have been funded by conservative foundations to support students who pursue these ideologies, making it financially feasible for them to influence the legal world upon graduation. Moreover, many of these students go on to clerk for prominent conservative judges, gaining crucial legal experience and connections that can propel them into influential positions.

Conservative judicial thought can be described as a business friendly ways to interpret the law. Much of the philosophy stems more from the economic manifesto of the Chicago school than of the United States Constitution. "Free market" economics plays an outsized role in their reasoning, often contradicting the views of the founding fathers.

Throughout the 1980s and 1990s, conservatives systematically built an infrastructure to support their judicial objectives. This included think tanks like the Heritage Foundation, which played a significant role in identifying and promoting judicial candidates. The creation of these networks ensured a steady pipeline of ideologically aligned judges who were committed to conservative principles. Backed by prominent conservative mega-donors like the Koch brothers, these institutions provide the intellectual framework for shaping legal thinking.

The Reagan and Bush administrations accelerated these efforts, appointing judges who were members or affiliates of the Federalist Society. These appointments marked the beginning of a deliberate shift in the judiciary, as conservative judges were strategically placed in key positions within the federal court system. The 5th circuit is a prime example that we'll look at later in the chapter.

The control of the Senate is crucial in the judicial appointment process, as it confirms presidential nominees. Recognizing this, right-wing activists have made concerted efforts to ensure Republican control of the Senate. This strategy was particularly evident during the Obama administration, when Senate Republicans, led by Mitch McConnell, obstructed numerous judicial nominations, leaving many vacancies unfilled.

The pinnacle of this obstructionist strategy came with the blocking of Merrick Garland's Supreme Court nomination in 2016. By refusing to hold hearings for Garland, McConnell gambled on a Republican victory in the upcoming presidential election. This gamble paid off with the election of Donald Trump, who would go on to appoint three Supreme Court justices, significantly shifting the Court's ideological balance.

The Trump administration marked an unprecedented acceleration in the conservative court-packing project. Picking from a list provided by the Federalist Society, Trump's judicial appointments were chosen for their youth, ideological purity, and commitment to "originalism"—a judicial philosophy that claims to be consistent with the framers' original intent, or their idea of what the original intent was or should have been.

Trump's administration, aided by a Republican-controlled Senate, confirmed over 230 federal judges, including three Supreme Court justices—Neil Gorsuch, Brett Kavanaugh, and Amy Coney Barrett. These appointments have had a transformative impact on the federal judiciary, ensuring a conservative tilt on key legal issues like abortion, gun rights, and religious freedom for generations to come.

The impact of this conservative judicial transformation is profound and multifaceted. Key rulings on issues such as reproductive rights, voting rights, LGBTQ+ rights, and executive power reflect the influence of the newly constituted courts and their intention to reshape the country in their idealogical image.

Conservative legal networks have also focused on 'strategic litigation' as a means of influencing policy. Groups like the *Institute for Justice*, the *Becket Fund for Religious Liberty*, and the *Alliance Defending Freedom* have been instrumental in bringing cases to court that challenge laws or regulations seen as infringing on conservative ideals. By bringing cases in conservative districts, they're able to effect the entire country often with dubious legal merit.

For instance, the Supreme Court's ruling in *Dobbs v. Jackson Women's Health Organization* effectively overturned *Roe v. Wade*, ending federal protection for abortion rights and returning the issue to individual states. This decision overturned 50 years of judicial precedent, even though during their confirmation hears before the senate, they swore under oath they would respect precedent and consider Roe settled law. This epitomizes what has been described as "moral fluidity" of the conservative judges.

The right-wing project to pack America's courts is a testament to the power of long-term strategic planning and the significance of the big money in shaping the judiciary and thus U.S. policies. Through this combination of 'strategic litigation', judicial appointments, and educational efforts, the right has successfully cultivated a generation of attorneys and judges who are deeply committed to reshaping American law in favor of conservative principles. Conservative activists have achieved a significant ideological shift in the American judicial system, with effects that will be felt for generations. Understanding this process underscores the outsized influence of the courts in American democracy and the enduring impact of judicial philosophy on the lives of every citizen.

Progressives have been slow to respond to these developments but are moving with increased urgency. Efforts to counterbalance the conservative judiciary include advocating for court reforms, such as expanding the number of Supreme Court justices, implementing term limits, and limiting jurisdiction.

The *Dobbs* decision has emphasized the importance of the judiciary in elections, urging voters to consider the long-term implications of judicial appointments when casting their ballots. Several "conservative" states have held votes on the issue of abortion and clear majorities have voted in favor of reproductive freedom.

The Federalist Society:
Leonard Leo, the most powerful man in America you've never heard of.

The Federalist Society has played an outsized role in shaping the judiciary in recent decades. Since 1982, the group has become a powerful force in the legal community, particularly in influencing judicial appointments. They have engaged in a concerted and well financed effort to pack the courts with ideologues, fundamentally altering the landscape of American jurisprudence. Here's a brief examination of the history and strategies employed to foster the ideological shift in the judiciary and their extreme right-wing agenda. The Federalist Society advocates an extreme vision for the justice system which favors business, christian nationalism and the billionaire class. Let's examine what this means and the broader implications are for the American justice system.

Established by a group of law students at Yale, Harvard, and the University of Chicago, dissatisfied with what they perceived as the liberal bias in American law schools and the judiciary. (Refer to "The

Democracy for sale

Great Myth" in earlier chapters.) The organization aims to promote an unique interpretation of the Constitution, which emphasizes the text's original meaning as understood at the time of its drafting. This seems absurd on its face because it basically advocates for the unwinding of 250 years of learning and advancements in the understanding of law, medicine, the environment and science. It also assumes that they, the Federalist Society, are the sole interpreters of the text of our constitution and what that means for the American people.

The society's influence on judicial nominations became particularly pronounced during the Reagan administration and has grown significantly under subsequent Republican administrations. Presidents George H.W. Bush, George W. Bush, and Donald Trump have all relied heavily on the Federalist Society to vet and recommend judicial nominees. Under Trump, this relationship became even more direct, with the society's executive vice president, Leonard Leo, selecting and promoting nominees for the federal judiciary, including the Supreme Court. Most Americans have never heard of Lenard Leo, or are aware of his role in building the conservative supermajority on the Supreme Court. He was responsible for the list of potential justices which Donald Trump released during the 2016 campaign when choosing his judicial appointments. He advised Trump on the nominations of Neil Gorsuch, Brett Kavanaugh and Amy Coney Barrett. Before that, he'd helped pick or confirm the court's three other conservative justices — Clarence Thomas, John Roberts and Samuel Alito.

Leo is also responsible for of advancement of Thomas Hardiman of the 3rd U.S. Circuit Court of Appeals who has ruled to loosen gun laws and overturn Obamacare's birth-control mandate. Leo had put Hardiman on Trump's Supreme Court shortlist and helped confirm him to two earlier judgeships. Leo also promoted Kyle Duncan and Cory Wilson to the 5th U.S. Circuit Court of Appeals, both were members of the Federalist Society for Law and Public Policy Studies, both deeply conservative libertarian lawyers and both fiercely anti-abortion.

The Federalist Society's strategy involves a meticulous and long-term approach to identifying and nurturing conservative legal talent. By sponsoring conferences, publishing legal scholarship, and fostering a network of like-minded lawyers and judges, the society has created a pipeline through which conservative lawyers can ascend to the highest echelons of the judiciary. This approach has resulted in the appointment of judges who are committed to radically reshaping our country through the legal system, often by outspending the more moderate or liberal candidates. With funding from corporations and billionaires, they wield significant influence in the law schools and in major law firms by which to promote the most extreme ideologues.

The Society's emphasis on "textualism and originalism" marks a significant departure in judiciary philosophy. Textualism focuses on interpreting the law based on its plain text, while originalism seeks to understand the Constitution's meaning as it was intended by the framers. Critics argue that these interpretive methods can be inflexible and fail to account for the evolving nature of society and the law. Proponents, however, argue that they provide a more stable and predictable legal framework. It's one thing to discuss these topics philosophically but when it comes to real world applications this creates a very unequal society.

On matters ranging from abortion rights and affirmative action to gun control and environmental regulations, the society's influence has led to more conservative rulings (meaning pro business). For instance, decisions by the Federalist justices on the Supreme Court have resulted in restricting reproductive rights, weaken labor unions, and roll back campaign finance regulations, overturn decades of establish law and decimated the government's power to regulate pollution and harmful products.

In 1992, the U.S. Supreme Court ruled in *Planned Parenthood of Southeastern Pennsylvania v. Casey* to uphold the constitutional right of women to an abortion. Anthony Kennedy, Sandra Day O'Connor and David Souter, the justices who wrote the majority's opinion, were all Republican appointees. The dilemma was that even conservative appointed justices could rule against the "agenda". So Leo and his allies set out to fix this problem. They needed nominees who remain stalwart through it all regardless of countervailing mainstream pressures. Leo and his allies concluded that they needed to identify candidates while they were young and nurture them throughout their careers. What they needed was a pipeline.

The takeover of the courts requires substantial resources and Leo became one of the most prolific fundraisers in American politics. Between 2014 and 2020, tax records show, groups in his orbit raised more than $600 million dollars. His donors include hedge fund billionaire Paul Singer, Texas real estate magnate Harlan Crow and the Koch family.

In the largest known political advocacy donation in U.S. history, worth $1.6 billion, industrialist Barre Seid, an elderly, ultra-secretive Chicago businessman, through a series of opaque transactions over the past two years, funded a new group run by Leonard Leo to aid efforts to reshape the American judicial system.

Leo's Federalist Society is not only focused on what they referred to as original constitutional interpretation, they are working with billionaires and corporate leaders to overturn regulations put in place to protect Americans from among other things, another financial collapse. According to research by the watchdog group, Accountable.US, Leo worked with attorneys general in at least three states regarding a legal challenge to Dodd-Frank, one of the most significant U.S. regulatory reforms since the Great Depression, which sought to reduce risk in the banking system. Leo had conference calls with the Oklahoma and Texas attorneys general at the time, Scott Pruitt and Greg Abbott, respectively, to discuss what they could do about Dodd-Frank. Oklahoma and Texas joined the bank's case as co-plaintiffs, then Montana joined, too. Leo called its newly elected leader, Republican Tim Fox, about the case. According to a person who worked in the Montana attorney general's office. Montana would not have joined the suit, this person said, if Leo had not called Fox. Lawrence VanDyke, then Montana's solicitor general, became an attorney of record on the case.

One of the biggest concerns about the Federalist Society's influence is the erosion of judicial independence. By promoting judges with a specific ideological bent, they are turning the judiciary into an extension of partisan politics. This undermines the principle of an impartial and independent judiciary, which is essential for maintaining a just legal system. The society's approach also poses a threat to established legal precedents. With the appointment of judges committed to textualism and originalism, there is a greater likelihood of overturning long-standing precedents that do not align with their vision for American jurisprudence. This creates legal uncertainty and can destabilize the legal framework upon which individuals and businesses rely.

The ideological shift in the judiciary has disproportionately affected marginalized communities. Decisions that roll back civil rights protections, weaken labor rights, and restrict access to healthcare disproportionately impact people of color, women, and the economically disadvantaged. By promoting judges who are less sympathetic to the concerns of these communities, the Federalist Society's influence exacerbates existing inequalities. This coupled with he fact that more than 50 percent of the congress are millionaires, intensify inequality not only in economics but also in the court where sentencing is already measurably harsher for people of color and those who can't afford high priced attorneys.

The Federalist Society's role in shaping the judiciary represents a disastrous development in American jurisprudence. While the society's advocates argue that it promotes a principled and consistent approach to legal interpretation, critics contend that it is packing the courts with ideologues and undermining the justice system's integrity. The long-term impact of this will depend on the judiciary's ability to maintain its independence in the face of increasing political pressure. As the debate continues, the fundamental principles of justice, equality, and impartiality must remain at the heart of the American legal system.

References
Pro-Publica, The American Prospect, Washington Post, NYT.

What's the matter with the 5th?

Traditionally, U.S. Courts of Appeals serve as gatekeepers to the U.S. Supreme Court, acting as a check on district court judges. Circuit court panels, typically comprising three judges randomly selected, commonly from a group of ideologically diverse jurists, are supposed to review district court decisions with procedural care. Most circuit courts maintain high standards when reviewing a case, especially when the outcome could profoundly affect the entire country. The U.S. Circuit Court of Appeals for the 5th Circuit, however, is a different animal altogether, and with disastrous results for the rule of law and the American people.

Corporate America and conservative activists love the 5th circuit court of appeals. The court that oversees Texas, Louisiana and Mississippi.

These states have played host to some major federal lawsuits with implications of national policy. In the Northern District of Texas, where some divisions have just one or two judges, appointed by Republican presidents, these judges have an outsized influence on

Democracy for sale

American law. The Amarillo division has only one judge, and so all cases there go to a Trump appointee, the ultraconservative, anti-abortion activist, Matthew Kacsmaryk. In the Fort Worth division, you get a choice of two judges: George W. Bush appointee Reed O'Connor, or Trump judge Mark Pittman. All of these judges actively promote their radically conservative version of the law. When their rulings are appealed, they end up at the Fifth Circuit, also stacked with partisan ideologues. This has created a pipeline that fast-tracks right-wing rulings to the Supreme Court—and creates endless delays for policies designed to protect and benefit the public.

This is known as judge shopping, and it's key to the right-wing project to politicize and capture the judiciary in order to aggressively enact unpopular policy priorities. According to studies, since January 2017, 63 percent of all U.S. Chamber of Commerce lawsuits challenging federal regulations have been filed at district courts within the Fifth Circuit.

Moreover, there are financial conflicts of interests, for example; Judge Don Willett is set to rule in a case involving The Consumer Financial Protection Bureau's cap on late fees, as part of the appellate panel, he holds significant amounts of stock in Citigroup, which could benefit from a ruling blocking the late fee cap. (He's not even the only judge involved in the case found to have credit card company stock.)

The 5th circuit has taken things to whole other level when it comes to challenging laws that might hurt business profits and benefit the public, stretching the bounds of its lawful authority in order to do so.

Unfortunately, the Fifth Circuit's aggressive moves to maintain jurisdiction has already succeeded. The Fifth Circuit is embroiled in a number of other ongoing venue fights. A suit filed by Elon Musk's SpaceX, challenging the constitutionality of the National Labor Relations Board. A different Texas judge dismissed a case involving the pharmaceutical industry's challenge of the Inflation Reduction Act's law allowing Medicare to negotiate drug prices, due to improper venue but the Fifth Circuit is hearing an appeal to that dismissal.

The Fifth Circuit is essentially litigating against other federal courts and even some of its own circuit colleagues over the right to hear high-stakes, politically charged cases. It's an unprecedented development that highlights the broader question of what can be done about partisan, rogue judges operating in service to raw power.

Some effects of the cases that the 5th Circuit has decided:

- To undermine the safety of domestic violence survivors by allowing abusers to have access to firearms.
- To restrict the use and availability of mifepristone, a 20-year-old drug used in more than half of all U.S. abortions, which has proven safer than Tylenol.
- To prohibit federal law enforcement and the Centers for Disease Control and Prevention from communicating with social media platforms on matters of critical public importance, including foreign disinformation campaigns.
- In multiple cases, to undermine much of functional governance at the National level.

Normally these cases should have been dismissed for a variety of reasons but with the 5th circuit packed with activist judges and actively seeking cases that will further their political ends, some of the most frivolous cases are not only being heard, but also doing real harm to the country.

Judge shopping should be banned, for the obvious reasons that it compromises the impartiality of our courts and circumvents the will of the people. Almost everyone condemns the practice, including the Supreme Court, Congress, the American Bar Association, and virtually every legal scholar that has studied the issue, but some judges are openly embracing the practice, potentially even overstepping their authority in order to do the bidding of business groups. Even worse, they have the full support of the Republican Party.

Sen. Mitch McConnell (R-KY), is one of the prime architects of the right-wing takeover of the courts. He and his allies have urged chief judges across the country not to change their case assignment practices. This has become the de-facto method to enact an unpopular and undemocratic agenda that would never make it through congress.

The decision to do something about judge shopping is entirely up to a panel of judges appointed by Chief Justice John Roberts. The *Judicial Conference* operates as a network of committees, led by the chief judges of all the federal circuit courts and headed by Roberts, who is officially the "Chief Justice of the United States," not just the Supreme Court. Roberts has sole authority to make appointments to the conference committees and to summon it into session; and very broad authority in deciding what comes before the conference. The Supreme Court settle these venue issues but the Supreme Court itself has been dealing with its own legitimacy crisis fueled by apparent partisanship and lavish gifts from billionaires.

Many constitutional law professors across the country are deeply concerned by the level of partisanship of this Supreme Court's decisions. In cases pertaining to abortion rights, gun laws, voting rights, labor unions, the separation of church and state, and affirmative action, the court has used flimsy legal theories to overturn decades of precedent—with the intended result of advancing right-wing political priorities.

Republicans ended the long-standing practice of vetting judges ' fitness via the so-called blue-slip policy, which allows home-state senators to block a judge they disfavor, and ignoring ratings from the American Bar Association, focusing instead on their approval by the Federalist Society and the Heritage Foundation.
Those moves have meant that many appointees who would never have been considered before President Trump's presidency are now on the bench, regularly deciding policies of national importance, and enjoying lifetime tenure. Democrats have failed to act in kind, meaning that Republican politicians can block the appointment of any judge in courts representing their states. This creates a one-way path where courts like the Fifth Circuit get more conservative, but never more liberal. Democrats are keen to fight back but the Republicans are determined to continue to packing the courts with ideologues.

Congress could act by passing legislation, to prevent some of the 5th Circuit's egregious conduct, requiring randomization of case assignments, this would not completely solve the judge shopping issues, but it is a good start. Other legislative solutions could also include limits to nationwide injunctive relief issued by one district judge by requiring a panel of multi-jurisdictional judges to hear those cases or allowing litigants to move the case to D.C. Circuit for review. The Supreme Court should explicitly call out the 5th Circuit's bad behavior but they seem to be in on the game.

References
Center for American Progress, The American Prospect, Washington Post, NYT

The Poisonous Influence of ALEC on Our Politics:

The American Legislative Exchange Council (ALEC) is an organization that wields considerable influence over American politics, yet remains relatively obscure to the average voter. Comprised of conservative state legislators and corporate representatives, ALEC's mission is to advance a specific ideological agenda, often through the drafting and dissemination of model legislation. The pernicious influence of ALEC on our political landscape is creating a country that's increasingly pro business and the American public know very little of its methods or its impact, and the broader implications for democracy.

Founded in 1973 by conservative activists, ALEC began as a small network aimed at promoting free-market policies and limited government. Over the decades, it has grown into a powerful force, shaping legislation at the state level across the United States. Its members include legislators and representatives from various industries, ranging from pharmaceuticals to telecommunications, who collaborate to draft model bills that align with their financial and political interests.

ALEC's primary tool of influence is its pre-drafted bills that legislators can introduce in their own states with minimal modification. These bills often reflect the interests of ALEC's corporate members, addressing issues like deregulation, tax policy, and labor laws. Legislators who attend ALEC conferences receive these model bills along with talking points and strategies for passing them.

ALEC's influence is augmented by substantial financial resources. Corporate members pay hefty dues and contribute additional funding to sponsor events and activities. This money flows into campaigns, providing direct support to ALEC-affiliated legislators. Furthermore, ALEC offers scholarships and travel stipends to lawmakers, ensuring their attendance at conferences where they receive training and indoctrination in ALEC's ideology. Lucrative positions are often offered to elected officials after they leave office, contributing to the revolving-door between government and these corporations.

The reach of ALEC's model legislation is extensive. For instance, the Stand Your Ground laws, which gained national attention following the shooting of Trayvon Martin in Florida, originated as an ALEC model bill. These laws, now enacted in multiple states, allow individuals to use deadly force in self-defense without the duty to retreat, often resulting in increased violence and racial disparities in their application. Black people who use stand your ground are almost

15 percent more likely to face a penalty for doing so than their white peers.

Another significant area of influence is voter ID laws. ALEC has promoted strict voter ID requirements that critics argue disenfranchise minority and low-income voters under the guise of preventing voter fraud. These laws have been enacted in many states, often resulting in lower voter turnout among marginalized communities. This is an example of a "solution without a problem". Voter fraud is so rare that statistically it doesn't exist and where there is actual cases, voter fraud is more likely to be committed by Republican voters. Because communities of color are more likely to vote democratic, they are the main targets of these restrictive laws.

In the realm of environmental policy, ALEC has championed legislation that undermines efforts to combat climate change. Model bills advocating for the rollback of renewable energy standards and opposing regulations on carbon emissions have been introduced and passed in various states, stalling progress on addressing environmental issues. ALEC's practices raise profound ethical concerns. The organization operates with limited transparency, keeping much of its activities and financial backers hidden from public scrutiny. This opacity prevents voters from understanding the extent to which corporate interests shape the laws that govern them.

Furthermore, the close relationship between lawmakers and corporate lobbyists facilitated by ALEC blurs the lines between public service and private gain. Legislators who rely on ALEC's resources may feel beholden to corporate interests rather than their constituents, eroding public trust in democratic institutions. The influence of ALEC represents a broader trend of corporate power infiltrating the democratic process. By providing ready-made legislation and substantial financial support, ALEC effectively outsources the lawmaking process to private interests. This dynamic undermines the principle of representative democracy, where elected officials are supposed to reflect the will of the people rather than the agendas of a select few. ALEC's mode of operation highlights the increasing polarization in American politics. The organization's focus on conservative policy goals contributes to the ideological entrenchment of its members, making bipartisan cooperation more difficult. This polarization is exacerbated by ALEC's framing of issues in binary terms, leaving little room for nuanced debate or compromise.

We can address the pernicious influence of ALEC in several ways: Increased transparency, lawmakers should be required to disclose their participation in ALEC and the model bills they introduce. Campaign finance reform is also critical to reduce the outsized influence of corporate money in politics. Public awareness and activism must play a pivotal role and educating voters about ALEC's activities and their impact on state legislation can mobilize opposition and encourage greater accountability. Supporting organizations and candidates that prioritize transparency and resist corporate influence can help shift the balance of power back toward the people.

The American Legislative Exchange Council's is not the only organization seeking to influence our politics, but the practice is both profoundly troubling and a potential threat to democracy. Through its model legislation, financial support, and strategic alliances, ALEC has managed to embed corporate interests deeply into the fabric of state governments across the country. This chapter has outlined the mechanisms by which ALEC operates, the significant impacts it has had on legislation, and the ethical and democratic concerns it raises. Countering ALEC's influence is imperative for restoring the integrity of our democratic institutions and ensuring that the voices of all citizens, not just the wealthy and powerful, are heard and respected.

Shock Politics: How the Right Seizes Power During Troubled Times:

The contemporary political landscape is often shaped by crises. From economic downturns to natural disasters, moments of instability provide fertile ground for radical political shifts. Naomi Klein's seminal work, "The Shock Doctrine: The Rise of Disaster Capitalism," outlines how such crises have historically been exploited to push through controversial policies that might otherwise be resisted. This chapter delves into how right-wing movements have adeptly used these "shocks" to seize and consolidate power, fundamentally altering the political and economic fabric of societies.

Klein's book posits that periods of collective trauma—be they economic collapses, terrorist attacks, or natural disasters—can be exploited to implement sweeping, often unpopular reforms. The core idea is that during a crisis, the general populace is too preoccupied with immediate survival to effectively resist or even notice the rapid implementation of policies that significantly alter their lives.

In this context, shock politics involves a series of strategic moves:

1. Exploitation of Crisis: Identifying or engineering a crisis to create a state of collective disorientation and fear.

2. Rapid Policy Implementation: Pushing through neoliberal policies such as privatization, deregulation, and austerity measures while the population is too distracted to mount significant opposition.

3. Control of Narrative: Using media and political rhetoric to frame these policies as necessary solutions to the crisis, often invoking themes of patriotism or economic survival.

4. Consolidation of Power: Strengthening the political power of those in charge, often through measures that reduce democratic oversight and civil liberties.

CASE STUDIES IN SHOCK POLITICS:

The Pinochet Regime in Chile:

One of the most striking examples of shock politics in action is the Chilean coup of 1973. Following the violent overthrow of President Salvador Allende, General Augusto Pinochet's regime, with substantial backing from the United States, implemented radical economic reforms inspired by the Chicago School of Economics. These reforms included widespread privatization of state-owned industries, deregulation of markets, and severe cuts to social spending. The shock of the coup and the subsequent repression — including widespread human rights abuses created an environment where dissent was stifled, many people who attempted to protest were summarily "disappeared", allowing the regime to impose its economic agenda with little resistance. The long-term effects included a deep scaring to the public psyche, massive inequality and the entrenchment of neoliberal policies that persisted long after Pinochet left power.

The Economic Crisis in Greece:
In the wake of the 2008 global financial crisis, Greece found itself on the brink of economic collapse. The European Union, particularly under the influence of Germany and other financially conservative member states, imposed severe austerity measures as conditions for bailout packages. These measures included drastic cuts to public spending, pension reductions, and tax hikes. The economic shock experienced by the Greek population was profound, leading to massive unemployment, widespread poverty, and significant social unrest. However, the crisis also provided an opportunity for right-wing parties to gain traction by promising stability and security. The austerity measures, framed as necessary to save the nation, fundamentally reshaped the Greek economy and society, often at the expense of the most vulnerable.

The attacks of 9/11 - The United States:
On September 11, 2001, terrorist flew two planes into the World Trade Center towers, a tragic event is known to most Americans alive today, but what's not known as well was the massive changes in law pushed through during the "shock" of the event. The "Patriot Act" had been rejected for years because it was viewed as too invasive and would compromise the rights of our citizens, but the bill passed shortly after the attacks by nearly unanimous votes, with only a single NO vote in the house of representatives. The Bush administration took further advantage of the shocked public to start an illegal and ill-advised war in Iraq. Planned long in advance, the war provided a

testing ground for extreme neoliberal policies. Under the leadership of L. Paul Bremmer, the policies of privatization and "free markets" failed miserably and cost the lives of over four thousand American soldiers and millions of Iraqi citizens.

More recently, the rise of authoritarian populism in various parts of the world exemplifies the use of shock politics. Leaders like Donald Trump in the United States, Jair Bolsonaro in Brazil, and Viktor Orbán in Hungary have capitalized on economic anxieties, cultural shifts, and security fears to consolidate power. These leaders often employ a narrative of crisis, whether it is immigration, terrorism, or economic instability, to justify authoritarian measures and curtail democratic norms.

Trump's rise to power, for instance, was significantly fueled by the lingering effects of the 2008 financial crisis and the subsequent disillusionment with the political establishment. His administration's policies, ranging from the aggressive deregulation of industries to the controversial tax cuts for the wealthy, were often framed as necessary to "Make America Great Again." Meanwhile, his rhetoric on immigration and national security created a climate of fear and division, further enabling the consolidation of power.

The utilization of crises to implement radical changes poses significant risks to democratic institutions and social equity. By capitalizing on moments of vulnerability, right-wing movements have not only reshaped economic policies but also altered the very fabric of democratic governance. The reduction of civil liberties, increased surveillance, and the erosion of checks and balances are common byproducts of shock politics. Moreover, the economic policies implemented during these times exacerbate inequality. Privatization and deregulation tend to benefit the wealthy and powerful, leaving the most vulnerable populations to bear the brunt of austerity measures and reduced social services.

Shock politics, as described in Naomi Klein's "The Shock Doctrine," reveals a troubling dynamic in modern governance. Crises, rather than being moments for collective solidarity and rebuilding, are often exploited to push through radical right-wing agendas that can reshape societies in profound and lasting ways. Understanding this dynamic is crucial for resisting such exploitation and striving for policies that truly serve the public good during times of crisis. The challenge remains to build resilient democratic institutions capable of withstanding the pressures of shock and to foster political awareness that can counteract the opportunistic use of crises for undemocratic ends.

The Corrupting Influence:
Corporate Approved - Politics, Education, and Science.

In contemporary society, "Think Tank" organizations are highly influential in shaping public policy, discourse, and opinion. However, the influence of right-wing think tanks such as the Cato Institute, The Heritage Foundation and the American Enterprise Institute (AEI) has been particularly contentious. These organizations have been accused of distorting politics, education, and science for ideological purposes, often prioritizing corporate interests over public welfare. These organizations promote libertarian and conservative ideologies, often emphasizing deregulation, tax cuts, and a reduction in government spending. While these ideas are not inherently corrupt, the methods used to achieve them can be.

Heritage, Cato and AEI produce a steady stream of policy papers, op-eds, and research reports that often find their way into the hands of policymakers. Through extensive lobbying efforts, they influence legislation in ways that favor their ideological and financial backers. This relationship between think tanks and lawmakers can create an echo chamber where policies that benefit the wealthy and corporations are prioritized over those that serve the public interest.

They also exert significant control over media narratives. Scholars and experts affiliated with these organizations frequently appear on news programs, write columns for major newspapers, and contribute to online platforms. Their pervasive media presence ensures that their perspectives receive disproportionate attention, often at the expense of more balanced or progressive viewpoints. More on the media in later chapters.

Education is another domain where the influence of right-wing think tanks has raised concerns. By using large donations to Universities and promoting certain curricula and educational policies, these organizations can shape the ideological leanings of future generations. They advocate for curricula that align with their ideological perspectives, emphasizing free market principles, American exceptionalism, and a limited role for government. They often support the inclusion of materials that downplay issues such as climate change, social inequality, and systemic racism, presenting a skewed version of history and science to students, creating an alternative reality in the minds of the students that favors neoliberal policies and the billionaire class.

These think tanks are strong proponents of charter schools and voucher programs, which they argue provide parents with more choices and foster competition in the education sector. However, critics contend that these policies siphon funds from public schools, exacerbating educational inequalities and undermining the public education system. Voucher programs when first introduced were seen as a way for the wealthy, who sent their children to private schools, the claw back money from an education system they weren't using.

Science is one of the most Orwellian domains, where they often challenge scientific consensus on critical issues such as climate change, public health, and environmental regulation. Their messaging is attempting and at some level succeeding in convincing the public that facts aren't facts and that we shouldn't believe what's right in front of our eyes.

One of the most significant areas of impact is the debate over climate change. Organizations like Cato and AEI have received substantial funding from the fossil fuel industry, leading them to question the validity of climate science and oppose regulations aimed at reducing greenhouse gas emissions. By promoting skeptical perspectives and amplifying the voices of a minority of (paid) contrarian scientists, they contribute to public confusion and policy delay.

The fossil fuel industry is a prime example of how corporate interests can stymie environmental progress. Despite overwhelming scientific consensus on the need to reduce greenhouse gas emissions, oil, coal, and gas companies spend millions lobbying against climate regulations and promoting misinformation about climate science.

Since renewable energy technologies threaten the market share of traditional energy corporations, these corporations often lobby against policies that would support renewable energy development, and create false narratives through their cronies who make ridiculous claims such as "global warming isn't real because it's cold outside". At the same time killing programs such as tax credits for wind and solar power or investments in grid modernization.

The Koch Brothers, Charles and David Koch (the later deceased), through their conglomerate Koch Industries and associated network of political organizations, have been influential in shaping conservative politics in America. Their spending has supported efforts to roll back environmental regulations, oppose healthcare reform, and influence state and federal elections. They are one of the major sponsors of what's referred to as "astro turf" movements, groups that appear to be locally created but in fact are funded and organized by corporations as we saw with the "Tea Party" movement.

In line with their broader deregulatory agenda, Cato and AEI often argue against environmental regulations that protect air and water quality, wildlife, and natural resources. Their influence has led to the weakening of critical environmental protections, prioritizing corporate profits over ecological and public health and using their money and resources to "muddy the waters" of scientific conclusions regarding the environment.

Public health events, as during crises, such as the COVID-19 pandemic, these organizations have often opposed government intervention measures, advocating for minimal restrictions and questioning the efficacy of vaccines and other public health tools. Their positions are counter to scientific understanding and can undermine public trust in health authorities by contributing to the spread of misinformation.

Big Pharma and Healthcare Policy

The pharmaceutical industry has a significant impact on healthcare policy through extensive lobbying and campaign contributions. This influence has contributed to high drug prices and the blocking of reforms that would make medications more affordable and accessible to the public.

At the heart of the corrupting influence of these think tanks is the intersection of money and ideology. The Heritage Foundation, Cato and AEI receive substantial funding from wealthy donors, corporations, and interest groups that benefit from their policy positions. This financial support creates a feedback loop where the research and advocacy work of these think tanks increasingly aligns with the interests of their funders, often at the expense of unbiased, evidence-based policy recommendations. In short, they are manufacturing consent.

PART 8:

The Media - Bigger is Better.

> *"Facts are stubborn things; and whatever may be our wishes, our inclinations, or the dictates of our passions, they cannot alter the state of facts and evidence."*
>
> John Adams

MYS-STORY.

In the early days, the media business was a different beast—especially the news media. The new technology had the power to transform the country in profound ways. No, I'm not talking about *Friends* reruns brainwashing an entire generation into thinking New York apartments are spacious. I'm talking about the ability to reach millions, shape public perception, and, ideally, serve the public interest.

To ensure that this powerful tool wasn't entirely hijacked for profit, the **Radio Act of 1927** put some guardrails in place, requiring broadcasters to serve the public interest. In 1934, the **Federal Communications Act** replaced it and created the **FCC**, the watchdog for America's airwaves. By 1949, the FCC interpreted its role to mean promoting fairness in broadcasting. Imagine that—broadcasters actually had to provide balanced coverage on controversial issues! Candidates for public office were even entitled to equal airtime. What a radical concept.

Congress tweaked the law in 1959, creating exceptions to equal airtime requirements but still insisting that broadcasters provide a *reasonable* balance of views on important public issues. Enter the **Fairness Doctrine**—a policy that, while not perfect, at least attempted to prevent the media from becoming a corporate megaphone. Naturally, some people weren't thrilled about that.

The Death of Fairness – Because Who Needs Balance?

Opponents of the Fairness Doctrine called it an attack on freedom—because, obviously, the First Amendment is *only* for billionaires and media conglomerates. The doctrine survived a Supreme Court challenge in **Red Lion Broadcasting Co. v. FCC (1969)**, but by the 1980s, the Reagan administration—always looking out for corporate interests—decided it was time to let media companies roam free. The **FCC repealed the Fairness Doctrine in 1987**, but for a while, a few remnants survived. Not to worry—by **2011**, the last scraps of fairness were finally thrown into the dustbin of history.

Then came the **1996 Telecommunications Act**, a masterpiece of deregulation that promised more competition, lower prices, and better services. In reality, it just allowed mega-corporations like **Disney, Comcast, and News Corp** to devour everything in sight. The Act eliminated restrictions on how many media outlets a single company could own, leading to a handful of corporate overlords controlling most of what we see, hear, and read. But hey, at least we got *cheaper cable and phone bills*! Oh, wait…

Overall, the Telecommunications Act of 1996 significantly changed the landscape of telecommunications in the U.S., leading to greater media concentration and altering the regulatory approach of the FCC.

Media Consolidation - Corporate Pac-Man:

The modern media landscape is a complex and influential environment where information is both created and disseminated to the public. With the proliferation of social media this landscape is increasingly shaped by a small number of powerful corporations, through decades of media consolidation, giving fewer and fewer individuals or organizations control of an ever increasing shares of the mass media. This chapter explores how media consolidation distorts reality, the rise of conservative outlets like FOX News, NewsMax and The Sinclair Broadcast Group and their role in propagating right-wing disinformation.

The concentration of media ownership can be traced to a shift to neoliberal deregulation policies, which is a market-driven approach. Deregulation effectively removes governmental barriers to allow for the commercial exploitation of media. Motivation for media firms to merge includes increased profit-margins, reduced risk and maintaining a competitive edge. It also reduces journalistic standards for the sake of increased profits.

There was a time when Walter Cronkite was the most trusted man in America but media consolidation has had a significant impact on the reliability of information available to the public. When only a few large corporations control the majority of media outlets, they have the power to shape public perception, influence political outcomes, and set the national agenda. This concentration of media ownership can lead to a homogenization of content, where a limited range of perspectives is presented, often reflecting the interests and ideologies of the owners rather than the facts that matter to the broader public.

> *"An educated citizenry is a vital requisite for our survival as a free people."*
> Thomas Jefferson

A corporate dominated news industry can suppress critical voices and marginalize populist or minority viewpoints. It also results in the dissemination of biased or incomplete information, which often misinforms the public and distort democratic processes. When media companies prioritize sensationalism, their own political agendas and shareholder value over objective, factual reporting, the public's ability to make informed decisions is compromised.

Sinclair Broadcast Group is one of the most prominent examples of media consolidation in the United States. With ownership of nearly 200 television stations across the country, Sinclair has a significant reach, influencing millions of viewers. The company has been criticized for using its vast network to propagate an ultra-conservative agenda, often through a practice known as "must-run" segments.

"Must-runs" are pre-packaged news pieces produced by Sinclair's national news desk, where the same story is aired across different stations, in which local stations are required to air the segments, often during prime viewing times. These segments are notorious for their right-leaning slant, frequently featuring commentary that aligns with conservative viewpoints or presents misleading information. They are particularly insidious because they use trusted local reporters to pass on misleading stories. This is simply propaganda by another name. This practice ensures that the same message is broadcast across a wide array of local stations, creating the illusion of widespread consensus and reinforcing conservative corporate narratives. Video clips of dozens of different news stations repeating the exact same message is a popular bit with late night comedians.

One of the most detrimental effects of Sinclair's "must-run" segments is the erosion of local journalism. By mandating the inclusion of content focused on their national agenda, Sinclair reduces the amount of airtime available for important local news. This not only deprives communities of important information but also may mislead people about issues that have dire consequences such as climate change, assistance programs or public health emergencies. This not only undermines the station's responsibilities to local population, but also harms communities with programming designed to facilitate distant corporate agendas.

Sinclair's "must-run" segments have been criticized for spreading right-wing disinformation. For example, during the 2020 presidential election, Sinclair stations aired segments casting doubt on the integrity of mail-in voting, echoing unsubstantiated claims made by former President Donald Trump and his supporters. This misinformation has a profound impact on public perception of reality, contributing to polarization and mistrust in democratic institutions.

By airing these propaganda segments alongside regular news programming, Sinclair creates an illusion of objectivity. Viewers may not realize that the content is mandated by the parent company and may perceive it as unbiased reporting. This blurring of the lines between opinion and fact-based journalism can mislead the public and distort their understanding of current events.

The dissemination of biased information poses a significant threat to our democracy. A well-informed public is essential for the functioning of a democratic society, and when media companies prioritize their agendas over factual reporting, the public's ability to make informed decisions is undermined. This can lead to an electorate that is misinformed or manipulated, weakening the foundations of democratic governance.

To counteract the negative effects of media consolidation, it is crucial to promote diverse media ownership. Diverse ownership ensures a plurality of voices and perspectives, which is essential for a healthy democracy.

Media consolidation poses a significant challenge to the integrity of journalism and the health of democratic societies. Deregulation and the use of corporate crafted messaging such as "must-run" segments to propagate right-wing disinformation highlights the dangers of concentrated media ownership and the erosion of local journalism. To safeguard democracy and ensure a well-informed public, it is imperative to address the issue of consolidated ownership and promote a diverse and independent media environment.

> *"The advancement and diffusion of knowledge is the only guardian of true liberty."*
> James Madison

The Great Shrinking of Investigative Journalism: Or How Media Got Sold to the Highest Bidder

Ah, the good old days when journalism was about uncovering the truth, not how many ads you can shove into a single clickbait headline. Nowadays, a small group of media conglomerates owns a *staggering* amount of outlets. Sure, this consolidation has brought about *efficiencies* and *economies of scale*—because who doesn't love a good monopoly? But at what cost? The quality and diversity of journalism have been flushed down the drain, all in the name of maximizing profits.

Investigative reporting, once the beating heart of real journalism, is now an endangered species. Why bother uncovering government corruption or corporate malfeasance when sensationalist celebrity gossip and "news" that barely qualifies as toilet paper filler rake in far more revenue? The sad truth is, media consolidation has made it perfectly clear: *public interest* is just an annoying obstacle when the bottom line is looking to climb ever higher.

So, while the rich get richer off your clicks, don't expect to see much digging into the stories that actually matter. Instead, sit back and enjoy the steady decline of investigative journalism as its slowly replaced by fluff and nonsense.

Investigative journalism is resource-intensive. It requires significant time, money, and personnel to conduct in-depth investigations, gather data, verify facts, and ensure legal compliance. Under media consolidation, the pressure to deliver high profit margins often leads to cost-cutting measures that undermine these resource-heavy projects. Investigative teams are among the first to face budget cuts, leading to fewer in-depth stories and a shift toward more profitable, less challenging content such as "opinion" segments.

As media companies merge, there is a tendency toward homogenization of content. This results in fewer unique perspectives and a reduction in the diversity of voices and stories also a greater risk of corporate and political influence on editorial decisions. Investigative journalism, which often challenges powerful interests and highlights underreported issues, suffers as the emphasis shifts to more universally appealing, less controversial content that is easier to produce and more commercially viable.

Investigative journalism that might expose wrongdoing or challenge the status quo is suppressed or diluted when it conflicts with the interests of the parent company or its affiliates. This compromises the independence and objectivity essential for robust investigative reporting. The Watergate scandal, uncovered by The Washington Post's investigative reporters Bob Woodward and Carl Bernstein, is a classic example of journalism's power to challenge the highest echelons of power. In today's consolidated media environment, it is questionable whether similar in-depth investigative efforts would receive the necessary support and resources.

One illustrative example is Tribune Media, it was one of the largest television broadcasting companies, owning 39 television stations across the U.S. and operating three additional stations through local marketing agreements. It owned national basic cable channel/superstation WGN America, regional cable news channel Chicagoland Television (CLTV) and Chicago radio station WGN. Investment interests included the Food Network, in which the company had a 31% share.

Prior to the company spinning-off the publishing division in August 2014 into Tribune Publishing, Tribune Media was the nation's second-largest newspaper publisher behind the Gannett Company, with ten daily newspapers, including the Chicago Tribune, Los Angeles Times, Orlando Sentinel, Sun-Sentinel and The Baltimore Sun, and several commuter tabloids.

In 2007, investors bought the company, taking on substantial debt. The subsequent 2008 bankruptcy of Tribune Company was the largest bankruptcy in the history of the American media industry. This is a common tactic among "Vulture Capitalists". They saddle the company with huge debt and pay themselves millions in salaries and bonuses, declare bankruptcy and leave the workers unemployed and with a raided pension fund. After Tribune emerged from bankruptcy they announced its sale to Maryland-based Sinclair Broadcast Group on May 8, 2017, but on August 9, 2018, Tribune cancelled the sale and sued Sinclair for breach of contract. In 2018, Nexstar Media group announced a merger with Tribune Media for $4.1 billion. This was the largest broadcast merger in U.S. history. Under Nexstar, The Tribune Company, which owns numerous newspapers including the Chicago Tribune and the Los Angeles

Times, has undergone multiple rounds of layoffs and restructuring. These cuts have severely diminished the investigative capacities of these once-venerable institutions.

Another example is the merger between Gannett and GateHouse Media in 2019 which created the largest newspaper chain in the United States. Despite promises of maintaining journalistic standards, the merger has led to significant staff reductions, with investigative reporters being among the hardest hit. For instance, The Arizona Republic, a Gannett newspaper that won a Pulitzer Prize for its investigative reporting on the border wall, has seen its investigative team decimated, crippling its capacity to undertake similar in-depth investigations.

Then there's Digital First Media, controlled by the hedge fund Alden Global Capital, who has gained a reputation for slashing newsroom budgets and staff to maximize profits. The Denver Post, once a beacon of investigative journalism, has seen its newsroom reduced to a fraction of its former size. In 2018, remaining staff members publicly protested against Alden's management, highlighting how the cuts had decimated their ability to produce quality journalism, including investigative work.

Local investigative journalism has been particularly hard hit. As media conglomerates focus on national and international news that attracts larger audiences and more advertising revenue, local issues are often neglected. This leaves many communities without watchdogs to uncover local government corruption, environmental hazards, or other critical issues.

Despite these challenges, there are notable examples where investigative journalism continues to thrive. Non-profit organizations and independent news outlets have stepped in to fill the void left by mainstream media. ProPublica, an independent, non-profit newsroom, has produced significant investigative work that has led to policy changes and public awareness. Similarly, smaller, independent outlets like The Texas Tribune and the Center for Investigative Reporting continue to produce high-quality investigative journalism by relying on alternative funding models, such as donations and grants. They have won numerous awards and exposed high level corruption both in local and national government as well as at the Supreme Court.

Technology has both exacerbated and mitigated some of the effects of media consolidation on investigative journalism. On the one hand, digital platforms and social media have disrupted traditional revenue models, contributing to the financial struggles of many news organizations. On the other hand, these technologies have also provided new tools for investigative journalists, from data analysis software to platforms that facilitate crowd-sourced investigations and whistleblowing.

Media consolidation has undeniably reshaped the landscape of journalism, often to the detriment of investigative reporting. The prioritization of profit over public interest, the homogenization of content, and the increased susceptibility to external influence have all contributed to the decline of this essential journalistic form. However, the resilience and innovation of independent and non-profit news organizations offers a glimmer of hope for the future of investigative journalism. To preserve the integrity and vitality of investigative reporting, it is crucial to support diverse, independent media and develop sustainable funding models that prioritize the public good over profits.

Regulatory measures, such as antitrust laws and policies that support independent media can help prevent the concentration of media ownership and promote a more balanced and inclusive media landscape. Consolidated corporate media ownership poses a significant risks to democratic societies and to reverse this trend, there must be a renewed focus on supporting independent journalism and safeguarding the editorial independence essential for a healthy democracy.

Opinion -

The founding father wrote into our constitution's 1st amendment:

"Congress shall make no law respecting an establishment of religion, or prohibiting the free exercise thereof; or <u>abridging the freedom of speech, or of the press;</u> or the right of the people peaceably to assemble, and to petition the Government for a redress of grievances."

At the time of the 1st Amendment's creation, the technology of the day was printed pamphlets, news papers and people shouting from atop of platforms in the town square. Modern media is very different, it uses technology and the public air-waves to reach tens of millions of people everyday. This is the most powerful communications tool in the history of mankind, it should also come with responsibilities, because the future of the U.S. as a free and democratic country depends on a well informed citizenry. We need to reinstitute the Fairness doctrine and require accurate fact based news reporting from corporations that have become so very wealthy from our public resources.

Consequently, a handful of conglomerates, such as Comcast, Disney, News Corp, and ViacomCBS, now dominate the media landscape. These large media conglomerates operate under significant commercial pressures. Their primary focus is on maximizing shareholder value, which often leads to prioritizing content that attracts the most viewers or readers, and therefore, the most advertising revenue. They are under no obligation to provide the facts and information the citizens need to make political choices. So now we elect actors and celebrities you are well known but lack the skills and temperament to lead the country.

How Corporate Media Has Abandoned Journalism for Sensationalism:

In an era dominated by 24-hour news cycles, social media proliferation, and intense competition for viewer attention, corporate media has increasingly shifted its focus from traditional journalism to sensationalism. This transformation has profound implications for public discourse, democratic processes, and the overall quality of information that reaches the populace.

The primary driver behind the shift from journalism to sensationalism is economic. Corporate media companies are primarily profit-driven entities. With advertising revenue being a major source of income, media outlets are incentivized to attract as many viewers, readers, and clicks as possible. Sensational stories, which often provoke strong emotional reactions such as fear, anger, or excitement, are more likely to capture and hold audience attention than straightforward reporting of facts.

In the digital age, ratings and clicks are paramount. The advent of social media has introduced new metrics for success, such as page views, shares, and likes. These metrics often reward sensational content where headlines are crafted to be clickbait, emphasizing shocking or scandalous aspects of stories to entice readers to click through. These headlines are designed to provoke curiosity and elicit an emotional response, often at the expense of accuracy. Phrases like "You Won't Believe What Happened Next" or "Shocking Truth About..." are common, drawing readers in with the promise of sensational revelations. Algorithms designed to push these sensationalized stories have resulted in a warping of our view of reality especially with childhood development, often inducing depression and anxiety, resulting in a massive rise in teen suicides.

Actual journalism, which requires significant time, resources, and expertise, and because In-depth investigations into corruption, environmental issues, and social injustices are expensive and time-consuming, sensational stories can be produced quickly and with fewer resources, making them more attractive to media companies focused on short-term gains.

Corporate media often employs emotional manipulation to engage audiences. Stories are framed to maximize emotional impact, using dramatic language, images, and music. This technique is particularly evident in television news, where visual and auditory elements are used to create a heightened sense of drama. "Is your canned tuna trying to kill you? Tune in at 11."

Crime and disaster stories are staples of sensationalist media. These stories are often given disproportionate coverage compared to their actual impact on society. The focus on violent crime, natural disasters, and other dramatic events appeals to primal fears and keeps viewers hooked. This often distorts the public's perception of actual statistical data creating a culture of fear.

Corporate media frequently focuses on the personal lives of public figures, celebrities, and politicians. Scandals, gossip, and personal controversies are highlighted, often overshadowing more substantive issues. This not only distracts from important topics but also fosters a culture of voyeurism and superficiality.

Sensationalism often exacerbates political and social polarization. Media outlets tailor their content to specific audiences, reinforcing existing beliefs and biases. This creates echo chambers where individuals are exposed only to information that aligns with their views, deepening divisions within society. FOX News is a classic example, in 2012, a Fairleigh Dickinson University survey reported that Fox News viewers were less informed about current events than people who didn't follow the news at all. This has become known as the Fox News effect. It conjures the image of Fox News as a black hole that sucks facts out of viewers' heads.

The quality of public discourse suffers when sensationalism dominates the media landscape. Complex issues are oversimplified, and nuanced debates are replaced with sound bites and sensational narratives. This reductionist approach impairs the public's ability to engage in thoughtful, informed discussions about critical issues. Our political discourse looks more like a reality show and the real loser is the American public.

A well-informed public is crucial for the functioning of a healthy democracy. Sensationalism undermines this by prioritizing entertainment over information. Tailoring the news to "what our audience wants" is a recipe for disaster as important issues such as policy debates, social justice, and scientific developments receive less attention, leaving the public less informed and more susceptible to misinformation.

The FOX "News":
A Propaganda Machine for the Republican Party.

> *"Those who stand for nothing will fall for anything."*
> Alexander Hamilton

How FOX News went from a fledgling cable news network to a powerful propaganda tool for the Republican Party and how it became a central force in shaping conservative discourse and advancing the political agenda of the Republican Party and the far right.

FOX News was launched on October 7, 1996, by billionaire media mogul Rupert Murdoch and Republican political strategist Roger Ailes. From its inception, FOX News positioned itself as a conservative alternative to what it characterized as a liberal bias in mainstream media. This positioning was not merely a market differentiation strategy but a deliberate ideological stance designed to attract a specific audience segment—conservative viewers who felt underrepresented by other networks, and to shape the political future of this country.

Roger Ailes, a former media consultant for Republican presidents Richard Nixon, Ronald Reagan, and George H.W. Bush, played a pivotal role in shaping FOX News' editorial direction. Ailes' experience in political communication and his understanding of television's power to influence public opinion were instrumental in creating a network that blended news reporting with partisan commentary.

Ailes implemented a format that mixed straight news with opinion shows featuring conservative pundits. This allowed FOX News to maintain a veneer of journalistic integrity while promoting a clear political agenda. Ailes 'approach was to appeal to emotions, emphasizing patriotism, fear, and anger, which resonated deeply with conservative viewers.

The 2000s saw the rise of influential opinion shows on FOX News, such as "The O'Reilly Factor," "Hannity & Colmes," and later "Tucker Carlson Tonight." These programs became platforms for conservative commentary and misinformation, often blurring the line between news and opinion. Hosts like Bill O'Reilly, Sean Hannity, and Tucker Carlson were not journalists but outspoken advocates for conservative causes.

These shows often framed news stories in ways that supported Republican policies and attacked Democratic initiatives. The repetitive reinforcement of certain narratives—such as the demonization of liberal politicians, the promotion of conservative cultural values, and the framing of complex issues in binary terms—helped solidify FOX News' role as a mouthpiece for the Republican Party.

Over time, the relationship between FOX News and the Republican Party became increasingly symbiotic. Republican politicians found in FOX News a reliable platform to communicate their messages unfiltered. The network's anchors and commentators, in turn, gained access to high-profile political figures, enhancing their credibility and viewership.

FOX News played a significant role in shaping public opinion on key issues. For instance, during the lead-up to the Iraq War in 2003, FOX News vigorously supported the Bush administration's arguments for invasion, mostly sidelining dissenting voices. The network's coverage contributed to building public support for the war, showcasing its ability to influence national discourse in favor of Republican policies. This is not to say that other corporate networks weren't also on the war bandwagon but FOX was an extreme example. After all, war is good for ratings.

The election of Barack Obama in 2008 marked a turning point for FOX News. The network became a hub for opposition to the Obama administration, amplifying criticisms and fostering the rise of the Tea Party movement, an astro-turf movement funded by the Kock

Brothers network. FOX News personalities like Glenn Beck played a crucial role in mobilizing conservative grassroots activism, which in turn pressured Republican politicians to adopt more hardline stances.

During this period, FOX News' content often mirrored the talking points of Republican leaders and Tea Party activists, creating a feedback loop that intensified conservative rhetoric. This alignment was evident in the network's coverage of healthcare reform, immigration, and other contentious issues, where FOX News consistently presented narratives that aligned with Republican opposition, even if they were blatantly false.

The 2016 election of Donald Trump brought FOX News' role as a Republican propaganda machine into sharp focus. The network's unwavering support for Trump, both during his campaign and his presidency, illustrated its complete alignment with the Republican agenda. Key figures at FOX News, including Sean Hannity and Jeanine Pirro, became vocal advocates for Trump, often defending his actions and policies regardless of controversy.

Under Trump, FOX News not only promoted the administration's policies but also engaged in disinformation and conspiracy theories, particularly during the 2020 election. The network's coverage of the COVID-19 pandemic and the presidential election was marked by the dissemination of false claims and the undermining of public trust in our democratic institutions. This cost News Corp, FOX's parent company, almost 800 million dollars when it settled a defamation lawsuit by Dominion Voting Systems for lying about the 2020 election. From the beginning, FOX was deeply aligned not only with the republican agenda, but Wall St. and its pro-business / anti-government stance on taxes, regulations and social welfare spending.

The transformation of FOX News into a propaganda machine has had profound implications for American society. It has contributed to the polarization of the media, where citizens increasingly gravitate towards outlets that confirm their preexisting beliefs. This has deepened partisan divides, making it challenging to find common ground on critical issues. When there are "facts" and "alternative facts" the right wing media exposes their true objectives, to distort the truth. FOX hosts have amplified racist, bigoted and misogynistic voices even flirting with fascist ideals.

Moreover, FOX News' success has inspired other media outlets to adopt similar strategies, further fragmenting the media environment and eroding journalistic standards. The network's influence on the Republican Party has also shifted the party further to the right, as politicians seek to align themselves with the narratives promoted by FOX News to secure their electoral base. The MAGA movement is the logical outcome of a decades long partisan misinformation campaign that underscores the consequences of media as a political weapon in America. By consistently aligning its content with Republican, neoliberal interests, FOX News has not only shaped political discourse but also redefined the role of news media in democratic society and as a Wall St. advocate. Understanding the broader dynamics of political communication and media influence in this country will be crucial if are are to avoid sliding into a fascist state.

The Right-Wing Echo Chamber:
When Repetition Creates "Truth".

In contemporary politics, an echo chamber is an environment where beliefs are amplified and reinforced by communication and repetition inside a closed system, often leading to the exclusion of differing viewpoints including the facts. This is particularly prominent within right-wing media and political spheres, where a sustained and concerted effort to propagate specific narratives can result in the transformation of misinformation or subjective opinions into perceived "truth."

The right-wing echo chamber operates through a network of media outlets, social media platforms, think tanks, and political figures who consistently disseminate and amplify certain political and social messages. These messages often align with the ideological stances of the right, focusing on themes such as nationalism, skepticism of journalism or science, and distrust of government institutions, among others.

The many right-wing media outlets like Fox News, Breitbart, and One America News Network (OANN) play a crucial role in creating the echo chamber. These outlets often present news with a particular spin that aligns with conservative values, selectively highlighting information that supports their narrative while downplaying or ignoring contradictory evidence. Right-wing radio dominated the talk radio sphere for decades with Rush Limbaugh leading millions of listeners down a misinformation rabbit hole and shaping the opinion of a vast swath of America. He and other shows like his were funded by corporate titans and billionaires in order to convince people to vote against their own best interests.

Social Media is an addictive drug and platforms like Facebook, X-Twitter, and Tic-Tok have been instrumental in the rapid spread of right-wing content. Algorithms on these platforms are designed to promote "engagement" where users are increasingly shown content that aligns with their existing beliefs and tend to create a negative emotional response, further entrenching their views and creating a feedback loop of reinforcement.

Think Tanks such as the Heritage Foundation and the American Enterprise Institute produce "research" and policy recommendations that support right-wing perspectives. These think tanks provide an intellectual veneer to the narratives being pushed, lending credibility and authority to otherwise dubious claims. These talking points tend to be repeated with religious fervor on the talk shows and from right-wing politicians.

Prominent right-wing politicians and influencers amplify these messages through speeches, social media posts, and public appearances. Figures like Donald Trump have mastered the art of repetition and hyperbole, ensuring that their statements are heard widely and frequently. When FOX or OAN repeat lies and misleading stories the corporate news media often picks up the story, even if it's to dispute the veracity of it, and by doing so add the disinformation echo chamber. If you have to argue that 2+2 dos not equal 5, you've already lost.

The Power of Repetition - The effectiveness of the right-wing echo chamber lies in its ability to repeat messages loudly and frequently. This strategy is rooted in the psychological concept known as the "illusory truth effect," which posits that repeated statements are more likely to be perceived as true, regardless of their factual accuracy. We see this played out with enthusiasm on the talk shows where Republicans and their allies can be seen fast-talking over their hosts or other guests in a loud, authoritative voice. Often promoting outright falsehoods but rarely being fact checked as the host end the segment with "we'll have to leave it there".

We all have biases, preconceived notions that effect what we believe and how we process new information. The human mind can be easily tricked into believing things that are demonstrably false but also taking actions that we would not have considered without the echo chamber playing on our inherent biases.

Cognitive Bias: Human cognition is susceptible to biases that can distort perception and judgment. When individuals are repeatedly exposed to the same information, they are more likely to believe it due to the mere exposure effect. This cognitive bias leads people to develop a preference for familiar information, which in turn becomes accepted as truth even if it's clearly false.

Selective Exposure: Individuals tend to seek out information that confirms their preexisting beliefs, a phenomenon known as selective exposure. In the context of the right-wing echo chamber, this means that audiences are more likely to consume media that aligns with their ideological leanings, further reinforcing the repeated messages.

Confirmation Bias: Once an individual has been exposed to a repeated message, confirmation bias can lead them to interpret subsequent information in a way that confirms their existing beliefs. This makes it difficult for contradictory evidence to penetrate the echo chamber, as it is often dismissed or reinterpreted to fit the established narrative. Facts become "Fake News!"

Several case studies illustrate the power of the right-wing echo chamber in transforming falsehoods into perceived truths.

The "Birther" Conspiracy, is one of the most prominent examples of repetitive misinformation, which falsely claimed that former President Barack Obama was not born in the United States. Despite being thoroughly debunked, the repeated assertions by right-wing media and political figures, most notably Donald Trump, led a significant portion of the American public to believe the falsehood.

The 2020 Election Fraud Claims: Following the 2020 U.S. presidential election, right-wing media and political figures perpetuated the unfounded claim that the election was stolen due to widespread voter fraud. Despite numerous court rulings and investigations finding no evidence of significant fraud, the constant repetition of this narrative convinced many Americans that the election results were illegitimate. Even after FOX News paid a massive $787 million dollar settlement to Dominion Voting Systems for spreading lies about their machines stealing the election. (Their audience were never told of the settlement.)

Climate Change denial is one of the most dangerous lies that right-wing media and politicians have long promoted the "skepticism" about the scientific consensus on climate change. By repeatedly casting doubt on the validity of climate science and emphasizing the uncertainty of models and predictions, they have succeeded in creating a substantial segment of the population that doubts or outright denies the reality of human-induced climate change. This is clearly driven by the Fossil fuel industry's lobbying efforts. Money, apparently can't buy happiness, but it can buy the "truth".

The right-wing echo chamber, with a constant stream of repeated falsehoods, undermines trust in essential institutions, including the media, scientific community, and government. The propagation of misinformation into perceived truths has significant implications for democracy, public discourse, and societal cohesion. When people believe that these institutions are inherently biased or corrupt, it becomes challenging to foster informed and rational public debate.

The echo chamber effect exacerbates political polarization by creating distinct and separate realities for different segments of the population. This division makes it difficult to find common ground or engage in constructive dialogue, as individuals are operating from entirely different sets of "facts." When misinformation becomes accepted as truth, it leads to misguided policy decisions and the downfall of our democracy.

The right-wing echo chamber demonstrates the potent combination of media, repetition, and cognitive biases in shaping public perception. By understanding the mechanisms at play, it may become possible to develop strategies to counteract misinformation and promote a more informed and cohesive society. Efforts to foster media literacy, encourage critical thinking, and promote diverse viewpoints are essential in mitigating the effects of echo chambers and ensuring that truth prevails over repeated falsehoods.

Manufacturing Consent:
How "Think Tanks" Purchase an Alternative Reality.

Right-wing think tanks have truly mastered the art of manufacturing reality. Organizations like The Heritage Foundation, The CATO Institute, and The American Enterprise Institute don't just dabble in influencing public opinion—they treat it like a well-oiled machine, flooding the media with carefully curated "truths" that just so happen to align with their interests. Their strategy? Pump the information sphere full of misleading articles, books, and media designed to shape the world exactly as they'd like it to be.

One of the most iconic moments in this grand tradition came when White House spokesperson Kellyanne Conway, with a straight face, introduced the world to "alternative facts" in response to reporters questioning Trump's blatant falsehoods. Because why settle for old-fashioned facts when you can just invent shinier, more convenient ones?

Think tanks are especially skilled at manufacturing intellectual credibility for their preferred narratives. They identify friendly scholars, journalists, or pundits—those eager to champion the wonders of deregulation, tax cuts for billionaires, and the magic of trickle-down economics. Once these eager messengers are found, the think tanks step in with generous support: paid research gigs, cushy funding for writing projects, and, of course, lucrative career opportunities. After all, nothing screams "independent thought" quite like a well-funded mouthpiece parroting corporate talking points under the guise of serious scholarship.

The success of books promoted by these think tanks is not merely a result of organic popularity but often the product of deliberate, strategic efforts. By leveraging their resources, networks, and influence, these organizations can significantly shape public discourse and ensure that specific books gain the prominence necessary to influence public opinion and policy debates.

Some Think tanks may generate "research" papers or reports that, lend these books an air of credibility and scholarly rigor. When often they are riddled with false assumptions and selective quotes, often out of context or edited from its original meaning.

Media Appearances and interviews for the author on sympathetic media outlets helps to build anticipation and interest in the book. One of the most effective strategies for ensuring a book becomes a best seller is through bulk purchases. Think tanks and their affiliated organizations may buy large quantities of the book, either to distribute to members, use at events, or provide as part of membership incentives. This practice can significantly boost a book's sales figures, propelling it onto best-seller lists.

Often, the promotion of a book is part of a broader campaign on a specific issue, by aligning the book with ongoing advocacy efforts, think tanks can create a synergistic effect where the book both supports and promotes an agenda that benefits them both financially and politically. This underscores the power and sophistication of corporate / billionaire think tanks in advancing their ideological agendas.

Anti-Social Media:
How Corporations Are Selling Our Souls for Profit.

The Social Dilemma:

With a cocktail of sophisticated algorithms, relentless data mining, and eerily precise targeted advertising, these companies have found the ultimate goldmine: *you.* Your likes, your dislikes, your political leanings, your late-night doomscrolling habits—it's all fair game. Forget selling products to consumers; why bother when you can just sell the *consumers* themselves?

Social media corporations have managed to commodify not just our attention but our very identities, repackaging us as neatly categorized data points for the highest bidder. The implications for American society? Well, let's just say when profit-driven algorithms determine what information people see, what they believe, and even how they vote, the future isn't hard to imagine—it just might not be one we like.

Data is often referred to as the new oil, and for good reason. Every click, like, share, and comment we make is meticulously tracked, analyzed, and stored. Social media platforms harvest vast amounts of personal data, creating detailed profiles of their users. These profiles are then sold to advertisers who can target users with unprecedented precision. What we once considered private is now a valuable asset in a global marketplace.

This commodification of personal data is fundamentally exploitative. Users are rarely fully aware of the extent to which their data is being collected and used. Privacy policies are often opaque, filled with legal jargon that obscures the reality of how our information is being utilized. As a result, we are often unwittingly complicit in the sale of our digital selves.

Social media platforms use algorithms designed to maximize user engagement. These algorithms prioritize content that generates strong emotional reactions, whether positive or negative. This has a profound effect on our perception of reality. By feeding us a steady diet of sensationalist and emotionally charged content, these algorithms distort our view of the world.

The consequences of this manipulation are far-reaching. Echo chambers form as users are continually exposed to information that reinforces their existing beliefs, leading to increased polarization. Misinformation and fake news spread rapidly, undermining trust in traditional media and democratic institutions. The algorithms that drive engagement are, in effect, sowing division and discord across the nation.

The pervasive surveillance by social media companies has led to a significant erosion of privacy. Our online activities are tracked across multiple platforms and devices, creating a comprehensive picture of our behaviors and preferences. This surveillance extends beyond social media; it encompasses virtually every aspect of our digital lives.From the gas station to the grocery store, every swipe, tap or scan is being recorded, profiled and sold to advertisers.

The implications of this erosion are profound. Privacy is a fundamental human right, essential for personal autonomy and freedom. The loss of privacy can lead to a chilling effect, where individuals censor themselves for fear of being monitored. This stifles free expression and inhibits the open exchange of ideas that is vital to a healthy democracy.

Attention is another valuable commodity in the digital economy. Social media platforms are designed to capture and hold our attention for as long as possible. This has led to the rise of the attention economy, where every second of user engagement translates into revenue for the platform.

The relentless pursuit of our attention has numerous negative consequences. It contributes to increased rates of anxiety, depression, and other mental health issues, particularly among young people. The constant barrage of notifications and the pressure to stay connected can lead to information overload and a diminished ability to focus on more meaningful activities.

The impact of social media on mental health cannot be overstated. Numerous studies have linked heavy social media use to a range of psychological issues, including anxiety, depression, and low self-esteem. The curated nature of social media content, where users often present an idealized version of their lives, can lead to feelings of inadequacy and envy.

Moreover, the addictive nature of social media exacerbates these issues. Platforms are designed to be habit-forming, using features such as infinite scroll and intermittent rewards to keep users engaged. This addiction can lead to a cycle of compulsive use, where individuals sacrifice real-world interactions and activities for time spent online.

Social media has transformed the way we interact with one another, often to the detriment of genuine human connection. Relationships are increasingly mediated by technology, where interactions are commodified and quantified through likes, shares, and comments. This has led to a superficial understanding of social bonds, where the quality of relationships is often secondary to the quantity of online interactions.

The commercialization of social interactions also has broader societal implications. It contributes to the fragmentation of communities, as individuals prioritize online engagement over local, face-to-face connections. This fragmentation weakens the social fabric, making it more difficult to build cohesive and resilient communities.

Social media has had a profound impact on democratic processes. The spread of misinformation and the manipulation of public opinion through targeted advertising pose significant threats to the integrity of elections. Foreign actors and malicious entities exploit these platforms to influence political outcomes, sowing discord and undermining trust in democratic institutions. It's been proven that Russian disinformation played a significant role in electing Donald Trump.

Furthermore, the echo chambers created by algorithmic content curation exacerbate political polarization. When individuals are only exposed to information that aligns with their existing beliefs, it becomes increasingly difficult to find common ground. This polarization hampers constructive political discourse and makes it challenging to address pressing societal issues.

The unchecked power of social media corporations calls for greater accountability and regulation. Our Governments and regulatory bodies have largely missed the boat when it could and should have regulated these platforms but through ignorance or an unwillingness to take action the damage has been done. Now they must step in to protect the public interest, ensuring that these platforms operate transparently and ethically. This includes enforcing data privacy regulations, combating misinformation, and promoting algorithmic transparency. These companies rely on public infrastructure such as data transmission lines, public airwaves and should be held accountable for operating responsibly.

In addition, there is a need for greater public awareness and digital literacy. Users must be educated about the ways in which their data is being used and the potential risks associated with social media use. Empowering individuals with this knowledge can help them make more informed choices about their online activities.

Social media has undoubtedly transformed the way we connect, communicate, and consume information. However, this transformation has come at a significant cost. The commodification of personal data, the manipulation of reality, and the erosion of privacy are all consequences of a system designed to prioritize profit over people. As we navigate this digital landscape, it is crucial that we remain vigilant, advocating for greater accountability and seeking to protect the fundamental rights and freedoms that are essential to a healthy, functioning democracy. The future of America depends on our ability to reclaim our digital souls from the grasp of corporate interests.

The Media's Obsession with "Both Sides-ism":

In contemporary journalism, the concept of "both sides-ism" has become a pervasive and often controversial practice. Rooted in the ideal of journalistic objectivity, "both sides-ism" refers to the tendency of news organizations to present two opposing perspectives on an issue as equally valid, regardless of the factual integrity or moral weight of either side. This approach, while seemingly fair and balanced, often distorts reality and contributes to public misunderstanding of critical issues.

The principle of objectivity in journalism emerged in the early 20th century as a response to the sensationalist and partisan press of the previous era. Journalists aimed to provide unbiased reporting, presenting facts without personal or editorial bias. This noble goal gave rise to the "both sides" approach, ensuring that diverse viewpoints were represented and that audiences could form their own opinions.

However, the media landscape has dramatically evolved since then. The rise of 24-hour news cycles, digital media, and social platforms has transformed how news is consumed and reported. In this new environment, the traditional model of objectivity often clashes with the complexities of modern issues, where not all perspectives hold equal weight in terms of evidence or ethical standing.

Both sides-ism manifests in various forms across different media platforms. In political reporting, it often appears as equal airtime for opposing political figures, regardless of the veracity of their claims. For instance, climate change debates frequently feature climate scientists alongside climate change deniers, creating a false equivalence between scientifically supported facts and unfounded opinions or purchased ones.

In coverage of social issues, both sides-ism can lead to problematic portrayals. For example, in discussions about racism or LGBTQ+ rights, journalists may feel compelled to include voices from groups espousing discriminatory views, thereby legitimizing harmful rhetoric and marginalizing already vulnerable communities.

The implications for public discourse are significant. By presenting all viewpoints as equally valid, the media can inadvertently misinform the public. This approach fosters a climate where facts are seen as debatable and where the truth becomes just one opinion among many. This confusion undermines informed decision-making and hampers democratic processes.

Moreover, both sides-ism often prioritizes sensationalism over substance. Controversial and extreme viewpoints generate more clicks and views, driving advertising revenue and viewer engagement. As a result, the media sometimes amplifies fringe perspectives, skewing public perception and inflaming societal divisions. The news business has a motto, "If it bleeds, it leads", which is to say that stories that are sensational such as fatal car crashes or murders, are promoted to the "top story" spots.

There is a difference between journalism and "reporting". Reporting can be as simple as standing in front of a burning build and stating the obvious that the building is on fire, it reports the facts but not the cause or the story behind the fire. "Journalism", on the other hand, should be the search for understanding of an issue based on evidence and deductive reasoning. If it looks like a duck, walks like a duck, quacks like a duck... It's probably a duck. I'm not suggesting that journalist make assumptions but it's necessary to make distinctions between facts and opinions.

One of the most glaring examples of both sides-ism is the coverage of climate change. For years, media outlets have given equal platform to climate scientists and climate change deniers, despite overwhelming scientific consensus on the issue. This false balance has hindered public understanding and delayed crucial policy actions to address the climate crisis. Compounding the problem are politicians who are supported by oil companies, amplifying false or misleading statements.

During outbreaks of vaccine-preventable diseases, media coverage often includes anti-vaccine activists alongside medical experts. This both sides approach has created doubt about vaccine safety and efficacy, contributing to lower vaccination rates and public health risks. Due to the massive amount of disinformation, public health officials have been threatened for trying to provide medical advice.

In political reporting, especially during elections, equal time may be given to candidates who make demonstrably false claims, creating a misleading narrative that both sides have legitimate viewpoints. This distorts voter perception and can influence election outcomes because equal time gives the perception of equal validity.

Journalists face a profound ethical dilemma with both sides-ism. The commitment to objectivity and balance must be weighed against the responsibility to report the truth. Upholding ethical journalism means recognizing that not all perspectives are created equal and that some viewpoints are grounded in falsehoods or harm.

The path forward requires a reevaluation of journalistic practices and standards. Media organizations must be made to adopt new, more rigorous standards for balanced reporting. This includes prioritizing fact-checking, contextualizing controversial viewpoints, and refusing to amplify baseless claims. Media outlets must distinguish between legitimate debate and false equivalency. Journalists should strive to provide a nuanced understanding of issues, emphasizing evidence-based reporting over superficial balance.

The obsession with both sides-ism in the media, while rooted in a historical commitment to objectivity, has significant drawbacks in the context of modern journalism. It often leads to misinformation, sensationalism, and a distorted public discourse. To uphold the integrity of journalism and serve the public good, media organizations must move beyond simplistic notions of balance and strive for truthfulness, accuracy, and ethical reporting. Only then can the media fulfill its role as a cornerstone of democracy, fostering an informed and engaged citizenry.

Deals with the Devil:
How Hedge Funds are Warping Journalism.

In today's media landscape, the once-sacred principles of journalism—truth, integrity, and public service—have been lovingly placed on a shelf to collect dust while corporate profits take center stage. News outlets, once tasked with holding power accountable, now answer to a different master: corporate conglomerates and hedge funds, whose guiding philosophy is less "seek the truth" and more "boost the quarterly earnings."

With profit-driven executives calling the shots, journalism has undergone a stunning transformation—one where sensationalism trumps substance, clickbait replaces investigative reporting, and critical coverage is conveniently softened when it threatens ad revenue. The result? A media industry that raises fewer tough questions for the powerful and more about how best to monetize outrage.

So what does the future of news look like? If current trends continue, it'll be less about informing the public and more about keeping audiences entertained, distracted, and, above all, profitable.

The media industry has seen a wave of consolidations, with large corporations acquiring smaller, independent news outlets. The 1980s and 1990s saw the emergence of media giants like Time Warner, Viacom, and Disney, who amassed a significant share of the market through mergers and acquisitions. Today the news is increasingly shaped by the interests of a few powerful entities rather than a diverse array of independent voices.

Hedge funds, with their vast resources and aggressive investment strategies, have turned their attention to media companies as lucrative targets. Unlike traditional media owners, hedge funds are primarily interested in maximizing short-term profits and shareholder value. This often involves cost-cutting measures, such as staff layoffs and reductions in investigative reporting, which can undermine the quality and depth of journalism.

The primary objective of both corporate media conglomerates and hedge funds is to generate profit. This profit motive has several detrimental effects on journalism:

Commercialization of News Content: To attract advertisers and maximize revenue, media companies increasingly focus on sensationalism and entertainment over substantive reporting. Stories that generate clicks and views—such as celebrity scandals, sensational crimes, and clickbait headlines—are prioritized over in-depth analysis and investigative journalism. Under pressure to deliver immediate financial returns, media companies often cut back on investigative teams, leading to a decline in the kind of reporting that holds power to account and informs the public on critical issues. When a handful of corporations control the majority of media outlets, the range of voices and viewpoints is diminished. This homogenization can lead to a narrow framing of news stories, influenced by the political and economic interests of corporate owners.

Journalistic integrity is under threat, reporters face pressure to avoid stories that could harm the interests of their owners or advertisers. This can lead to self-censorship and a reluctance to pursue stories that are critical of powerful entities, including those with financial ties to the media company.

Some examples of the consequences of corporate ownership: Alden Global Capital, a hedge fund known for its aggressive cost-cutting strategies, has acquired numerous local newspapers across the United States. The fund's ownership has often led to significant newsroom layoffs, reduced publication frequency, and a decline in the quality of local journalism. Communities that once relied on these papers for vital information are left with a lack of reliable news sources.

As mentioned earlier, Sinclair Broadcasting, owner of numerous local TV stations, has been criticized for imposing a conservative editorial slant on its news coverage. This top-down approach to content control undermines the editorial independence of local newsrooms and has eroded public trust in media as an impartial source of information.

When audiences perceive that news coverage is driven by profit motives rather than a commitment to truth and accountability, they become skeptical of the information presented to them. This erosion of trust is exacerbated by the rise of misinformation and "fake news," further complicating the media landscape.

What can be done when 80% of media outlets are owned by the largest corporations in the world?
Nonprofit news organizations, funded by foundations, grants, and public donations, can provide an alternative model that prioritizes public service over profits. These outlets can focus on investigative

journalism and in-depth reporting without the pressures of commercial revenue targets. Example: Pro-Publica is an award winning non-profit practicing legitimate journalism and breaking important stories.

Government support for public broadcasting and subsidies for local journalism can help ensure the survival of independent news outlets. By providing financial assistance, governments can help maintain a diverse and vibrant media landscape. Also, by reversing the decades long attack on public television and radio we can help balance the corporate media landscape.

Regulatory policies that limit media consolidation and promote competition can help preserve a diversity of voices in the media. Regulations that ensure transparency in media ownership and editorial independence are also crucial. Bringing back some form of the "fairness doctrine" liken to truth-in-advertising. Also Personal Privacy legislation to protect people from commodification and shielding children from exploitation.

The intersection of corporate media and hedge funds represents a "deal with the devil" that threatens the very foundations of journalism. The relentless pursuit of profit, at the expense of journalistic integrity and public service, has profound implications. To safeguard the role of journalism in a democratic society, it is imperative to prioritize the public good over corporate profits. Only then can journalism fulfill its essential mission of informing the public and holding power to account.

The Merchants of Doubt:
Corporate PR Campaigns and the Distortion of Truth.

In today's so-called "age of information," where facts are supposed to speak for themselves, reality has proven to be a bit more... flexible. As Naomi Oreskes and Erik M. Conway expose in *Merchants of Doubt* — both the book and its documentary adaptation — corporations have long understood that when the facts aren't on your side, the next best thing is to manufacture confusion.

Enter the public relations industry, a well-oiled machine designed to muddy the waters, distort the truth, and keep the public just misinformed enough to maintain the status quo. These tactics have been deployed across industries with stunning success — whether it was Big Tobacco insisting cigarettes were *totally* safe or fossil fuel giants spending decades convincing the public that climate change is just an elaborate hoax dreamed up by meddling scientists.

The result? Public discourse and policy decisions shaped not by evidence or the public good but by corporate interests with deep pockets and an allergy to accountability. After all, why let pesky things like science or reality get in the way when there's money to be made?

The concept of manufacturing doubt can be traced back to the tobacco industry in the mid-20th century. As scientific evidence began to link smoking with cancer and other serious health issues, tobacco companies faced a looming threat to their profitability. In response, they didn't seek to disprove the science directly but rather to create the illusion of uncertainty. By casting doubt on the scientific consensus, they aimed to keep the public skeptical and undecided, thereby protecting their market.

One of the key strategies was the hiring of public relations firms to orchestrate campaigns that emphasized the idea that the science was not settled. As Oreskes and Conway detail in "Merchants of Doubt," companies such as Brown & Williamson and Philip Morris engaged in deceptive tactics, employing strategies that would later be adopted by other industries facing similar challenges.

Oreskes and Conway outline a recurring playbook used by these industries:

1. Hire Experts: Corporations would fund scientific research that contradicted mainstream findings. Often, these studies were conducted by scientists with questionable credentials or were misrepresented in ways that exaggerated uncertainty.

2. Magnify Disagreements: By highlighting any dissent within the scientific community, even if minimal, PR firms could suggest that there was no consensus on the issue. This tactic was particularly effective because it played into the public's lack of deep scientific understanding.

3. Shift the Focus: PR campaigns often shifted the debate from the substance of the scientific findings to questions of individual rights and freedoms. For example, the tobacco industry argued that smoking was a personal choice and that regulation was an overreach by the government.

4. Deploy Front Groups: These groups, often with innocuous or positive-sounding names, would advocate for corporate positions under the guise of grassroots movements. This created the impression of widespread public support for their stance. This can be seen during the "Tea Party" movement, backed by Kock Brother's funding and direction, they attempted to appear "grass roots".

5. Media Manipulation: By placing op-eds, sponsoring media events, and using other forms of strategic communication, these firms ensured that their messages reached a wide audience. They exploited the media's preference for balance, which often resulted in false equivalency between scientific consensus and fringe theories.

The tobacco industry's campaign is perhaps the most infamous example of manufacturing doubt. The industry's PR efforts were remarkably successful for decades, delaying regulation and public awareness about the health risks of smoking. As Oreskes and Conway document, this campaign included funding research that questioned the links between smoking and cancer, creating front groups like the Tobacco Institute, and running extensive media campaigns that argued smoking was a matter of personal freedom.

The tactics honed by the tobacco industry found new life in the debate over climate change. Fossil fuel companies, faced with mounting evidence of their contributions to global warming, employed similar strategies to sow doubt about climate science. PR firms were once again instrumental, creating front groups such as the Global Climate Coalition and funding studies that questioned the severity or even the existence of global warming. Prominent figures in the climate denial movement were often the same individuals who had previously worked for the tobacco industry. This continuity highlights how the strategies of doubt manufacturing became a blueprint for various industries.

The campaigns to manufacture doubt have had profound impacts on public opinion and policy. By creating a false sense of scientific controversy, these campaigns have delayed regulatory action on critical issues, from tobacco control to climate policy. Public opinion has been swayed to view these scientific matters as unsettled or exaggerated, leading to political inaction. The political right has fully embraced these tactics and have used misinformation and false stories to cloud the issues and provide cover when they are actually doing the lobbyist's bidding.

Case Study: The Tobacco Industry Research Committee (TIRC)
In 1954, the tobacco industry formed the Tobacco Industry Research Committee (TIRC), later known as the Council for Tobacco Research (CTR). The TIRC's stated purpose was to fund independent research on smoking and health, but its real goal was to generate skepticism about the link between smoking and disease. The TIRC published advertisements in major newspapers claiming that there was no scientific proof that smoking caused lung cancer, thereby confusing the public and delaying regulatory actions.

The delay in addressing climate change, for instance, has had dire consequences. Storms are becoming much more powerful and frequent and the decades of inaction have exacerbated the crisis, making the necessary interventions more urgent and more costly.

Similarly, the delay in tobacco regulation has resulted in millions of preventable deaths and continues to affect public health.

As early as the 1970s, oil companies like Exxon (now ExxonMobil) conducted research indicating that burning fossil fuels contributed to global warming. However, this information was kept from the public, and the companies instead funded efforts to dispute climate science. Oil companies have a long history of misleading the public about the environmental and health impacts of fossil fuel consumption. Despite internal knowledge of the risks associated with carbon emissions, these companies have actively worked to undermine climate science.

Oil companies have financed think tanks, advocacy groups, and scientists who promote climate change skepticism. By creating a network of seemingly independent voices questioning the reality and severity of climate change, they sought to delay policy responses that would limit fossil fuel use and threaten their profits.

In response to increasing public concern about climate change, oil companies have engaged in greenwashing, portraying themselves as environmentally responsible through advertising campaigns that highlight minimal investments in renewable energy or carbon offset projects, while their core business continues to heavily rely on fossil fuels.

Chemical companies have often misled the public about the safety of their products, ranging from pesticides to industrial chemicals. By obscuring the harmful effects, they have managed to continue profiting from substances that pose significant risks to human health and the environment. Chemical companies have been known to manipulate or suppress data that demonstrates the toxicity of their products. This includes selectively publishing favorable studies while burying those that show negative effects.

Through extensive lobbying and legal challenges, chemical companies have sought to influence regulatory frameworks to favor their interests. This includes weakening safety standards, delaying the banning of harmful substances, and reducing the burden of proof required to demonstrate a product's danger.

Similar to tobacco and oil companies, chemical firms have invested heavily in public relations campaigns that emphasize the benefits of their products while downplaying or ignoring the risks. They have portrayed themselves as innovators providing essential services to agriculture, industry, and consumers, masking the associated health and environmental impacts.

Case Study: Monsanto and Glyphosate
Monsanto, the producer of the herbicide glyphosate (commonly known by the brand name Roundup), has been embroiled in controversy over the safety of this chemical. Despite evidence linking glyphosate to cancer and other health issues, Monsanto has aggressively defended its product. The company has been accused of ghostwriting scientific papers, influencing regulatory assessments, and discrediting critics. Internal documents have revealed strategies to manipulate public perception and regulatory processes to maintain market dominance.
"Merchants of Doubt" offers a stark examination of how corporate interests have manipulated public understanding and policy through

sophisticated PR campaigns. By revealing these tactics, Oreskes and Conway challenge us to scrutinize the sources of our information and to be vigilant against efforts to distort scientific truths for corporate gain. As the battle over facts and truth continues in various domains, the lessons from these historical cases remain profoundly relevant.

The deceptive practices of tobacco, oil, and chemical companies reveal a pattern of prioritizing profits over public health and environmental safety. By funding biased research, engaging in extensive lobbying, and employing sophisticated public relations strategies, these industries have managed to obscure the harmful impacts of their products. This not only endangers individual health and the environment but also undermines public trust in scientific and regulatory institutions.

Understanding these manipulative strategies is crucial for fostering a more informed and discerning public, capable of resisting these misdirection campaigns and supporting policies grounded in scientific reality. It may be too late as the damage has already been done. As of this righting, some of the largest corporations and media outlets still refuse to call out politicians and corporate talking heads for lying to the American people, and the public is deeply divided on whether the facts are facts.

References

- Oreskes, Naomi, and Erik M. Conway. *Merchants of Doubt: How a Handful of Scientists Obscured the Truth on Issues from Tobacco Smoke to Global Warming*.
- Merchants of Doubt - Directed by Robert Kenner, Sony Pictures Classics, 2014.

PART 9:

On Sale - Everything Must Go!

Owning Knowledge:
How Journals and Public Research became a profit center.

Despite a narrow audience, scientific publishing is a remarkably big business. With total global revenues of more than 20 billion dollars. With a profit margin of upwards of 36%, higher than Apple, Google, or Amazon. A small number of astute publishers, often with very few connections to the academic or scientific community, saw an opportunity in the vast amount of funding pouring into universities.

The public started funding research in a big way during the Cold War but neglected to put funding and planning into the process of dissemination. Policymakers and scientists had faith that their system of peer review and publication, which largely happened through scholarly societies, would be enough. We didn't anticipate how the volume of papers would overwhelm the small-scale journal operations run by the scholarly societies, or how anyone would work out a way to make money from them.
The publishing of academic journals and public research has become a highly lucrative, concentrated industry controlled by a small number of companies that have found ways to monetize knowledge that was once freely accessible or publicly funded. Among the first to recognize the potential for profit in scientific publishing was Robert

Maxwell, a British media mogul whose methods laid the foundation for the monopolistic model that now dominates the field. Maxwell's pioneering strategy in the academic publishing business shifted the landscape dramatically, transforming journals into profit centers for publishing companies and creating structural challenges that affect the cost, access, and integrity of academic research to this day.

The Birth of Profit-Driven Academic Publishing: Maxwell, originally the owner of Pergamon Press, was one of the first to realize the untapped potential in scientific and technical journals. Founded in 1948, Pergamon Press published specialized scientific journals and, through Maxwell's direction, adopted a model that monopolized academic journals on niche subjects, establishing a network of highly profitable publications. By obtaining exclusive rights to publish research in fields that were often highly specialized and understudied, Maxwell's company could dictate prices for subscriptions, setting a trend for the industry that placed the financial burden on university libraries, government agencies, and research institutions.

His success inspired other publishers to adopt similar practices. By leveraging exclusivity agreements and creating brand loyalty in highly specialized academic communities, Maxwell demonstrated that academic journals could generate substantial revenue without relying on a broad readership. This focus on niche markets allowed Maxwell to build Pergamon's portfolio into one of the largest collections of academic journals in the world.

Concentration of Power: Maxwell's innovations created a blueprint for the industry, inspiring future publishing giants like Elsevier, Springer, Taylor & Francis, and Wiley—often referred to as the "Big Four." These corporations expanded on Maxwell's model, purchasing smaller publishers and securing exclusive rights to vast amounts of academic research. The mergers and acquisitions that followed resulted in an unprecedented concentration of academic content under a handful of powerful companies. Today, these corporations control a vast portion of the world's scientific publications, with Elsevier alone accounting for over 2,500 journals across nearly every scientific discipline.

The Big Four's market consolidation enabled these companies to enforce high subscription fees, creating what is now known as the "serials crisis," where universities and public libraries struggle to afford access to academic journals. Subscription costs have risen significantly, often at rates that outpace inflation, and because researchers rely on these journals for information and career advancement, they are left with few alternatives. In a vicious cycle, academics conduct research, submit it to these journals (often at their own cost), and are then required to buy back access to their own work, making knowledge both inaccessible and unaffordable to those outside elite academic circles.

The publishing industry's monopolistic tendencies have led to a "financialization of knowledge," where access to research is treated as a product rather than a public good. By securing rights to academic work, publishers can control access and impose steep fees, even on research funded by taxpayers. Despite the digital age reducing the cost of distributing information, major publishers continue to raise prices, driving record profits. Through a practice known as "bundling," publishers sell entire collections of journals rather than allowing libraries to choose individual subscriptions, pushing costs even higher. This practice often leaves smaller institutions, particularly those in less wealthy countries, unable to afford subscriptions. Meanwhile, companies benefit from copyright laws that allow them to maintain exclusive rights to academic articles, limiting the distribution of knowledge and effectively locking research behind paywalls.

In addition to subscription fees, publishers have turned to "article processing charges" (APCs) in open-access publishing, where authors pay fees to make their research publicly accessible. While open access was initially proposed as a solution to increase access to knowledge, the high APCs now required by some journals continue to restrict access, especially for researchers without significant funding.

As publishers increasingly focus on profit, concerns have emerged about the quality and integrity of the research published. The pressure for profit can lead to prioritizing quantity over quality, with publishers encouraging researchers to submit articles as frequently as possible to maximize the number of publications. In some cases, this has led to a phenomenon known as "salami slicing," where researchers publish minimal findings across multiple papers rather than consolidating comprehensive results, diluting the quality of available research.

The journal "impact factor"—a metric reflecting how often a journal's articles are cited—has become a standard measure of quality but is often manipulated to boost journal prestige and attract submissions. This creates a system where researchers are incentivized to aim for high-impact journals, which often favor trendy or sensational topics, sometimes at the expense of rigor and scientific relevance. Such pressures have increased instances of research misconduct, including data fabrication and manipulation. The integrity of peer review is also compromised by the drive for profits. Rapid publishing schedules leave little time for rigorous review, and the rise of "predatory journals"—publications that exploit the open-access model by charging authors high fees with minimal review—further undermines trust in the scientific record.

In response to the growing commercialization of academic publishing, a global movement advocating for open access to research has emerged. Researchers, universities, and public agencies are increasingly supporting open-access journals, preprint repositories, and new publishing models that bypass traditional publishers. Initiatives like Plan-S, backed by several European funding agencies, require publicly funded research to be published in open-access formats, challenging publishers 'grip on scientific knowledge.

While open-access publishing provides a promising alternative, challenges remain. Many open-access journals still rely on APCs, creating barriers for underfunded researchers. Some universities and funding bodies have begun to cover these costs, but the dominance of major publishers has yet to significantly decline. Open-access models must find sustainable funding mechanisms that do not shift costs to researchers if they are to serve as a true alternative to the traditional publishing model.

The commercial strategies initiated by Robert Maxwell transformed scientific publishing into a profit-driven enterprise, one that places knowledge in the hands of a few powerful corporations. This concentration has led to rising costs, restricted access, and, in some cases, a decline in research integrity, leaving students, researchers, and the public with limited access to the scientific record. Efforts to democratize access to knowledge through open science and alternative publishing models provide hope but face structural challenges given the entrenched power of academic publishers. Addressing these issues will require a systemic shift in how we view and fund the dissemination of knowledge, recognizing that public research serves a social good and should not be commodified as an elite product.

Vulture Capitalism:
A System Feeding on the Vulnerable.

This book would not be complete without mentioning one of the most vile of all business practices:

"Vulture capitalism" is a term used to describe an especially predatory form of capitalist investment, where profit is pursued through the aggressive acquisition and restructuring of companies, often at the expense of employees, communities, and even the long-term health of the acquired businesses. Unlike traditional venture capital, which seeks to invest in companies to foster growth, or private equity, which can focus on building sustainable returns, vulture capitalism is likened to a vulture scavenging from the weak. It targets companies that are distressed or struggling, acquiring them at low costs with the primary objective of extracting maximum value, often without regard for the company's future.

Over the past few decades, vulture capitalism has shifted from a peripheral, albeit profitable, approach to a dominant and highly lucrative strategy in sectors like retail, healthcare, and even education. This shift has led to profound economic and social impacts, laying bare the harsh realities of a system that incentivizes profit over people and raises fundamental questions about the ethics of capitalism itself.

The methods employed in vulture capitalism are distinct and typically follow a predictable sequence:

1. Targeting Vulnerable Companies: Vulture capitalists focus on businesses in financial distress, often facing bankruptcy, declining revenues, or management issues. These companies, unable to resist a takeover due to low share prices or high debt levels, are acquired at bargain prices.

2. Aggressive Cost-Cutting: Once acquired, vulture capitalists rapidly implement cost-cutting measures. These often include massive layoffs, closing departments, selling off assets, and shuttering stores. The aim is to quickly boost profit margins and maximize cash flow, but these cuts often dismantle the very components that made the company successful or sustainable.

3. Debt-Loading and Asset Stripping: To fund acquisitions, vulture capitalists may take on massive debt in the target company's name, making it responsible for repayment. This practice often saddles the acquired company with unsustainable debt, leading to an inevitable downturn. Vulture capitalists may also strip the company of valuable assets, including real estate, patents, or brand rights, selling them off to third parties for a quick return.

4. Extracting Short-Term Gains: After restructuring, vulture capitalists frequently pay themselves and their shareholders with dividends or hefty "management fees." These actions divert resources away from long-term investment and toward instant profit extraction, leaving the company weakened and financially unstable.

5. Disposal or Bankruptcy: When there's little left to extract, vulture capitalists either sell off what remains of the business or let it collapse into bankruptcy. Workers, communities, and consumers are often left to deal with the fallout, while the investors walk away with their profits intact. The government (tax payer) are often required to bail out the de-funked pensions through the Pension Benefits Guaranty Corporation.

Several cases illustrate the destructive impact of vulture capitalism on industry and community welfare:

One of the most infamous examples of vulture capitalism was the acquisition of Toys "R" Us by private equity firms in 2005. They loaded the iconic retailer with $5 billion in debt, creating a crushing financial burden. Despite its historic brand strength, Toys "R" Us struggled under the debt, unable to reinvest in its stores or compete with online retailers. In 2017, the company declared bankruptcy, leading to the closure of hundreds of stores and the loss of thousands of jobs.

Sears and Kmart: Once giants in the American retail landscape, Sears and Kmart were acquired by a private equity firm in the early 2000s. Their acquisitions followed a similar pattern: loaded with debt and stripped of assets, Sears and Kmart were left unable to modernize or effectively compete. Thousands of jobs were lost, and many communities, particularly in rural areas, saw their primary retail options vanish.

Healthcare Providers: This practice has had severe consequences in healthcare, with some investors targeting hospitals and nursing homes. By cutting essential staff, reducing services, and focusing on short-term profits, these investors often undermine the quality of care patients receive. In some cases, the result has been a decline in patient outcomes, as overburdened healthcare workers struggle to meet demand with inadequate resources.

The rise of vulture capitalism has left a trail of economic and social devastation. While investors reap profits, workers are left with stagnant wages, unemployment, and reduced benefits. The communities dependent on these businesses suffer as well; local economies weaken, property values fall, and residents often find themselves without essential services. These are not the mere collateral damage of an efficient capitalist system but rather the byproducts of a ruthless and short-sighted business model that prizes shareholder wealth over sustainable development.

The "winners" of vulture capitalism—often a small group of high-net-worth investors—grow wealthier at the expense of the public. This wealth disparity exacerbates existing social inequalities and creates widespread cynicism toward capitalism as a system that should ideally reward productive investment and long-term growth.

In classic "capitalist" theory, investment and growth are seen as the pathways to societal prosperity. When functioning well, capitalism drives innovation, rewards productivity, and raises standards of living. Vulture capitalism, however, undermines these values. Rather than fostering growth, it exploits vulnerability; rather than creating long-term value, it seeks only short-term gain. This approach erodes public trust in our system and fosters social and economic instability.

The destructive practice of vulture capitalism have prompted calls for reform from various quarters, including lawmakers, labor unions, and economic theorists. Reforms should include, Regulation of Leveraged Buyouts: restricting debt-loading practices that burden acquired companies and limiting the amount of shareholder dividends paid out after acquisition. Institute Employee and Community Protections: Policies that give employees and communities a voice in acquisition decisions, as well as protections against the adverse impacts of aggressive restructuring. Transparency and Accountability: Mandating greater transparency in private equity acquisitions and holding firms accountable for the long-term outcomes of their acquisitions.

Reforming or restraining vulture capitalism would represent a crucial step toward preserving the positive aspects of investment capitalism while minimizing its destructive potential. By emphasizing sustainable growth over quick profits, the broader capitalist system can better serve society and avoid the reputational and economic risks posed by unchecked predation.

Vulture capitalism, another force unleashed by the "free-market" ideals that prize minimal regulation, has shown itself to be unsustainable and dangerous for the very people and institutions that capitalism should ideally support. Without meaningful intervention, it risks transforming not only individual companies but the fabric of society itself, reshaping it into a landscape stripped bare for profit and leaving devastation in its wake.

What's the Matter with U.S.?
Why People Vote Against Their Own Best Interest.

Voter behavior often appears paradoxical, particularly when people vote for policies or candidates that seem to contradict their personal or economic interests. This raises crucial questions: Why do people make voting decisions that seem counterproductive to their well-being? What beliefs or motivations drive these choices? Thomas Frank's "What's the Matter with Kansas?" provides an insightful exploration of this issue, especially within the context of working-class Americans who vote for conservative agendas that may not economically benefit them.

In "What's the Matter with Kansas?", Frank examines how conservative ideology gained a foothold among Kansas's working-class population, a demographic that would seem more aligned with economic policies of the left, given issues like wage stagnation, job outsourcing, and healthcare concerns. Historically, Kansas was a populist stronghold, with a political landscape marked by progressive stances. However, as Frank argues, the state saw a conservative shift driven not by economic policies but by cultural and social issues.

This shift occurred as political operatives reframed political debates around "values" rather than economics, emphasizing issues like abortion, gun rights, and family values. These topics resonated emotionally and culturally with many voters, who began to prioritize these issues over their economic interests. Frank points out that conservative leaders effectively persuaded voters to see themselves as part of a moral struggle, framing liberal economic policies as harmful to their way of life. This strategy redirected voter frustration from corporate power or wealth inequality to cultural elites or "liberal" values, thereby securing loyalty to conservative candidates.

The idea that cultural identity often supersedes economic interests in voting behavior suggests that Kansas's shift toward conservatism reflects a broader American phenomenon where voters prioritize their cultural identities over class-based or economic self-interest. Conservatives have crafted a narrative portraying themselves as the defenders of "real" American values, aligning themselves with a sense of tradition and resistance to liberal "elitism" while their actual policies reflect more the priorities of the rich and powerful.

This shift toward identity-based voting wasn't coincidental—it was strategically cultivated by conservative leaders who saw an opportunity to mobilize working-class and rural voters through a shared sense of cultural grievance. Conservative messaging painted Democrats as disconnected urban elites who disregard the values and concerns of "ordinary" Americans. The resulting cultural and ideological identification enabled many voters to view economic policies—like tax cuts for the wealthy or deregulation—as secondary concerns to cultural issues.

Religion plays a powerful role in shaping political ideology in regions like Kansas. Evangelical and other religious groups became central to conservative coalitions, linking religious values with policy positions. Through churches and religious networks, conservatives were able to frame policies in moral terms, thereby creating a deep loyalty among religious voters who viewed support for conservative politicians as a moral duty.

These appeals to religious values and moral authority became effective tools for mobilizing conservative voters, who began to see policy positions as intertwined with their faith. Economic policies, particularly those benefiting corporations or wealthier classes, were tolerated or even supported because they were packaged alongside moral and religious imperatives that resonated with these voters' identities.

Another key factor is the American ideal of individualism and self-reliance. The cultural appeal of economic individualism suggests that hard work, not government intervention, is the path to success. This framing supports policies like tax cuts, deregulation, and reduced government welfare, which ostensibly provide individuals with greater freedom to pursue economic success, although this rarely manifests in reality.

The conservative narrative positioned government assistance as antithetical to the American Dream, labeling it as a "handout" that undercuts hard work. In Kansas and beyond, this rhetoric found support among working-class and rural voters who feared that government intervention would erode their self-reliant ethos. By tapping into this ideal of economic individualism, conservatives shifted the conversation away from structural inequalities or corporate power, instead focusing on personal responsibility as the explanation for economic struggles. The Democratic party's embrace of Neo-liberalism may have provided fertile ground for these ideas to grow with things such as NAFTA and "free trade" policies that moved American jobs off-shore.

Frank also highlights the impact of conservative media and targeted political messaging in shaping voter perceptions. Conservative talk radio, television networks, and publications amplified messages of cultural threat and economic individualism. They portrayed Democratic policies as intrusive, out-of-touch, and even un-American. This media ecosystem allowed conservative leaders to promote an ongoing narrative of cultural struggle, reinforcing distrust of liberal or progressive candidates and policies.

Through carefully crafted rhetoric and media channels, conservative leaders nurtured a distrust of government programs aimed at redistributing wealth or regulating industry. Even policies like the minimum wage increase, which could directly benefit working-class voters, were framed as government overreach, suggesting that they would ultimately harm the economy or undermine personal freedoms.

As Thomas Frank elucidates in this book, cultural and identity-based voting is a powerful propaganda tool that can override economic self-interest. By framing political issues as moral or cultural battles, conservative leaders effectively mobilized voters around a shared sense of identity, loyalty, and grievance, displacing economic concerns in the process. These dynamics reveal how deeply embedded narratives around culture, religion, and individualism can profoundly shape voting behavior. This paradox, voting against one's own best economic interest, is less perplexing when considering the complex web of identity, culture, and ideology that shapes modern American political behavior.

In the 2024 election we saw the fruits of decades of cultural and identity politics in the MAGA movement. They have not only convinced a large portion of the voting public to vote against their own financial interest but have convinced them to support a deeply flawed, unreligious, authoritarian who is openly threatening the very system our founding fathers created. I guess the many years of right wing talking points and outright false or misleading statements have cultivated a public where facts are flexible and subservient to ones beliefs.

The Consequences of a Corporate-Driven Society:

Over the last 100 years there has been a concerted effort by corporations to minimize the government's role in protecting our citizens from corrupt and unfair business practices. Through regulation and oversight, we the people, have forced the business elite to change some of their most destructive and deadly behaviors, but the struggle has not been an easy one nor has it been consistent. Franklin Delano Roosevelt and the "New Deal" moved the needle towards justice in a major way, creating millions of jobs for Americans that were suffering from a massive failure of the business community to self-regulate, and building the most powerful economic country on earth, but since then, there has been a concerted, organized effort to roll back progress and seize back the power from the people. The decisions made in the board rooms have little concern for what happens in the real world or compassion for the people who are effected by those decisions. If we are honest with ourselves, when we examine the major problems in the world, large corporations are often at the heart of the problems.

The climate crisis has largely been driven by fossil fuel companies refusing to acknowledge the harm their product was doing and actively trying to confuse the issue.

The global health crisis, during the pandemic, pharmaceutical companies used government research and money to develop vaccines and then refused to make them available to needy countries adding greatly to the death of tens of thousands of people. These are the same companies that collude to keep drug prices high here in the

U.S. through extensive lobbying while raking in massive profits from government programs.

Chemical companies, including plastics manufacturing, are one of the biggest polluters and a major cause of cancer and other serious illnesses but because of the business lobby's relentless efforts, they are rarely held accountable. The medical costs resulting from their dangerous products and sloppy management of them are often shifted to the public through higher insurance prices or government subsidies.

Factory animal farms are a major source of pollution and of food born diseases but because there are only about four companies who control 90% of the market, they use their market power to maintain poor working conditions and low pay and their lobbyists resist regulations that would save lives and genuinely help improve the nation's food supply.

The constant drive for increased profit and "growth" creates an attitude that anything goes as long as its pushes share prices higher and adds to the bottom line even when the cost is environmental degradation and loss of human life. The current compensation model for CEOs have exacerbated the situation and creates incentives to do whatever necessary to raise the share price and thereby increase their own compensation. With stock options and bonuses being the major CEO pay structure, it has set the stage for catastrophic effects on a global scale. When we consider that according to recent data, the top 10% of Americans own around 89% of all stocks. This reveals how the stock market does a poor job of indicating the financial health of our economy but rather shows how the wealthy have captured the levers of power and are using them to inflate their profits.

Wealth distribution may be a better method of determining the health of our nation. At the time of this writing the U.S. is experiencing the greatest wealth inequality in our history. The top 10% control more wealth than the bottom 50%. This is a stark example of how successful the billionaire business class has been at rigging the system in their favor, but this has come at a terrible cost. Up until the 1980s businesses paid a majority of the tax burden, with taxes high on profits, companies where better off investing in new factories, equipment and paying good wages with benefits. This created an economy that built what many call the "American Dream", where workers were paid enough to raise a family, buy a house and could afford the things that made life good. This created the strongest economy on the planet because, despite what the pundits on the financial shows like to say, corporations are not the job creators. Jobs are created by demand, demand for products and services. Companies don't hire people out of the goodness of their heart, they hire people to makes things that sell. When people have money in the pockets, they buy things, store that sell those things, hire people, those employees have money to spend and so on and so on. Corporations like to refer to themselves as job creators but they wouldn't pay a dime to keep people that weren't making them money and they are quick to layoff workers when there's a slow-down in the economy or a new technology that improves "efficiency".

It was said that "the government should do what business is unable or unwilling to do" but I would add that We the People have an obligation to look out for each other, as well as the planet we depend on. I'm not advocating a "managed system" but when it comes to necessities such as food, medicine, or housing it's necessary to regulate and correct the distorting effects of "free markets". We've seen the effects of weak regulations, in 2008 when the home loan industry went "free market" it literally crashed the world economy. Recently we've seen food prices spike due to greed-flation, companies taking advantage of lax oversight to raise prices. This had devastating effects on the working poor, many were forced to choose, pay rent or skip meals. during both of these examples the majority of the people suffered, but the wealthy elite became a hell of a lot richer.

Part 10:

Some Bright Spots

Media that Matters.

In an era dominated by corporate media conglomerates and profit-driven news cycles, non-profit news organizations have emerged as essential forces for democratic integrity, investigative rigor, and public accountability. Platforms like Democracy Now!, ProPublica, and similar non-profit news organizations offer models of journalism that prioritize truth, depth, and impact over advertising revenue. Non-profit news organizations provide a crucial alternative to commercial media by creating a more informed citizenry and fostering a healthier, more transparent society.

Non-profit news organizations are not bound to the conventional profit motives that drive much of the mainstream media, allowing them to focus on issues that are often overlooked or downplayed. Funded by donations, grants, and foundational support, non-profit news organizations are insulated from the pressures of corporate advertisers and shareholders, which can create conflicts of interest in traditional, for-profit media. For-profit news networks are often beholden to advertisers and parent companies whose interests can color editorial choices and coverage priorities.

Democracy Now! and ProPublica have emerged as leaders in non-profit news, building large followings and a reputation for uncompromising journalism. Founded in 1996 by Amy Goodman and

Democracy for sale

Juan González, Democracy Now! operates with the mission to provide an independent voice on issues of justice, politics, human rights, and the environment. Similarly, ProPublica, founded in 2007 by Paul Steiger, aims to pursue investigative journalism in the public interest, exposing abuse of power and promoting accountability.

Democracy Now! has frequently covered stories that receive scant attention in mainstream media, such as environmental injustices, human rights abuses, and indigenous rights. This freedom allows it to highlight voices from underrepresented communities, voices often sidelined by mainstream networks. ProPublica, known for its hard-hitting investigative work, has published critical exposés on a range of issues, from financial misconduct to healthcare abuses. Its independence allows it to confront powerful interests without fear of losing advertising revenue or shareholder support.

ProPublica's investigation into "patient harm" in hospitals—a series called "Deadly Deliveries"—exposed serious shortcomings in maternal care across the United States, resulting in improved hospital practices and awareness of maternal mortality risks. By bringing these issues to light in a thorough, comprehensive manner, non-profit journalism serves as a powerful force for public accountability and societal improvement. Their reporting on police misconduct in the United States has led to policy changes and increased public awareness of police accountability.

Democracy Now! frequently features interviews with grassroots organizers, indigenous leaders, activists, and experts from around the world, offering perspectives that contrast sharply with the more establishment-oriented viewpoints often found on commercial networks. Democracy Now!'s coverage of the Dakota Access Pipeline protests brought national attention to the plight of indigenous communities facing environmental degradation, which galvanized widespread support and advocacy.

The success of non-profit news organizations signals a growing recognition of the need for alternatives to commercial media. As for-profit news outlets consolidate and become more homogenized, non-profit journalism offers a counterbalance that prioritizes the public good over profits. This dedication to diversity in perspective helps non-profit news organizations provide a more complete and nuanced view of complex issues. In this way, they promote a more inclusive public discourse and empower communities that may otherwise lack a platform to share their stories and experiences.

The resilience of non-profit news organizations rests in their commitment to their missions, the trust of their audiences, and the tangible benefits they bring to society. They serve as a reminder that journalism, at its core, is a public service—a means of educating, informing, and empowering citizens to engage with the world around them. As public interest in unbiased, investigative journalism grows, non-profit news organizations will continue to play a vital role in shaping a more informed and just society.

It's Funny but True!

Traditional media often struggles to maintain public trust and relevance, Last Week Tonight with John Oliver (LWT) has carved a unique niche as an educational platform disguised as a late-night comedy show. This HBO series, hosted by British comedian and writer John Oliver, not only entertains but also provides an in-depth exploration of a wide range of social, economic, and political issues, many of which are overlooked or underreported by mainstream media. Through a combination of humor, investigative journalism, and narrative storytelling, Oliver's show has become a powerful vehicle for educating the public in ways that often surpass conventional news outlets and even formal education.

While many see LWT as a comedy show, the series is also a forum for public education. Each episode opens with a brief monologue, touching on the week's notable news items, before moving into an extended main segment that focuses on a specific topic, often one that is complex or technical, like net neutrality, civil asset forfeiture, or municipal debt.

In many ways, LWT functions as a crash course in current events, employing a pedagogical structure that includes:

1. Introduction and Background: Oliver provides an overview of the topic, detailing its history or essential background information. This groundwork ensures viewers with no prior knowledge can engage with the material.

2. Exploration of Key Concepts: Through real-world examples, statistics, and case studies, the show unpacks the complexities of issues, illustrating how they affect individuals, businesses, and society as a whole.

3. Critical Analysis and Perspective: the show often goes beyond just presenting facts. The show critically analyzes issues, highlighting

contradictions, systemic flaws, and historical contexts that may not be readily available in traditional news sources.

4. Engagement and Call to Action: Many episodes conclude with actionable insights or recommendations, encouraging viewers to think critically or even take action. For example, episodes on voting rights or the census have often motivated viewers to participate in these civic activities.

This humorous approach is pedagogically effective; it keeps viewers entertained and receptive while also helping them retain complex information in ways that a traditional news segment does not.

Oliver and his team conduct in-depth research for each segment, sometimes taking months to investigate topics fully. Unlike traditional news outlets constrained by the immediacy of the 24-hour news cycle, LWT operates on a weekly schedule, allowing the team to delve deeper into issues. The show's writers and researchers draw from academic research, government reports, and interviews with experts to compile well-rounded, fact-checked content.

The rigor of this research often rivals that of investigative journalism. The show's segment on FIFA, for instance, explained the corruption within international soccer's governing body in a way that few mainstream networks had done, resulting in massive public awareness of FIFA's internal issues. Similarly, LWT's coverage of net neutrality included comprehensive explanations that were widely praised for helping viewers understand an otherwise complex and obscure topic.

LWT's emphasis on educating the public about issues of social justice and civic engagement also topics like voting rights, gerrymandering, and criminal justice reform are covered not only to entertain but also to inspire public awareness and action. John Oliver's episodes on immigration policy have highlighted the human impact of policies like family separation, providing viewers with data, personal stories, and context that foster empathy and understanding. After an episode on net neutrality, the Federal Communications Commission (FCC) was flooded with comments from viewers spurred to action by Oliver's clear explanation of the issue. His exposé on the abuses within the bail bond industry also motivated some state governments to reconsider their policies on bail reform.

In a media landscape often accused of spreading misinformation or sensationalism, Last Week Tonight with John Oliver is an example of how entertainment can be harnessed to educate and inform the public.
As media continues to evolve, the success of LWT suggests that the future of education may well be interdisciplinary and hybrid, involving humor, storytelling, and creative engagement to break down complex topics for a broad audience. John Oliver and his team have redefined what an educational program can be, suggesting a model that, far from trivializing serious issues, proves that an informed and engaged public can also be entertained.

Business Unusual: Yeah, we built that!

In the shifting landscape of modern business, one of the most compelling success stories comes from employee-owned companies. Defined by their unique ownership structures where employees hold significant or majority shares, these organizations have sparked interest among economists, policy-makers, and corporate leaders alike. Not only do they present an alternative to traditional shareholder-owned structures, but they also highlight the potential for businesses that prioritize employee welfare alongside profitability. Let's explore the mechanisms behind the success of employee-owned companies, the benefits they bring, and the challenges they face.

Employee-owned companies have a long, storied history, but it's in recent decades that they've gained prominence. The growth in the employee-ownership movement began in the mid-20th century, as companies sought to find new ways to incentivize workers, reduce turnover, and increase loyalty. Today, the structures of employee ownership vary widely, ranging from cooperatives and Employee Stock Ownership Plans (ESOPs) to profit-sharing and stock options. These models give workers a vested interest in the company's success, fostering a culture of inclusivity, accountability, and commitment.

The advantages of employee-owned companies are numerous and well-documented, both in terms of financial success and social impact. Key benefits include:

1. Enhanced Productivity and Innovation: When employees have a stake in the outcome, they are often more motivated to perform at higher levels. Studies show that employee-owned companies typically exhibit higher productivity and efficiency than their conventionally-owned counterparts. This is due in part to the alignment of individual incentives with company goals, leading to greater innovation and a stronger work ethic among employees.

2. Increased Job Satisfaction and Reduced Turnover: With ownership comes responsibility and pride, which translates into higher job satisfaction. Employee-owned firms often see reduced turnover rates compared to traditional companies. This reduction in turnover saves on recruitment and training costs and fosters a more stable and cohesive work environment.

3. Long-Term Profitability: Contrary to the belief that employee ownership might limit a company's financial success, data suggests that these businesses often outperform traditional firms in profitability. Employee-owned firms tend to prioritize sustainable growth and long-term planning over short-term gains, which can yield more stable financial returns over time.

4. Wealth Creation and Economic Equity: Employee-owned companies can help bridge income inequality by distributing wealth more equitably across an organization. As employees accumulate shares over time, they benefit from the company's success, building wealth that might otherwise be inaccessible in a traditional corporate structure.

5. Community Impact and Economic Resilience: Employee-owned companies are more likely to be rooted in their local communities and less likely to outsource jobs. They contribute to local economic resilience, as workers who have a stake in the company are also invested in the health of the surrounding community.

Examples:
1. *Publix Super Markets, Inc.*

Publix, the largest employee-owned grocery chain in the U.S., is a sterling example of the potential for success in employee-owned companies. With a robust ESOP, Publix employees, or "associates," own a substantial share of the company. This has translated into a highly motivated workforce, a reputation for excellent customer service, and consistent profitability. Publix's success shows how employee ownership can work effectively at scale in a highly competitive industry.

2. *New Belgium Brewing*

Known for its flagship Fat Tire Amber Ale, New Belgium Brewing was one of the most well-known employee-owned companies in the craft beer industry before its acquisition in 2019. During its employee-owned years, New Belgium maintained a culture of transparency and shared responsibility, which fueled its rise to become one of the most respected breweries in the U.S. While New Belgium eventually sold to an external company, the employee-owned model was crucial to its growth and success.

3. *WinCo Foods*

A lesser-known success story, WinCo Foods is an employee-owned grocery chain that competes with industry giants like Walmart and Costco. Its unique model allows employees to accrue significant retirement savings, with some long-term employees reportedly retiring as millionaires due to the company's ESOP. WinCo's success demonstrates how employee ownership can provide competitive advantages even against much larger corporations.

While the benefits are numerous, the employee-owned model is not without its challenges:

Transitioning to an employee-owned model requires a significant financial investment, often involving the purchase of shares by employees or the establishment of a trust. For some companies, this initial hurdle can be difficult to overcome, particularly in capital-intensive industries.

Employee-owned companies face unique governance challenges, as decision-making can be slower due to the need for consensus among stakeholders. This requires a careful balance between empowering employees and maintaining effective management practices. For companies without a clear leadership structure, this can lead to internal conflicts and inefficiencies.

In difficult economic periods, employee-owned companies may be more vulnerable, as employees' livelihoods and retirement savings are tied to the company's performance. This creates additional pressure on management to ensure sustainable operations even in lean times.

Employee ownership requires a degree of financial literacy that some employees may lack. Effective education and training are necessary to ensure that employees understand their roles as stakeholders and can make informed decisions about the company's future.

The trend towards employee ownership appears to be gaining momentum, fueled by the need for sustainable business models and the growing emphasis on social equity in the workplace. With more businesses recognizing the benefits of employee ownership, the model is likely to expand in the coming years. Governments and policymakers are beginning to take note as well, with some introducing tax incentives and supportive policies to encourage the growth of employee-owned companies.

Employee-owned companies offer a blueprint for a more equitable, resilient, and productive form of capitalism. They demonstrate that prioritizing employees' well-being and fostering a sense of ownership can lead to impressive financial success, increased job satisfaction, and stronger community ties. While the model presents its challenges, the successes of companies like Publix, New Belgium Brewing, and WinCo Foods suggest that employee ownership is not only viable but perhaps essential to building a more inclusive and sustainable economy.

The success of employee-owned companies reveals a promising alternative to the traditional corporate structure. These organizations challenge the idea that wealth must be concentrated at the top and show that shared ownership can drive both profitability and social benefits. While not a one-size-fits-all solution, employee ownership offers a path forward for businesses looking to balance the needs of their workers with the demands of the marketplace, proving that when employees are given a stake in their work, the possibilities for success are boundless.

Guaranteed Basic Income or UBI:

Universal Basic Income (UBI) is a social and economic policy proposal aimed at providing all citizens or residents of a country with a regular, unconditional sum of money from the government. The main idea behind UBI is to ensure that everyone has a basic level of financial security, regardless of their employment status or other income sources.

Key Features of UBI are Unconditional Payments that are made without any requirements related to employment, income level, or other conditions. Payments are made on a consistent basis, typically monthly. They are Universal, because everyone receives the payment, regardless of income or wealth.

The objective of UBI is Poverty Reduction, by ensuring everyone has a minimum income, UBI aims to lift people out of poverty. UBI could simplify or replace existing welfare systems by reducing bureaucracy and administrative costs. Provide Economic Stability, a consistent source of income can help people better manage economic challenges and fluctuations. Empowerment and Freedom, UBI can offer people the freedom to pursue education, entrepreneurship, caregiving, or other activities without the pressure of immediate income needs.

The benefits of UBI are it reduces poverty and helps and the poorest segments of society to avoid falling into homelessness. It can stimulate the economy by increasing consumer spending and encourages Innovation. With financial security, people may feel freer to pursue creative projects or start businesses.

It can help address the challenges of job loss due to automation and technological advancements such as A.I..

Some of the challenges of UBI are its cost and the resistance to raising taxes on the wealthy. Some argue that UBI could reduce the incentive for people to work, although there's little evidence of this, or possible Inflation. There are concerns that an influx of money could drive up prices, offsetting the benefits of the income.

An alternative might be a means-tested program such as a guaranteed minimum income that provides a base level of income, if any citizen falls below that level, then their income would be supplemented up to the minimum level. This would greatly simplify the process and give people a financial safety net. Combine this with basic health insurance and it could drastically improve the lives of tens of millions of people as well as stabilize the boom-bust cycle that our economy has been on since the deregulation spree began.

Some examples of UBI trial programs:

- Finland (2017-2018): The government ran a pilot program giving unemployed citizens a monthly payment of 560 euros. Results showed increased well-being and a slight increase in employment among participants.

- United States: Some cities, such as Stockton, California, have experimented with UBI through privately funded programs, showing positive impacts on financial stability and mental health improvements.

In *"Davos Man: How the Billionaires Devoured the World"* by Peter S. Goodman, the author explores how global elites have shaped policies and economies to favor their interests, often at the expense of broader societal well-being. While the book covers a range of economic and social policies, one notable case Goodman discusses is Finland's experiment with Universal Basic Income (UBI) and its subsequent termination.

Goodman argues that the decision to stop the UBI trial in Finland was influenced by a prevailing narrative among economic and political elites that emphasizes fiscal conservatism and market-driven solutions. The trial, which ran from 2017 to 2018, involved giving 2,000 unemployed Finns a monthly income with no strings attached. The purpose was to study the effects on employment, well-being, and the efficiency of a social safety net that didn't penalize people for working while receiving benefits.

Despite some positive outcomes, such as improved mental health and reduced stress among participants, the trial ended without being expanded. Goodman points out that this was partly due to pressure from conservative policymakers and financial skeptics who believed that unconditional cash transfers could encourage idleness or become fiscally unsustainable. These arguments align with broader resistance from the Billionaire class who often push for social policies that do not challenge entrenched wealth structures or require redistribution.

The book suggests that such experiments often face opposition from those who see them as a threat to the prevailing economic order. The issue is that many powerful interests are more inclined to promote solutions that maintain their influence and avoid systemic shifts toward greater economic equality. Critiques often stymie progressive policies like UBI, framing them as impractical or unsustainable, even when evidence suggests they could offer substantial societal benefits.

Overall, UBI remains a topic of active debate among economists, policymakers, and the public. It represents a shift from traditional welfare systems to an approach that provides guaranteed income for all, aiming to promote economic security and social welfare.

Choices, Choices, Choices!

Ranked-choice voting (RCV) has become a popular alternative to the traditional "first-past-the-post" (FPTP) system due to its potential to improve democratic processes, reduce polarization, and more accurately capture voter preferences. This chapter explores the key benefits of RCV and highlights regions where it is currently in practice.

One of the most compelling advantages of RCV is that it ensures the elected candidate has broader support from the electorate. In FPTP, our current systems, candidates can win with a mere plurality, even if a majority of voters oppose them. In RCV, voters rank candidates in order of preference. If no candidate receives a majority in the first round, the lowest-ranked candidates are eliminated, and their votes are reallocated according to the voters' next preferences. This process continues until one candidate has over 50% of the vote, resulting in a winner with majority support. This feature helps to legitimize elected officials and aligns more closely with democratic ideals.

RCV tends to reduce negative campaigning, as candidates benefit from appealing to a broader base. Under this system, candidates are incentivized to be voters' second or third choice, not just their first, which encourages more respectful and issue-focused campaigns. In traditional voting systems, attacking opponents is often a tactic to sway the base, but with RCV, candidates who attack opponents too aggressively may alienate potential supporters. San Francisco, where RCV is used in local elections, has seen a decline in divisive campaigning due to this dynamic.

RCV allows voters to support their favorite candidate without the "spoiler" effect. In FPTP systems, voters might shy away from voting for a less popular candidate they truly support, or a "third" party fearing their vote might be "wasted" or inadvertently help elect their least preferred candidate. With RCV, voters can rank a diverse set of candidates without this risk. This has led to greater representation of women and minority candidates, as seen in places like Minneapolis and San Francisco, which have both reported more diverse candidate pools in RCV elections.

Because RCV encourages candidates to seek broader support, it can reduce the political polarization that often arises in winner-takes-all elections. Candidates in RCV elections are more likely to adopt centrist positions or focus on shared community values to appeal across a wide spectrum. Maine, the first state to adopt RCV for statewide elections, has seen a positive shift in candidates 'focus on policy issues that resonate with broader constituencies rather than catering exclusively to the extremes of their parties.

RCV has been associated with increased voter engagement and turnout because it provides voters with more choices and the feeling that their votes have greater influence. In New York City's 2021 municipal elections, RCV was credited with encouraging voter turnout and engaging a larger portion of the electorate. Voters reported feeling empowered by the ability to rank multiple candidates rather than selecting just one, leading to a more invested and participatory democratic process.

In traditional voting systems, close races often require additional runoff elections, which can be costly and result in lower voter turnout. RCV provides an instant-runoff mechanism that eliminates the need for a separate runoff election. This saves time, resources, and reduces voter fatigue. Cities like San Francisco, Oakland, and Minneapolis have saved significant sums by eliminating the need for additional elections and experienced more seamless transitions to office.

Ranked-choice voting addresses several of the common issues in electoral systems, fostering candidates with majority support, reducing negative campaigning, and encouraging diverse candidate representation. Its implementation in U.S. jurisdictions such as Maine, Alaska, New York City, San Francisco, and Minneapolis serves as evidence of its potential to create a more inclusive, representative, and efficient democratic process. By enhancing voter choice and diminishing the influence of divisive campaigning, RCV offers a promising reform for modernizing and revitalizing democratic elections.

Increased funding for the IRS.

I know it sounds crazy to cheer for the IRS but even though they are often seen as a burden, especially around April 15, they have been the victim of a political smear campaign for decades. Going back to the 1980s there has been an effort to curtail tax enforcement on upper income Americans. Bill Clinton declared a "kinder, gentler IRS", but what really happened was the lost tax revenues from wealthy tax dodgers had to be made up by going after the little guys. The lack of funding for the IRS has gutted the agency, leaving it unable to do its job. Tax enforcement, or the lack of it, has led to uncollected taxes of more than 500 Billion Dollars each year. Collecting taxes from high income tax cheats is an expensive endeavor, it requires experts in all the ways that people avoid paying taxes, through offshore account and shell companies etc. President Joe Biden and the democrats increased funding for tax enforcement by 65 billion dollars to hire people like forensic tax auditors to uncover the money that is owed to the American people. This is not increased taxes, this is just what is owed under current law. The deficit that we face is largely due to reduced revenue, corporate taxes have been slashed, the use of tax havens and shell companies, as discussed earlier, have flourished and yes, out of control military spending has lead to a massive deficit. The revitalized IRS could start leveling the playing field between the working Americans and the ultra rich tax cheaters, if it can survive the Republican politicians that are already calling to defund the IRS.

How to be Grassroots: Joining the Fight for Reform

One of the most satisfying things I've ever done was joining fellow activists fighting for our environment. Becoming a part of something larger than ourselves and taking an active role in trying to make the world a better place can be transformative. We all have a part to play in the fight ahead but it doesn't have to be struggle, we can approach this with joy and enthusiasm, knowing that we are making a positive contribution to the future of this great country.

Grassroots movements play a crucial role in countering corporate influence. Activists and community organizations work to raise awareness, mobilize voters, and push for policy changes that reflect the public interest rather than corporate agendas.

There have been notable successes in the fight against corporate influence. For instance, campaigns to increase transparency in political spending, impose stricter lobbying regulations, and promote public financing of campaigns have gained traction in various states and municipalities.

Solutions for Reclaiming our Democracy.

Campaign Finance Reform

Reforming campaign finance is essential to reducing corporate influence. Measures such as public funding for elections, limits on campaign contributions, and enhanced transparency requirements can help level the playing field. When money equals speech then the wealthy have enough "speech" to drowned out all of us.

Strengthening Lobbying Regulations

Stronger lobbying regulations, including stricter revolving door policies and greater disclosure of lobbying activities, can help mitigate the undue influence of corporate lobbyists on policy-making. Outside groups have both bribed and / or threatened our elected officials into playing by their rules. Some PACs, political action committees, have spent tens of millions of dollars in recent elections to defeat candidates who worked to level the playing field for working class. They have been buying our politicians and that must stop.

Corporate Accountability

Holding corporations accountable for their political activities is critical. This includes enforcing existing laws on corporate political spending, as well as implementing new regulations to ensure that corporate actions align with the public good. We can't allow the peddlers of lies and misinformation to continue to muddy the water so they can continue to profit off the harm that they cause. There must be real consequences for their action including jail. Corporate decisions can and do effect people's lives in profound ways including killing them. When corporate executives knowingly endanger the public for profit, they must be held accountable and pay more than just a "slap on the wrist" fine that adds up to nothing more that a small percentage of their quarterly profits.

Conclusion:

The selling of our democracy to corporate interests is a grave threat to the integrity of American governance and the health of our planet. However, it is not an irreversible trend. Through an informed citizenry engagement, robust activism, and comprehensive policy reforms, we can reclaim our political system and ensure that it serves the needs of all the people, not just the wealthy few. We face serious obstacles when it comes to correcting the financial coup that corporate billionaires have been enacting over the last fifty years. As was once said "The Revelation will not be Televised" so that leaves it in the hands of citizens to see beyond the corporate "yoga babel" and "green washing" about how they're doing right by the planet. We must overcome the algorithms that feed us a non-stop supply of outrage and anger and demand evidence based information from our media. Only by a concerted effort can "We the People" stop what is literally killing us, but we must act soon before it's too late. The future of our democracy and our planet depends on our ability to rise to this challenge.

Some might assume reading this that I am anti-business but that would be missing the point. If business is to thrive we need a robust regulatory system to ensure a fair playing field and when large businesses and billionaires pay higher taxes (or any taxes at all) all business thrives because citizens have more money to spend. For as long as we've been a country there has been a battle between the powerful, who would use their wealth to create unfair advantage for themselves at the expense of the public, and those who believe in the promise of this country, that all men are created equal and that we are granted inalienable rights to pursue life, liberty and happiness.

Thank you and may we all be healthy, happy and free.

Addendum:

As this book is going to print Donald Trump has won the 2024 election. Media pundants are scrambling to diagnose where the Democrats went wrong and to place blame on the progressive wing of the party. It seems incredibly arrogant that the corporate media that has treated the former president's constant, almost pathological, lying and threats to his political opponents as just another day at the office while grilling Vice President Harris on the smallest of details, now points it's finger at the people who were correct all along. I believe this exemplifies the overall bias of corporate media towards the right. After all, Donald Trump is good for business even if he destroys our democracy.

Project 2025: The Coup in a Suit and Tie.

It started with denials. "Project 2025? Never heard of it," said the usual suspects in Trump's orbit—right before details surfaced proving that his allies had spent years quietly crafting a blueprint to gut the federal government and install a regime of unaccountable, ideological loyalists. It's like watching a magician botch a trick, insisting the rabbit isn't in the hat while its ears poke out.

How to Kill a Government in 4 Easy Steps.

Back in the Trump administration's glory days of deregulation, cronyism, and breathtaking corruption, one of their favorite pastimes was dismantling government agencies from the inside. The Environmental Protection Agency (EPA)? Hand it over to a coal lobbyist. The Department of Education? Put a billionaire who's never set foot in a public school in charge. The Post Office? Let a logistics tycoon cripple its operations. It was like watching a corporate raider strip a company for parts—except the company was the U.S. government, and the shareholders were, well, all of us.

Project 2025, cooked up by the Heritage Foundation and other right-wing think tanks, is a continuation of this grand tradition. It lays out a plan to replace tens of thousands of career civil servants with ideological warriors willing to do Trump's bidding without hesitation. The goal? To purge the so-called "Deep State" (read: competent professionals) and replace them with people who treat the Constitution like a toilet paper.

The New and Improved Authoritarian Playbook.

Project 2025 isn't just about swapping out bureaucrats. It's about reshaping the government into an unrecognizable entity that answers solely to an authoritarian executive. Some of the juiciest details include:

A Politicized Department of Justice – The plan calls for putting loyalists in charge of prosecutions and law enforcement, effectively ensuring legal immunity for Trump and his cronies while targeting political opponents. (See: Washington Post)

The End of the Regulatory State – Agencies that oversee environmental protections, labor laws, and consumer protections would be hollowed out. Say goodbye to pesky things like workplace safety and clean air. (See: New York Times)
Total Executive Power – With expanded use of the Insurrection Act and a Justice Department bent to his will, Trump 2.0 would wield unprecedented power to suppress protests and silence dissent. (See: ProPublica)

Government: The Last Counterweight to Corporate Power. While Trump and his allies rail against "big government," they conveniently ignore that government regulations are often the only thing standing between the public and corporate abuses. Billion-dollar companies have endless resources to lobby, litigate, and rewrite laws in their favor, but government agencies like the EPA, OSHA, and the FDA exist to ensure that corporations don't poison the air, exploit workers, or sell hazardous products. Without these regulatory bodies, corporations would be free to cut corners on worker safety, pollute without consequence, and price-gouge consumers into oblivion. (See: The Atlantic, Mother Jones)
But the war on regulations isn't about freedom—it's about power. By weakening the federal government, corporations gain unchecked authority, and the public loses any means of holding them accountable.

Elon Musk and the War on Oversight:
Enter Elon Musk, billionaire tech mogul and self-styled free speech absolutist—except when it comes to government agencies investigating his businesses. Musk, a vocal critic of government

intervention, has made it a personal mission to undermine the very agencies that regulate workplace safety, environmental practices, and consumer protections. His latest creation, the so-called Department of Government Efficiency (DOG-E), is little more than a PR stunt designed to push deregulation under the guise of streamlining bureaucracy. (See: Bloomberg, ProPublica)

From defying labor laws at Tesla factories to skirting FAA regulations at SpaceX launch sites, Musk has repeatedly shown disdain for oversight. Reports have documented unsafe working conditions at his factories, aggressive union-busting tactics, and environmental concerns over SpaceX's rocket debris. Yet, rather than comply with regulations, Musk has used his influence—and Twitter rants—to attack regulatory agencies, painting them as corrupt and inefficient. (See: New York Times, The Verge)

Deny, Destroy, Dominate - For months, Trump's team played dumb about Project 2025, treating it like some rogue document floating in the ether. But then, as the details became unavoidable, they switched tactics: deny it's real, then execute it anyway. Classic authoritarian strategy. Just ask Viktor Orbán, who methodically gutted Hungary's democratic institutions while claiming to protect them. Or look at Putin, who turned Russia's government into a rubber stamp for his personal rule.

The parallels are alarming. In Turkey, Erdoğan purged thousands of government workers after a failed coup attempt (sound familiar?). In Brazil, Bolsonaro tried to rig government agencies to serve his agenda, much like Project 2025 aims to do. And here in the U.S., we have a movement hell-bent on making sure the next Trump presidency is less chaotic, more efficient, and dangerously effective at consolidating power.

The Frog Is Boiling

The Trump administration's first go-around was messy—a scattershot assault on government institutions where incompetence occasionally slowed the damage. But Project 2025 is different. It's calculated, methodical, and designed to ensure that next time, there's no undoing the damage.

There has been a worldwide political shift towards the right. This may be a sign that the massive inequality created by neo-liberalism, and the billionaire class it serves, has finally met the preverbal immovable object. As many of us struggle to understand how a twice impeached, convicted felon and orange tinted con-man convinced a majority of Americans that he was the solution and not the problem it may just be that the people are sick and tired of being treated as nothing more than servants of corporate profit. The public may not be well informed but most people can tell when the system isn't working for them and for decades both parties have catered to their corporate donors and neglected the vast majority of American citizens. Is it any wonder that people are disengaged and disinterested in politics? Our country's founding principle, a government of the people, by the people and for the people, may not be worth the paper they're printed on as our democracy is being sold for corporate profit.

Thank you for reading.

Acknowledgements:

The world is a much better place thanks to people who work hard and sacrifice much to improve the lives of people they will never meet. What makes it even better are people who share the gift of their knowledge and wisdom with the world. Thank you to everyone who strives to learn, grow and help others.

To all the individuals I have had the opportunity to meet, to learn from, or to pass on what I've learned. I want to say thank you for being the inspiration and foundation for this work and my life.

Without the experiences and support from my family, friends and my peers, this book would not be possible. You have given me your time, resources and the wisdom of your experience to help me become a lover of life and of learning, and to care deeply about the people I share this amazing planet with.

Thank you to Mom, Dad, my brothers, sister, and all my soul family. To my Santa Monica brothers for 40 plus years of friendship and laughs. To my mentors John Roger, Robert Razz, Joey Hubbard, Michael Beckwith, my sensei Brian Hawkins, Jeff Speakman and Jimmy Diggs. To all the amazing people I've had the honor of meeting, Jane Goodall, Nelson Mandela, Tom Hanks and many others, in your own way you have made me want to make a difference in the world.

To the many authors referenced in this book, and those not sited here but who set the foundation of my work.

Howard Zinn for *"A People's History of the United States"*.

Erik M. Conway and Naomi Oreskes for their books *""The Big Myth: How American Business Taught Us to Loathe Government and Love the Free Market"* and *"Merchants of Doubt: How a Handful of Scientists Obscured the Truth on Issues from Tobacco Smoke to Global Warming"*.

Donald Cohen and Allen Mikaelian for *"The Privatization of Everything: How the Plunder of Public Goods Transformed America and How We Can Fight Back"*.

Thomas Frank for *"What's the Matter with Kansas? How Conservatives Won the Heart of America"* and *"Listen, Liberal: Or, What Ever Happened to the Party of the People?"* and many other great reads.

Peter S. Goodman for *"Davos Man: How the Billionaires Devoured the World"*.

David Cay Johnston for his many works about the corruption of Donald Trump.

Jeremy Scahill for *"Blackwater - The Rise of the World's Most Powerful Mercenary Army"*.

Anand Giridharadas for *"Winners Take All: The Elite Charade of Changing the World"*.

Thom Hartman for his many *"The War On"* books and his uncanny knowledge of the history of the United States.

Democracy Now and Amy Goodman for the many decades of quality journalism.

Other References:

The Guardian (multiple references)

The Washington Post (multiple references)

The New York Times (multiple references)

The Stamford Advocate (multiple references)

U.S. Supreme Court rulings (e.g., Citizens United)

The Library of Congress

Historical texts on corporate influence and governance

Recommendations:

Scott Galloway - *Adrift: America in 100 Charts*

Ta-Nehisi Coats - *Between the World and Me*

Yuval Noah Harari – "*Sapiens: A Brief History of Humankind*" as well as "*Nexus: A brief history of information networks*".

ABOUT THE AUTHOR

Robert Cain is a world traveler and Renaissance man. In his current incarnation, he's a director, cinematographer and editor. He's also a still photographer, technical supervisor, graphic designer, storyboard artist, carpenter, designer and author. He has worked as a stockbroker, rebuilt classic cars, surfs and holds a black belt in Kenpo Karate, he has worked with world leaders and celebrities. He's an avid reader and an ordained minister. As a political activist and policy junkie, he co-founded the upcoming podcast On-Point, a resource for living well, and the Democracy4Sale podcast for citizen engagement